Volume I

REMINISCENCES

of

Admiral U. S. Grant Sharp

U. S. Navy (Retired)

PREFACE

These two volumes contain the transcript of eleven taped interviews with Admiral U.S. Grant Sharp, U.S.N. (Retired). They were conducted by Commander Etta Belle Kitchen, U.S.N. (Retired) for the Oral History program of the U.S. Naval Institute and were held at intervals from September 20, 1969 to June 7, 1970 in the Admiral's home in San Diego, California and at the Naval Training Center, San Diego.

These interviews cover a very distinguished naval career. They are particularly important for Admiral Sharp's detailed chronicle of his years as CincPac (1964-68). It was precisely in those years that the United States dealt with a crescendo of involvement in the military and political events of Vietnam. It was in the selfsame years that we witnessed a barrage of enemy propaganda that had echoes throughout the civilized world.

I am confident that historians will find most valuable these recollections of Admiral Sharp. He worked carefully with available documents in the preparation of his interviews. The memoir was read and cleared for classified material by officials of the Navy, the JCS and the State Department.

A subject index has been prepared and is to be found at the end of each volume.

Volume I incorporates Interviews 1-6 (pages 1 through 331); Volume II incorporates Interviews 7-11 (pages 332-659).

John T. Mason, Jr.
Director of Oral History
March, 1976

ADMIRAL U. S. G. SHARP, USN, RETIRED

Admiral Sharp was born in Chinook, Montana, April 2, 1906. He attended high school at Fort Benton, Montana, and was graduated from the U.S. Naval Academy, Annapolis, Maryland, on June 3, 1927.

After graduation from the Academy, he served for a year on board the battleship USS NEW MEXICO. From 1928 until 1932, he was assigned to the transport USS HENDERSON, and the destroyers USS SUMNER and USS BUCHANAN, and for two years thereafter in the aircraft carrier USS SARATOGA.

He returned to Annapolis in 1934 for the Operating Engineering course at the Postgraduate School, and was graduated in June 1936. For the next two years, he served in the Engineering Department of the cruiser USS RICHMOND and in the destroyer USS WINSLOW as the Engineer Officer.

In May 1940, when a Lieutenant Commander, he reported to the Bureau of Ships, Navy Department, Washington, D.C., where he served until May 1942. He then commanded the high-speed destroyer-minesweeper USS HOGAN (DMS-6) on convoy duty in the Western Atlantic and Caribbean as well as in the invasion of North Africa.

In January 1943, he took command of the destroyer USS BOYD in the Pacific, and for nearly two years participated in strikes against Wake Island, Nauru, The Marianas, the Bonins, Mindanao, Cebu, Negros, Luzon, Truk, and Hollandia, New Guinea. His ship also took part in the first strikes against Okinawa and Formosa, and the occupation of the Gilbert Islands. On June 19-20, 1944, Admiral Sharp's ship participated in the Battle of the Philippine Sea.

While commanding the BOYD, Admiral Sharp, then a commander, was awarded two Silver Star medals for gallantry in action against the Japanese. On December 8, 1943, after a bombardment of the Japanese-held Nauru Island, northeast of Australia, the destroyer BOYD was ordered to search for an aviator reported downed off the island. Commander Sharp headed his ship for Nauru at 25 knots while U.S. aircraft circled about two miles off the island, watching the spot where their colleague had gone down.

Since the pilot was reported to be down at a position within point-blank range of the shore batteries, Commander Sharp knew that the BOYD would have to effect a high speed rescue. Upon reaching the reported location of the downed aviator, he backed down on his engines when a lookout reported a man in the water.

"Unfortunately, the lookout report was in error," Admiral Sharp recalls. "The 'man in the water' was in fact an aircraft float light that had been mistaken for a man waving."

As the BOYD began to slow, a pair of six-inch shells slammed into her forward engine room. This meant she would have to run the gauntlet for several miles with only one of her two engines before she could be clear of the enemy guns.

Despite the partial loss of power, Commander Sharp managed to regain the open sea, steering a zig-zag course which brought his ship safely through the heavy barrage.

"Knowing that the gunners would attempt to correct their fire after each miss," he said, "I decided to chase the fall of the shot."

As each Japanese shell landed near the BOYD, Commander Sharp would steer the ship toward the splash, literally weaving to safety through the shells.

BOYD made it back to port under her own power. After repairs, the ship returned to action in the Pacific war.

In November 1944, Admiral Sharp returned to the U.S., and in January 1945, joined the staff of Commander Cruiser-Destroyer Force, U.S. Pacific Fleet, as Combat Information Center and Tactical Radar Officer.

He remained on this staff until July 1948, when he became Commanding Officer of the Fleet Sonar School, San Diego, California.

Admiral Sharp next attended the Naval War College, Newport, Rhose Island, and in June 1950, assumed command of Destroyer Squadron FIVE and deployed to waters off Korea. During part of this period, Admiral Sharp was temporarily attached to the staff of the Commander SEVENTH Fleet, serving as Fleet Planning Officer for the Inchon invasion.

In January 1951, Admiral Sharp reported to the Commander SECOND Fleet on the U.S. east coast for duty as Operations Officer, and, in October 1951, as Chief of Staff and Aide.

In August 1953, he assumed command of the cruiser USS MACON.

One year later, Admiral Sharp reported to the Commander in Chief, U.S. Pacific Fleet, for duty as Deputy Chief of Staff for Plans and Operations. In 1955, during this assignment, he was promoted to Rear Admiral.

In July 1956, Admiral Sharp became Commander of Cruiser Division THREE. In October 1957, he was assigned to the Office of the Chief of Naval Operations, Navy Department, where he served as Assistant Director, Strategic Plans Division, until November 1958, when he became director of that division.

Adm. U. S. G. Sharp, USN, Ret.

In February 1959, Admiral Sharp became Commander, Cruiser-Destroyer Force, U. S. Pacific Fleet. On April 30, 1960, he reported as Commander U.S. FIRST Fleet, and was promoted to Vice Admiral. He commanded the FIRST Fleet until July 1960, when he became Deputy Chief of Naval Operations (Plans and Policy), Navy Department. In this latter capacity, he was deeply involved in planning for naval operations, including those during the Cuban crisis of 1962. For his service as Deputy Chief of Naval Operations (Plans and Policy), he was awarded the Distinguished Service Medal.

He was promoted to Admiral on September 27, 1963, and became Commander in Chief, U. S. Pacific Fleet, on September 30.

With headquarters at Pearl Harbor, Hawaii, Admiral Sharp commanded approximately 265,000 Navymen and Marine Corps personnel serving in the world's largest naval command.

Admiral Sharp directed the movements of some 450 combatant and support ships of the FIRST and SEVENTH Fleets, operating from the west coast of the U. S. and throughout the Pacific and Far East. In addition, he directed approximately 2400 first line combat and support aircraft, plus two Marine ground divisions and associated Marine air wings.

Admiral Sharp became Commander in Chief Pacific, on June 30, 1964. With headquarters at Camp H. M. Smith, Hawaii, he directed the largest of U.S. unified commands and United States operations in the U.S. Pacific Command. He had more than 940,000 military personnel of the Army, Navy, Marine Corps, and Air Force under his command, in addition to more than 7,500 operational aircraft and 560 major ships. His Pacific Command responsibility extended on the West Coast of the Americas and extended some 8000 miles across the Pacific into the Indian Ocean and from the Aleutian Islands down to the area of the South Pole--an area encompassing 85 million square miles.

As Commander of all U. S. Armed Forces assigned to the Pacific, he was responsible directly to the Joint Chiefs of Staff. He was also the U.S. Military Advisor to the Southeast Asia Treaty Organization (SEATO), U.S. Military Representative to the Philippine-United States Representative to the Australia-New Zealand-United States Council (ANZUS), and Military Adviser and Member of the United States - Japanese Security Consultative Committee.

Part of the Paficic Command's mission is to defend the U.S. from attack through the Pacific, and to support and carry out U.S. policy in this area. An example of Pacific Command preparedness to carry out its mission occurred in the Gulf of Tonkin off Vietnam in August 1964, when U.S. Navy ships were targets of an unprovoked attack from North Vietnamese torpedo boat bases.

Admiral Sharp, believing the U.S. should respond to the attack

Adm. U. S. G. Sharp, USN, Ret.

with more than protests, recommended to the Joint Chiefs of Staff that the U. S. strike the offending torpedo boat bases.

The Secretary of Defense and the President agreed. The U.S. decision to retaliate was translated into swift and appropriate air strike action by units under Admiral Sharp's Pacific Command.

Since the first Gulf of Tonkin incident, Pacific Army, Navy and Air Force personnel have executed a number of precisely planned actions in the Vietnam theater. As CINCPAC, Admiral Sharp had the responsibility for directing these and other U. S. military operations in the vast Pacific area.

"For exceptionally meritorious service... from June 30, 1964 to July 31, 1968..." he was awarded a Gold Star in lieu of the Second Distinguished Service Medal.

On August 1, 1968 he was transferred to the Retired List of the U.S. Navy.

In addition to the Distinguished Service Medal with Gold Star and the Silver Star Medal with Gold Star, Admiral Sharp has the Bronze Star Medal with Gold Star, the Commendation Ribbon with two Bronze Stars and Combat "V", the American Defense Service Medal with Fleet Clasp, the American Campaign Medal, the European-African-Middle Eastern Campaign Medal with seven stars, the World War II Victory Medal, the Navy Occupation Service Medal, Europe Clasp; the National Defense Service Medal with bronze star, the Korean Service Medal with three stars, the United Nations Service Medal, the Vietnam Service Medal with three stars; and the Philippine Liberation Ribbon with one star. He also had the Korean Presidential Unit Citation Badge and the Republic of Vietnam Campaign Medal with Device.

Admiral Sharp's brother, Lieutenant Commander Thomas F. Sharp, USN, was lost in the USS PICKEREL when that submarine failed to return from war patrol in the Western Pacific in May 1943.

Mrs. Sharp is the former Patricia O'Connor of San Diego, California. Admiral and Mrs. Sharp have two children, Patricia (Mrs. Russell F. Milham) of Los Angeles, California, and Grant, a 1960 graduate of the U.S. Naval Academy. Grant is a Navy Lieutenant.

25 November 1968

DECLARATION OF TRUST

The undersigned does hereby appoint and designate as his (her) Trustee herein, the Secretary-Treasurer and Publisher of the United States Naval Institute to perform and discharge the following duties, powers, and privileges in connection with the possession and use of a certain taped interview between the undersigned and the Oral History Department of the United States Naval Institute.

1. Classification of Transcript.

    ( )a. If classified OPEN, the transcript(s) may be read or the recording(s) audited by the qualified personnel upon presentation of proper credentials, as determined by the Secretary-Treasurer of the U. S. Naval Institute.

    ( )b. If classified PERMISSION REQUIRED TO CITE OR QUOTE, the user will be required to obtain permission in writing from the interviewee prior to quoting or citing from either the transcript(s) or the recording(s).

    (X)c. If classified PERMISSION REQUIRED, permission must be obtained in writing from the interviewee before the transcribed interview(s) can be examined or the tape recording(s) audited.

    ( )d. If classified CLOSED, the transcribed interview(s) and the tape recording(s) will be sealed until a time specified by the interviewee. This may be until the death of the interviewee or for any specified number of years.

2. It is expressly understood that in giving this authorization, I am in no way precluded from placing such restrictions as I may desire upon use of the interview at any time during my lifetime, nor does this authorization in any way affect my rights to the copyright of my literary expressions that may be contained in the interview.

Witness my hand and seal this 24th day of April 1970

[signature]
Adm USN (Ret)

I hereby accept and consent to the foregoing Declaration of Trust and the powers therein conferred upon me as Trustee:

[signature] R E Bowker Jr

Interview #1

Admiral U.S. Grant Sharp

September 20, 1969 at 876 San Antonio Place, San Diego

Interviewed by Etta-Belle Kitchen

Q: This is the first in a series of biographical interviews with Admiral U.S. Grant Sharp at his home, 876 San Antonio Place, San Diego. Good morning, Admiral.

Sharp: Good morning.

Q: I feel, and the Navy, of course, feels that you are the most distinguished naval officer that I have certainly been able to interview and that has existed today and we are very fortunate to have you participate in the Institute's program. So if it's agreeable with you, I'd like to start at the beginning.

In the first place, I am interested in how you got your name.

Sharp: Well, I got my name from my father. Actually, I am a Junior. My father got his name from U. S. Grant, of course. He was born just after the battle of Vicksburg in 1863. My father's mother was Mrs. U. S. Grant's sister. The General, when he heard that my father was born, asked that my father be named after him. That's where the name came from.

Sharp #1 - 2

Q: I notice that in your cabinet in the little morning room there is a mug with the name of U. S. Grant on it, and what's the inscription above that?

Sharp: Gee, I don't know.

Q: "To my godson," I think.

Sharp: Yes, I guess it's . . .

Q: "To my namesake."

Sharp: Yes, my namesake. That was given to my father by U. S. Grant.

Q: So you have a fitting military background, I guess, to begin with.

Sharp: Well, that's generally. I think -- well, we'll get into that a bit later. Now, what else did you want to get into?

Q: I think where you were born and how you happened to go to the Academy.

Sharp: Well, I was born in Chinook, Montana, on the 2nd of April 1906. My mother was a school teacher who went from

Pennsylvania to Montana and taught school in Chinook, met my father there. My father was a merchant in Chinook. They were married, I guess, it was in 1904 or '05. I was born in 1906. My sister, Margaret, was born in 1908 and about 1910 or maybe '11 my family moved to Fort Benton, Montana, and lived there until about 1931 or '32, I guess it was, when they went to California.

I went to school -- grammar school and high school -- at Fort Benton and graduated from high school there. During my senior year in high school I took a competitive exam for the Naval Academy. Fortunately, there was very little competition.

Q: How did you happen to choose the Navy when actually your background is Army?

Sharp: Well, my background is Army _and_ Navy. I have relatives in the Army. However, my father's brother graduated from the Naval Academy in 1870, I think it was, and I think that's where the impetus to go into the Navy came from. He was in the Navy until he died. He had a son, Alexander Sharp, Jr., who graduated from the Naval Academy in 1906. I also had a cousin who graduated from the Naval Academy in 1924.

Q: Oh, so you really did have both.

Sharp: The cousin came from Montana, from Fort Benton. He

lived right close to us. So there was a Navy tinge to the family right along.

Q: I guess you carry out the fact that the finest naval officers come from inside the United States who probably never saw the ocean before they went to the Academy.

Sharp: Well, a lot of them do. That's right. I had never seen the ocean before I went to the Academy. Well, anyway, to go on -- I just did get by, I just did pass the competitive exam because of little competition I won an appointment to the Naval Academy and was appointed to the Naval Academy by Thomas J. Walsh, the famous Senator from Montana.

Now, a question. Do you want to get into any detail about the school life?

Q: I would think if you had any anecdotes or any comments on the Academy as you experienced it . . .

Sharp: Oh, the Academy. Now we get into the Academy.

Q: Unless you have anecdotes that you want of your high school days.

Sharp: I think we might just note that in the little town of Fort Benton there were two graduates in the Class of '24 at the Naval Academy -- one of them, my cousin, retired as a captain and then, of course, was rear admiral because of combat decorations. Another class of '24 graduate there was G. C. Towner, who became a vice admiral. Then there was a high school graduate from Fort Benton named Raymond C. Curtis, who went to West Point in the Class of '27 and he retired as a major general.

Q: Isn't that interesting for such a really small town!

Sharp: And then there was another person before us named Hoover who retired as a vice admiral.

Q: You mean the Admiral in charge of Air in the South Pacific?

Sharp: That's right. And also, there was a Marine major general named Karl Luther -- all around the same time. So we had a pretty good representation.

Q: Have you ever stopped to think what might have been the motivating idea in this really small group to have so many illustrious people in the military?

Sharp: I think, except for Admiral Hoover -- I don't know what turned him toward the Navy and he was before our time -- but the rest of us were more or less influenced by my uncle, Alexander Sharp.

Q: I see. Was there a military fort near? Well, of course, Fort Benton had been a fort, too.

Sharp: Fort Benton was an old fort in frontier days.

So I guess we started at the Naval Academy. Another lad who graduated from high school, a classmate of mine named D. B. Overfield, went to the Naval Academy. We were roommates at the Naval Academy. He graduated in the class of '27 and he died as a commander.

Q: How many people were in the Academy when you were?

Sharp: Well, there were around 3500, I guess. Our class was a very large class. The class of '27 was the biggest class they had had up to that time. We entered with over 1,000 and graduated with 585. 585 were commissioned.

My brother also went to the Naval Academy and graduated in the Class of 1935. He was lost on the submarine Pickerell in World War II.

So we get on to the Naval Academy, I guess. In 1923, early July, the first or second of July, I went down and reported in to Annapolis, took my physical exam, and they told me I was too light -- I weighed 109 pounds at that point. They said go out and over the weekend -- this was Friday -- they said go out and over the weekend and eat as many bananas as you can and drink a lot of water and come in on Monday.

Q: I didn't know bananas would put a lot of weight on you.

Sharp: Well, I ate bananas and drank water and ate as much as I could and went in on Monday and I weighed 107 pounds.

Q: Oh, no!

Sharp: So they told me I was too light and couldn't get in.

Q: What did they want you to weigh?

Sharp: Something like 120 -- I don't know what it was. Maybe 115. But I went up to Washington and talked to an uncle of mine who was a major general in the Army named Dennis Nolan. He called up the Surgeon General of the Navy whom he knew and said he had a problem with a cousin who wanted to get into the Navy. So I got a waiver from the Chief of Medicine and Surgery and went back and went in on the waiver. I think when I graduated from the Naval Academy I didn't weigh any more than about 118 or 119.

Q: You don't weigh much more than that now, do you?

Sharp: Oh yes, I weigh 150.

Q: Do you really! How tall are you?

Sharp: About 5' 7" -- 5" 6 3/4". I remember one time I was trying out for the boxing team. I was, of course, the lightest weight, what they called the "fly weight" or something like that. I remember one time Spike Webb, the boxing coach said, "You go out and put on some weight." I was probably the only man on the team he said should take on some weight.

So, my Naval Academy plebe year was distinguished by difficulty in staying SAT. I had a tough time staying SAT in math -- chiefly math, I think it was. The schools in Fort Benton weren't very good so I had poor preparation for the Naval Academy and I had quite a struggle of keeping SAT plebe year and to a certain extent third class year. I think that lack of preparation sort of gave me trouble right through the Naval Academy. I graduated on the bottom of the top third of the class. I certainly didn't star.

Q: Were you interested in athletics besides boxing?

Sharp: Well, I really was not a very good boxer. I ended up boxing on the class and company teams. I didn't amount to anything really. I also ran track on intramural activities in track and cross-country.

Q: Did you think the Naval Academy courses fitted you or were adequate for your later days in the Navy?

Sharp: I think it was a good education. I think, like anything else, it's only a starter to education. You've got to keep on working at it. I thought it was quite adequate at that time. The courses now are much more difficult than they were then. They cover a lot more ground, and they cut out some things that were good to have if you had the time. Courses change to keep up with the times. But I thought it was good for me. I enjoyed it by and large. Of course, in those days we who lived in Montana didn't get back except for our summer leave -- September leave -- after . . .

Q: After your cruise?

Sharp: After your cruise you went off on leave.

Q: Did you take any interesting cruises?

Sharp: Yes. Our first cruise was to Europe in a coal-burning battleship and I guess the first one was in the Utah or the Wyoming, I guess was the first one -- a coal burning ship. I used to, because of my light weight -- they used to put me up in the bunkers to strike down coal. That was where they put the lightweights.

Q: To break it loose so it could go in . . .

Sharp: Shove it down to where the stoker could get it. That

was a very interesting cruise. Coaling ship, of course, was an experience that people don't get now that we did get then. In coaling a ship, you just get the whole ship completely dirty and it's almost impossible to seal it off. So then the day after you coal the ship, you start from the top and scrub it down completely.

Q: How long did that last? One coal?

Sharp: One coaling -- you get it done in a day.

Q: But then how long did the ship go before it had to have another?

Sharp: If they're underway, they could go ten or twelve days and they'd have to coal again. Of course, if you stay in port you don't have to coal so frequently. And we'd coal about three or four times on a cruise -- three times, I guess it was. It was a fairly rugged experience. Then our next cruise, I think, came to the West Coast and we went off the coast. And our last cruise, I believe, was, as I recall it, was on the East Coast. We didn't go far. All those cruises were in coal-burning battleships. The very last cruise, because our class was so large and the next class was so small -- the Class of '28 was very small -- so we had most of the manpower. On my first class cruise, I was up in the bunker stoking down the coal.

Q: At least you knew how the other half lived at that point, didn't you?

Sharp: Yes, I sure did. That was a nice experience. First class year when they picked the midshipmen officers I was -- in the final selection, I was a second-class petty officer. That's as low as you can get.

Q: Oh, not really.

Sharp: Yes, that's as low as you can get. We had an interesting -- in that connection, we had an interesting get-together in Honolulu one time. Admiral Tom Moorer, General Vic Krulak, Vice Admiral B. J. Semmes -- I don't remember who the others were -- but all of us were second-class petty officers in our first class year. So I guess it must show that you don't have to have four stripes your first class year in order to be successful in the Navy.

Q: I'm sure it doesn't. At least for you. I'm sure, too, that all the men who were famous and carried the brunt of the war were all in Annapolis with you at that same time.

Sharp: Carried the brunt of which war?

Q: World War II.

Sharp #1 - 12

Sharp: World War II, yes. Well, most of the people who were in the Academy with me were squadron commanders of aircraft squadrons and skippers of destroyers and that sort of thing.

Q: Did you ever have any desire to go into flying?

Sharp: Oh, I thought about it at one time when I was on duty in the old Saratoga for two years as a gunnery officer. I thought about going to Pensacola but, I don't know, I think I took the physical exam and found that my ears weren't up to it or something like that. It killed what little desire I had. I really didn't have any burning desire.

Q: It didn't wreck you emotionally that you weren't able to go.

Sharp: No, it didn't bother me a bit. So we get through the Naval Academy with graduation on the 3rd of June, 1927 and go back to Montana -- no, first we had what they called familiarization training or something like that. Or maybe that was second class year. No, I think it was after we graduated, I guess, that we had this familiarization air training at the Naval Academy and flew around in these old flying boats, F5Ls or something like that, for a couple of weeks and then we went home to Montana and stayed there on 25 days leave or something like that and then reported to the battleship New

Mexico in July or August of '27. Now, let's stop this a moment . . .

In other words, I'm not going to try to do this to make a good tape out of it because if you did you'd almost have to organize your thoughts and then do it, you see.

Q: Then you'd have to have a run through and then do a final on that. That's the purpose of this really and then you'll get your manuscript back.

Sharp: That's right. So we're really going for a manuscript, not a tape.

Q: True. As a matter of interest -- I'm going to let this run just while I tell you -- of all of the tapes in oral history the experience has been that if people want to do research that maybe only ten percent of them are interested in the tapes because the manuscript is much easier to handle.

Sharp: Sure. Okay. So I report to the New Mexico in August of 1927 as an ensign. I was assigned to the main engine division of the ship and stayed in that position until I left the ship in June of the next year, June of 1928.

Q: Where was the New Mexico?

Sharp: She was in the Pacific during the time I was aboard. I reported to her in San Francisco. We came back to San Pedro, as I recall it and cruised around up and down the West Coast, but we didn't go anyplace away from the West Coast.

Q: Just part of the battle force, battleship force.

Sharp: Right. Aboard the New Mexico as a junior grade lieutenant -- no, I guess he was an ensign when I was aboard -- was George Towner, one of the lads from Fort Benton and my roommate, Basham Overfield, went to the New Mexico also. So there were three of us from Fort Benton aboard that ship at that time.

Q: I'm sure you had some interesting shore leaves together.

Sharp: We did. Right. Next, I was detached in June 1928 and went to the USS Henderson, an old transport. I was ships officer. Really my primary duty was officer of the deck and I had a division. While I was aboard the Henderson we made three trips to the western Pacific. What we did normally was leave San Francisco or Los Angeles, go to Honolulu, stay there a couple of days, then we'd go to Guam, stay there a couple of days, go to Manila, we'd stay there a couple of days, and we'd pick up families and enlisted men and officers who were going up to China -- you know, were going to ships up there. We'd stop in Hongkong and stay a couple of days and we went to Shanghai and then we'd normally go on up to Tsingtao and to Takubar.

Q: I don't know that name.

Sharp: Well, Takubar is where we let people off who were going up to Peking. And then we'd go on up to Chefu which is where the destroyers were based and then we'd make a circuit back again and come back to San Francisco.

Q: That was pleasant, wasn't it?

Sharp: Yes, it was a lot of fun. We had a lot of interesting times there. We'd haul people that I had met and met people there that we had known for a long time.

Q: This was your first experience in the Orient, wasn't it?

Sharp: Yes, it was. It was a great experience to go into Hongkong and Shanghai. Of course, Shanghai -- we used to go in there at least twice every trip. So I had been in Shanghai six times, I guess, at least before they closed it down. And in those days it was quite a city. I remember when we used to go ashore, we had a place that we used to go and gamble with what little money we had. We got $125 a month so we weren't gambling very much, you know.

The old Henderson made about 11 knots so it was pretty slow.

Q: Well, the term "shanghai" actually came from Shanghai, did it not? A sailor being shanghaied?

Sharp: Yes.

Q: So there must have been some wild goings-on in those days.

Sharp: Oh no, it was pretty calm then. Shanghai was well under control. It was a fine city, actually. It was the nicest city in the Orient by far. Hongkong was really second rate in those days. It was smaller and it was kind of stuffy. We didn't care much for it then.

Q: Who was the commanding officer of the Henderson or the New Mexico, do you recall?

Sharp: Let's see, the commanding officer of the New Mexico. I don't remember.

Q: So many times I've found that men when they were very young officers had commanding officers who became very famous.

Sharp: Well, of course, Admiral Blandy -- he was a commander aboard the New Mexico. He was the gunnery officer. Of course, he became very famous. Admiral Low was the fire control officer. He became a vice admiral and I served with him when he was ComCruDesPac. Towner became a vice admiral. There were four or five.

In the Henderson -- Adams was the skipper of the Henderson and there were three or four officers aboard the Henderson that I saw a good many times after that. So the Henderson lasted a year until July of 1929 and then I went to the Sumner which was an old four-pipe destroyer, a four-stack destroyer. I was aboard the Sumner and the DD-131 -- No, that was . . .

Well, anyway I went aboard the -- and I think this is right -- (phone rang) . . .

So from the Henderson I went aboard the Sumner which was DD-333, an old four-stack destroyer. I was aboard that ship for a short time and then they started putting that ship out of commission and putting the Long in commission to replace the Sumner. In the meantime, I went to Torpedo School over at North Island in San Diego. This was a three or four month course, I guess.

I should go back to the Henderson. Actually, I should go back to the New Mexico and say that in the fall of 1927 I came down here and took this what they called elimination flight training, where they gave us about 15 hours of instruction. At the end of the instruction you were supposed to solo if you passed it. They didn't let us solo because they said they didn't have enough airplanes to solo. But anyway, I was passed being qualified for further instruction or something like that. So that was the last of the flight training. I got a good enough standing to go ahead through if I wanted to but I never did do it.

Q: Was this training something they gave you whether you asked for it or not?

Sharp: Yes, everybody took it.

Q: I see. Did you enjoy it?

Sharp: Oh yes, it was fun. We had a lot of fun.

Q: Did you find later that it came in -- it was wise to have been knowledgeable even as much as you did?

Sharp: O yes, it was very useful. And, of course, as I go on, I'll show you later I served two years aboard the Saratoga. All of this, of course, was during prohibition. At flight training I remember we had a bootlegger who used to come down and supply us with that horrible stuff we drank. As a matter of fact, I remember one time going back to the Naval Academy, my roommate liked his liquor pretty well. He had a pint of moonshine when we left Fort Benton. The two of us had polished that off by the time we got to Minot, North Dakota, I think it was. The train was stopping twenty mintues in Minot so we decided we better see if we could get another bottle of moonshine. Well, we got a taxi driver at the station and said, "Do you know where we can get some moonshine?" He said, "Oh, yea, across town."

So he drove across town and drove up to a house. He went in and came out with a bottle in a brown paper bag and the moonshine was hot. It was just off the still. So that was age 0. And we drank it.

Q: I went through those days, too.

Sharp: Did you?

Q: Through the prohibition days.

Sharp: Yes, they were pretty rugged. But anyway, one time coming back aboard the Henderson we had a whole lot of Marines that were coming back from Peking and one of the dependents was General Smedley Butler's daughter. At the end of the trip she gave me the name of a girl to look up. The gal was Patricia O'Connor, who subsequently became my wife.

Q: You met her here in San Diego?

Sharp: I met her here in San Diego, yes. She was living in

San Diego and through Ethel Butler I called her up and had a blind date and we started going together then.

Q: That's a beautiful picture of her there on the wall.

Sharp: This one here? Did you see the one in the living room?

Q: Yes, I did.

Sharp: It's a beautiful one. Well, so now we're aboard the Sumner and detached and going to torpedo school. All this time I'm going out frequently with Patricia O'Connor. I proposed to her during the time I was at Torpedo School so we were to get married on the 2nd of August. We had it all set that we were going to get married just as the Torpedo School course ended then I would report aboard my next ship. Everything was pretty much settled as far as the ceremony was concerned. We were going to be married in the Catholic church and all that sort of thing, although I was an Episcopalian, she was Catholic. So her mother got it arranged to be married in the church and everything was all set. The wedding party was planned. And I was detached from the Torpedo School, I think is was probably on Wednesday or Thursday, and reported to this new ship which I was going to, which was the Buchanan (DD-131), another four-pipe destroyer.

Well, I reported aboard, I guess it was a Friday, and I was going to get married the next day. They told me that I had the weekend duty.

Q: Oh no.

Sharp: Well, that was a big crisis there for a few minutes until another lad that I came to know very well, Lieutenant (jg) H. P. Webster, said that he would take my duty so that we could get married.

Q: You were a j.g. now.

Sharp: No, I guess I was still an ensign in the Buchanan. Yes, I think I didn't take my exams for junior grade lieutenant; this was July of 1930 when I reported aboard the Buchanan and I didn't take my exams until after I got the Buchanan. So we were married on the 2nd of August, 1930 and I was still an ensign. We had a little apartment up in San Diego. It must have cost us $40 a month and you probably couldn't get it now for $150.

Q: Oh, I'm sure not.

Sharp: Well anyway, we were married on Saturday and I reported back aboard ship on Monday morning and we left for San Francisco.

Q: So you didn't have much of a honeymoon.

Sharp: We didn't have too much of a honeymoon, no. As a matter of fact as I recall it now, my wife and her sister and another wife drove up to San Francisco. But anyway, no honeymoon. So I stayed aboard the Buchanan then and we lived in San Diego and we generally operated around San Diego.

Q: Was that ComCruDesPac in those days? What was she part of?

Sharp: No, it was called the Destroyer Force I think, as I recall.

Q: It was here . . .

Sharp: Here in San Diego.

Q: And the battleship force was up in San Pedro.

Sharp: That's right.

Q: What were your duties aboard the Buchanan?

Sharp: I was torpedo officer and I guess I was communication officer, too.

Q: You must have taken the last service-wide exam, didn't you, in 1930? No. The last service-wide exam for promotions was late in '30, wasn't it?

Sharp: Actually, I took it late. I took it in August of 1930 or something like that, maybe it was September. So I was taking it later than usual. And I was aboard the Buchanan then from July of 1930 until July of '32. I remember aboard that ship we went on out to Honolulu escorting, plane guarding the old Saratoga or Lexington. Old Lexington, I guess it was. I remember we left one Sunday evening or Monday morning at one minute after midnight Sunday and we went out and joined the carrier and we started off at something like 24 knots or something like that aboard this old four-piper. It was rough as the dickens. That was the only time in my naval career that I ever got seasick. Everybody was seasick.

Q: You had to make that speed because of the carrier, of course.

Sharp: Yes, we had to keep up with the carrier and the carrier pushed it pretty hard and it was a rough trip the whole way. But anyway, that was my one experience with being seasick.

Q: I'm sure one was enough, wasn't it?

Sharp: One was enough -- that's right. Then in July of 1932 I was detached from the Buchanan and went to the Saratoga, the old Saratoga. There I was a division officer and I had the first division, I guess, it was the second division where I had the 8-inch guns. I guess I had one battery, only one turret of the 8-inch guns. We stood deck watches and, of course, I had a great big slice of the ship to take care of. It was a very interesting duty. There I met a whole lot of aviation officers and I got well acquainted with carrier operations. The exec was Richmond Kelly Turner. The first exec was a fellow named Douglas, who made rear admiral I think, and Richmond Kelly Turner, of course, was an admiral. Commander Spencer was the air officer. He was Wally Simpson's first husband. At that time he was married to the girl who subsequently was Admiral Radford's wife. Commander Spencer died later.

Then there was Lieutenant Commander Hedding. He was the hangar deck officer, I guess he was, and he became a rear admiral or a vice admiral.

Q: Who was the skipper?

Sharp: The skipper was George Steele first and then he was relieved by Rufus Zaugbaum. I remember one time aboard the Saratoga we were doing runs for short-range battle practice and all the gunnery officers were at their gun stations. At that time I had a five-inch division and we were stationed up on an anti-air control platform along with most all of -- a lot of the senior deck officers, senior people who were officers of the deck. Well, the ship was steaming along off of Long Beach and we thought it was getting, just from our seaman's eye, thought it was getting kind of close to the beach. We got one of the senior watch officers up there, after all of us talking about it -- he called up and told the officer of the deck who was the navigator -- he and Captain Steele were in the pilot house -- he told the navigator that the next time they turn they should turn out to sea because if they turned in, they were getting into too shallow water. He didn't do it. He turned in the next time they turned to go by the target and went aground.

Q: Was it bad? Were they able to get out of it under their own power?

Sharp: It was a sandy bottom and they ran the ship pretty well aground though. This was about three o'clock in the afternoon. The old Saratoga was solid aground so they got out tugs and the battleship Colorado I think it was and all these ships out pulling on the old Saratoga. They finally got her off some time in the evening, eight or nine o'clock.

Q: She had such a deep draft I would think it would almost instinctively know to stay away from the beach.

Sharp: Well, he wasn't a very good navigator, obviously. Anyway, that was one happening. So after that, Captain Steele I guess got court-martialed and he was relieved by Captain Zaugbaum.

Q: What happened to the navigator?

Sharp: Well, he was relieved, too. I don't remember whether he got court-martialed or not.

Q: Being on the Saratoga and still in these years lots of naval officers who hadn't grown up with accepting aviation had an antipathy toward the air branch of the Navy. Did you ever have any feelings of that sort at all?

Sharp: No, I can't say that I did. I had a lot of friends that were aviators and, of course, in the Saratoga you were thrown with aviators all the time. I remember on one cruise my roommate was W. B. Davis from the Class of '24 who became a vice admiral. He was DCNO for Air at one time.

Q: With your later responsibilities it would have been a real lack if you hadn't had this experience.

Sharp: It was fortunate that I had it because it gave me an insight into carrier operations that I wouldn't have had if I hadn't been aboard and they were a lot of fine people, too.

One other thing that happened during that period in March of 1933, they had the Long Beach earthquake. The Saratoga was in port. I was ashore. Pat and I had the upstairs apartment in a duplex on I guess it was First Street in Long Beach. We were sitting on the couch when this happened with our daughter sitting between us. She normally played over in front of the big window but she just happened to be sitting between us that day. We were having cocktails just before dinner. This shake happened and the window that she normally sat in front of fell in and there was not too much damage to the apartment actually. Actually, the biggest damage we had -- I had -- at that time, of course, we were still in prohibition and I was making home brew. Out in the kitchen I had just bottled a whole lot of home brew and when the earthquake happened, it all fell over and some of it exploded. So I had home brew all over the kitchen floor. But other than that, we had very little damage.

Well, anyway, we ran out in front and stood out in the street while we had a lot more shock and then decided that we couldn't stay there because the gas was off and the lights were off and the place was still shaking pretty badly. So we decided to get in our car and to to Los Angeles where my mother and father were living at that time. So we went up there and stayed there overnight. We came back the next day and went aboard ship -- I went aboard ship. Pat used to go down to the apartment and sit outside until I was ready to come back.

Q: Had the ship had any feeling of it at all?

Sharp: The ship had some feeling and, as a matter of fact, the officer of the deck was so alarmed he thought it was some kind of an explosion or something. There was a sort of vibration in the ship and the noise and he didn't know what it was. A lot of people went out to the ship and stayed aboard the ship that night.

Q: I thought that's what you were going to say. Did they take any dependents aboard?

Sharp: Yes, they took some dependents aboard. Then they had dependents there for two or three days afterwards.

Q: Did the ship contribute any light or power to the city?

Sharp: No. They had to send a lot of parties over to help in controlling the situation -- shore patrol and things like that.

Q: It was pretty devastating.

Sharp: Oh yes, it was a bad earthquake, very bad. It was lucky that it happened when it did. It if had happened when school was in session, there would have been many children killed because some of the schools just collapsed.

Q: I think that was one of the reasons why so much earthquake legislation was passed in building codes as a result of that Long Beach . . .

Sharp: One of the big schools in Long Beach just was a complete ruin. Fortunately, there were no children in it. It had happened at five minutes of six or something like that in the evening.

Q: What kind of planes were they flying on the Saratoga then?

Sharp: They had the bi-plane torpedo planes, I remember, and the righters were bi-planes, too. As a matter of fact, the first Grumman monoplane was tried out aboard the Saratoga. It was brought aboard and they ran some landings with it. On one of the landings -- this was a heavier plane than they had used before and it was faster -- and on one of the landings the landing wire broke and flew across the deck and cut one man's legs off and killed another man. It was a pretty disastrous affair.

I also remember one time when I was officer of the deck

and we had a flight of torpedo planes up there -- about ten or twelve of them. They were up about twenty minutes when the first pilot said, "My engines stop and then start again. I'm going to ditch." Within about ten minutes we had about six planes in the water.

Q: What was that from?

Sharp: They got water in the gasoline. They just went so far and then the water came up and so the engine died.

Q: Had the gasoline been taken on aboard the ship?

Sharp: Yes.

Q: And you had water in it?

Sharp: Yes. You see, in those days, they used a water displacement system and as the gas tank was emptied -- I mean, as the gasoline was drained off, it was drained off by water pushing it up.

Q: And they took it off too close to the top. Were there any developments aboard the Saratoga in catapults or planes or arresting gear or deck covering or anything that you recall while you were on her?

Sharp: No, I don't . . . They used catapults, of course. They had this one casualty with the arresting gear which, of course, probably was the forerunner of making heavier and heavier arresting gear. But at that time, the arresting gear wire was maybe half an inch in diameter and, of course, now it's almost two inches in diameter. That was another interesting experience I had aboard the Saratoga. Admiral Kelly Turner, then Commander Kelly Turner, the exec called me down to his office and said, "What do you know about baseball?" I said, "Well, I played a little bit in high school but I'm really not a baseball fan." He said, "Well, you're the manager of the baseball team." So I managed the baseball team for a year. That was quite an experience. We had a real good baseball team.

Q: Where did you play?

Sharp: We played mostly in San Pedro and Long Beach. We had some fancy games. The baseball players in those days -- that's about all they did -- play baseball.

Q: Is that so?

Sharp: Yes. During the baseball season they practiced every afternoon and we had a game at least once a week, maybe more frequently.

Q: They didn't have to do any other duty?

Sharp: Oh, they had other duties but during the baseball season they weren't much help. They mostly played baseball. There were some real characters playing on that baseball team. Every now and then one pitcher's wife would make a crack about another pitcher and the wife would overhear it and they would start having heavy words and we'd have to calm that down. We had time with them.

Q: Did the officers and men all participate?

Sharp: Yes. I had, fortunately, a junior grade doctor who was a very good baseball player. He was the coach and also played. So I didn't have the problem of trying to coach this outfit. I really wasn't that good.

Q: I forgot to ask on the aviators, were you able to pick them up? The ones that ditched?

Sharp: Yes, we got them all back.

Q: How did you pick them up?

Sharp: The destroyer picked them up. Well, let's see, I guess we got to the Saratoga and then in 1934 . . .

Q: Oh, I forgot to ask you, excuse me -- how about Admiral Turner's temper in those days? Did he give signs of his future nickname?

Sharp: He had a pretty husky temper. He was very good, of course, a very good officer. And he did a lot for that ship and the ship needed him. He did a good job as exec.

Q: Do you have any for instances?

Sharp: No. I mean, it just turned out to be a very fine ship and he tightened it up a lot from what it was before he arrived.

Q: Was he aboard -- he was when it went aground, wasn't he?

Sharp: No, I don't think he was. I think he was not the exec then. I'm pretty sure he wasn't.

Well, let's see now. Next. We're not progressing very fast. The Saratoga went around to the East Coast in May or June of 1934 and while we were in New York, I was detached and reported in to Postgraduate School. Pat, my wife, and another wife drove across the continent with the one child we had then. I don't know whether the other woman had children or not. But they went across the continent.

Q: That was quite an achievement in 1934, as I recall.

Sharp: That was a pretty good deal. I remember at that time we had a Studebaker which we had bought used. They got across all right though. They did a good job.

Q: The PG School was in Annapolis, wasn't it?

Sharp: In Annapolis at that time, right. We lived first in an old house in Annapolis that belonged to a landlord named Mr. Hart, who was a sort of a very, very tough landlord. He had a lot of property and we had to live in this old wreck of a house for one year. This was during the time when -- this was during the depression, of course. Our pay was cut, as I recall it, after we arrived there. You know, they reduced everybody's pay. Or actually what they did was . . . did they reduce it or . . .?

Q: They speak of having it as a cut in pay.

Sharp: Yes, I guess it was a cut in pay. Anyway, we had a cut in pay and at the end of '35, I guess it was, the pay cut was restored. The landlord said, "Since your pay cut's restored, I've got to raise the rent."

Q: Did he cut it?

Sharp: No, he didn't cut it.

Q: He didn't cut it while it was lower but he raised it when you got it back.

Sharp: So we decided we had had enough of him and we found another house over in Eastport which was considerably nicer and the landlord was certainly nicer, of course.

Q: Do you think maybe personnel felt the depression as civilians did even though the pay was small?

Sharp: No, I don't think they did. The pay was pretty small, of course, but, I mean, we still had a pay coming in every day - every month. The civilians, of course, had a terrible time. No, I think we were pretty well off. The pay cut, of course, was tough because we didn't have much to start with. But nevertheless, we were a lot better off than most people.

Q: People didn't lose their jobs, at least.

Sharp: No. So I spent two years there at the Postgraduate School taking operating engineering.

Q: What did that mean?

Sharp: Oh, it was a two year engineering course. You had to take a three year course to get a degree, to get a Master's degree.

Sharp #1 - 36

Q: Because you already had your B.S. actually in engineering when you graduated.

Sharp: Yes. And this was a two year course. What it really was was just qualifying you to be an engineer aboard ship, but not trying to get you qualified to be a technical engineer or a design engineer or something like that.

Q: Did you find it stimulating?

Sharp: Yes, it was very good. I must say I found out what math was all about.

Q: I was going to ask. Did you learn math then at the time in the engineering, did you feel?

Sharp: Yes, I found out -- yes, I caught onto math much better then. The math course was a pretty heavy course at postgraduate school but anyway it was a good course and the whole thing was very useful. I was happy to have the opportunity.

Q: Just as a philosophical comment, have you ever learned anything that wasn't helpful later in your life?

Sharp: No, I think generally speaking most of the stuff that we were taking was useful. I think one of the most useful things I ever did -- one time I was in high school, a junior in high school or something like that and we had come back to school. When the school year starts, why you look over the teachers and here was a real good-looking teacher that's teaching typing and commercial courses. So a whole lot of us decided we would take typing. And we took typing. I learned to do the touch system, you know, and that's one of the best things I ever did. I just fell into it because of a good-looking teacher.

Q: Well, I like to hear you say it. As it happened, I did the same thing, not because of the good-looking teacher, but I took it in high school, too. And I've made my living sometimes when there wasn't any other way to do it because I took typing.

Sharp: Well, it's turned out, at postgraduate school, for example, to be a real help because I could type and we always had a typewriter and I still type. A good many times when I've wanted something turned out in a hurry and the yeoman has gotten flustered I'd say, "Get out, get away, and let me sit down and do it." Of course, that sort of shakes them up.

Q: I bet it does.

Sharp: So the Postgraduate School lasted for two years and

then I remember toward the end of the course we got our assignments to where we were going to go next. Well, I wanted to be engineer on one of these new destroyers.

Q: I forgot to ask you. Did you request engineering school?

Sharp: Yes, I think I asked for it. I had two or three choices. This was one of my choices. When the thing came out where we were going to go, they had me lined up to go to one of the old battleships. I think it was the Nevada which was an old reciprocating engine type, the oldest style ship you could possibly find.

Q: And you have learned all these new, modern things.

Sharp: I had learned these modern things and I wanted to go to a destroyer. So this is the first time that I objected to any orders that I had had. I went to Washington and told them I didn't want to go to this ship. I wanted to go to a ship where I used the knowledge that I had gained and would be useful to me and further along engineering. Alexander Sharp, Jr., was a commander, I guess, at that time -- maybe a captain -- in the detail office. So I got him to give a little pressure. So then I got ordered to the Richmond, one of the old light cruisers, with the idea that I stay aboard the Richmond for a year or so and then I'd be qualified to go to a destroyer. It's a commentary on how different things are now. In those days, here I was. I had had a year of engineering in a battleship. I had had a postgraduate course in engineering but I wasn't sufficiently qualified to go to be an engineer of one of their new destroyers because I hadn't had enough experience. Nowadays, they'll take somebody right out of reserve officers training or OSC and give them a four months' course in engineering and put them aboard these much more complicated ships.

Q: Well, they had the time and the people.

Sharp: They had the time and the people -- that's right. And you really had to have a lot of training before you got these jobs. Of course, as a result, everything, I must say, things worked better than they do with less experienced people.

I also remember one incident during postgraduate school. Our class was up for selection to lieutenant and the list came out and my name wasn't on it. This was a Saturday morning that this list came out and my name wasn't on it. So I called Alexander Sharp and said, "What in the world has happened to me here. This lieutenants list is out and I'm not on it." He said, "Of course you're on it." But when he looked, he verified that I was on the list but my name had been omitted from the list that came down to the Naval Academy.

We went to a cocktail party that afternoon after I found out that I was on the list. It was a funny thing. Everybody was sort of shying off . . .

Q: Feeling sorry for you.

Sharp: Feeling sorry for me. They didn't know what to say.

Q: How did you handle it? Did you let them go ahead and feel sorry for you?

Sharp: Oh no, I just told them it was a mistake. So I got aboard the Richmond in June 1936. It was July of '36 and I was the assistant engineer. It was a rather uneventful year. We'd cruise up and down the West Coast.

Q: How did you get from Annapolis to the West Coast?

Sharp: We drove across country.

Q: What was the Richmond part of? What force?

Sharp: She was part of the cruiser force. It wasn't cruiser-destroyer force then. I think it was called Scouting Force or something like that.

Q: And you were living again in San Diego?

Sharp: We were living again in San Diego, right.

Q: So your ties really are pretty much here except for the fact that you were born in Montana.

Sharp: Yes. So we were living in San Diego and I was aboard the Richmond for a year and we went off on some fleet exercises and stuff like that. Then in December of 1937 I was transferred to the Winslow which was DD-359, that was one of the new destroyer leaders, they called it.

Q: Leader?

Sharp: Destroyer leader, yes. It was a big destroyer for those days. I went aboard her as an engineer officer and stayed there for about two or three years. Yes, I stayed there until May of 1940, two years and a half. Each year I won the engineering "E". There was a lot of heavy competition.

Q: Did you ever have to cheat?

Sharp: No, I didn't have to cheat. But we really watched everything. We had to watch everything like mad.

Q: Who was it that said there is first place and then all the rest of the guys and you could do anything you had to do in order to get that first place?

Sharp #1 - 42

Sharp: Well, we really had to watch things. We didn't waste any juice or we didn't waste any steam or water and that sort of thing and we had to have the plant in good shape.

Q: You were well prepared for your job, surely.

Sharp: Yes, pretty well. I had a good crew. I remember one time we were fueling from the Idaho while at sea and we got gyped in the fueling. That really hurt us and we always sounded our tanks very carefully before and after fueling to be sure that we actually got what they said. Well, we thought we got gyped around ten or twelve thousand gallons which was quite a blow. Alexander Sharp was skipper of the Idaho so I sent him a message saying that we had been robbed. He really tore the Engineer Officer apart.

Q: They actually had tried to short . . .

Sharp: I don't know whether they tried to or not but they did and we griped about it over the telephone. So I sent him a message and things really happened and very shortly we got a message saying, "You tell us what you received and we'll take that." And that's what we gave them.

Q: For their records.

Sharp #1 - 43

Sharp: Yes.

Q: Did Admiral Stroop ever tell you his story that when he went out on the Saratoga they almost didn't make it because, according to the engineering officer they had been short-fueled?

Sharp: No. Is that right?

Q: I had never heard of it and he said he was sure it wasn't in the history books but when they went out after Pearl they had been requested to steam an extra night so that they would come in in the morning and the engineering officer went up to the bridge and he said, "We can't make it because that so-and-so always has cheated me . . ."

Sharp: He didn't have as much fuel as he thought he had. No, I never heard that. In a ship as big as the Saratoga they just didn't know what they had. They had so darn many fuel pumps.

Q: So you got the engineering "E" every year you were the engineering officer.

Sharp: Yes. So then in May of 1940 -- I guess it was February 1940 I was told that I was going to be Inspector of Engineering at Milwaukee, Wisconsin. I wrote back to the detail officer and said I didn't want the job. I didn't want to be isolated from the mainstream of the Navy at a time when I was in this stage and wanted to make use of my postgraduate course in some better place.

So as a result of that, I was ordered to the Bureau of Ships. I was to be the Destroyer Engineering Maintenance Officer. This is another time where not accepting orders that you don't like or you didn't think was good for you turned out to be a very useful thing to me because I was ordered then to a good job.

Q: I would have thought that would be a terrible job just to go in some isolated spot.

Sharp: Well, somebody has to take it, but I wasn't going to take it if I could avoid it.

Q: Yes, if you had to go, Okay, but otherwise.

Sharp: Then we drove across continent again and got a house in Arlington from a classmate of ours that was leaving. I stayed in the Bureau of Ships until after World War II broke out. I had destroyer maintenance in what was then the Bureau of Engineering and while I was there they combined engineering and construction and repair and made it the Bureau of Ships. So I had the destroyer machinery desk and the lad that had the destroyer hull desk was R. K. James, who subsequently became the Chief of the Bureau of Ships.

Q: Oh yes, of course.

Sharp: We struck up a friendship that lasted for a long time.

Q: How many destroyers were you responsible for?

Sharp: All the destroyers in the Navy. I don't remember how many there were.

Q: A thousand?

Sharp: Oh no, not that many.

Q: 500?

Sharp: Maybe 500. At that time Admiral, then Lieutenant Commander Rickover was in the electrical division. The head of that division was Commander Libby -- I guess he was Lieutenant Commander Libby -- who is here now and retired. He became a Vice Admiral. There were any number of people in the Bureau at that time who became admirals.

The second year that I was there -- oh no, it was early 1941 we started, or maybe late '40, we started a turnover of 50 destroyers to England and we had to pick out the destroyers that were going to go and get them ready. So there was a lot of planning around about that.

Q: How did you go about selecting?

Sharp: Oh, we selected the ones that were in fairly good shape but still we tried not to take our very best ones.

Q: They weren't necessarily the oldest?

Sharp: Not necessarily the oldest, no. There were a whole stack of old ones that we had to put in when we got into the war. These were not that old, the oldest type. We had a lot of work to do that we were very busy with in getting those ships ready. One thing I remember, we were working hard and there were some British there, you know, sort of working with us to get ready. They would leave for lunch about 11:30 and they'd get back about two o'clock or something like that, having had whatever they drank for lunch.

Q: Too many of whatever it was . . .

Sharp: They weren't much help the rest of the afternoon. And, of course, one of the things we had to do with these ships to get them ready was to have a liquor locker for them. Then we had to separate the living compartments, the crew's living compartments, because they separated their engineering and their deck rates. They had to have more divisions in the thing than we had.

Q: Their enlisted rates had to live in separate quarters?

Sharp: Yes.

Q: One would wonder why.

Sharp: It was just the custom in their Navy and they wanted to stick to it.

Q: Where were these fifty ships turned over?

Sharp: It seems to me they were taken over in Boston and Norfolk and maybe New York. I don't remember.

Q: Not all in one spot.

Sharp: I know there were a lot of them at Boston.

Q: Were you aware of the -- well, of course, you were -- but I was going to ask you what build-up you felt in the Bureau of Ships during this limited emergency for the American Navy, in the numbers or plans for destroyers?

Sharp #1 - 48

Sharp: Well, there was a building program going on, you know, that was a pretty good building program. Roosevelt was in office and he was strong for the Navy, of course.

Q: Were you aware that there was going to be the war? Did you talk about it?

Sharp: Well, there was a war on, of course.

Q: I know.

Sharp: Our ships were participating in escort of convoys in early '41, you know.

Q: I was going to ask. When did that start that we began escorting? It wasn't until after we got in the war, was it?

Sharp: No, it was before we got into the war.

Q: It was?

Sharp: It was in early '41 or mid '41 or something like that. Then December 7th of '41 I was home. Somebody called up and asked if we had been listening to the radio. We hadn't. He said that Pearl Harbor had been attacked. So the first thing we had to do was dig out our uniforms and wear uniforms because we hadn't been wearing them. And then, of course, we went on a much heavier schedule.

Q: How did you feel when you heard the word?

Sharp: Oh, it was just hard to believe, of course, and the information was pretty sketchy and it stayed sketchy. It never did really get filled in on very well. Not like it is now where they cover everything they have. Censorship was pretty darned heavy then. So then things really started to boil and we got busy pushing all the ships, getting them in commission as fast as we could and all that sort of thing. My class at that time was beginning to get command of the older destroyers, the old four-stack destroyers.

Q: You were a lieutenant commander by this time, I guess.

Sharp: Yes, I think I made lieutenant commander in '41 or something like that. I was appointed lieutenant commander for temporary service on 24 December 1941. And then 6 March of '42 I was made a lieutenant commander. Apparently there was temporary service and permanent then. So then in March of -- well, to go back a little bit, almost as soon as the war started I tried to get out of BuShips to get command of a ship. Well, I had a hassle with the Engineer Detail Officer. He wanted me to be engineer of one of these new cruisers that was coming along and I didn't want it. I wanted to be skipper of a destroyer. So I got asked about three times,

"How would you like to be engineer of this ship?" One of them was the <u>Atlanta</u>, one of these lighter cruisers, and I turned all of them down because I was trying to get a destroyer. I was having a heck of a time trying to get broken loose from the engineering routine.

Finally in March of '42, a classmate of mine, Red Yaeger, came to see me one time and said they were forming up a new force called the amphibious force and "I'm going to be the admiral's flag lieutenant, I guess, how would you like to be the flag secretary?" Well, it looked like that was a chance to get out of Washington and get off of this engineering slate so I said, "Okay, I'll do it." So in March of '42 I went down to Norfolk as aide and flag secretary to Commander Amphibious Force, Atlantic Fleet. We had only been there about a month and a half when somebody was killed -- I can't remember. But anyway, an admiral was killed. I think he was swept overboard.

Q: In the Atlantic?

Sharp: Yes, in the Atlantic. And our admiral was detailed to relieve him.

Q: I don't remember an admiral being swept overboard.

Sharp: I can't remember his name now but there was one. And our admiral, Admiral Barnard, I think it was -- so this admiral was killed and Admiral Barnhard had to go to relieve him. And then Admiral Hewitt came along and Admiral Hewitt had his flag secretary so that gave me an opportunity to get sprung. Then, I think it was in May of '42, I got to be skipper of the Hogan. The Hogan was an old, one of the poorest of the old four-pipers that was converted into a minesweeper and I can remember going aboard this thing and remembering that this was one class of ship that we thought we'd never put into commission because they were so poor. They were the Union Iron Works destroyers and they were notorious for being a very poor machinery plant.

Q: You probably wished you had given this one to the British.

Sharp: Yes. Actually, they were a class that we weren't giving to the British because they were so bad.

Q: Where had it been?

Sharp: It had been laid up.

Q: It had been laid up and they re- . . .

Sharp: Yes, and it was being put in commission and made a minesweeper. So we put this old crate into commission in a big hurry and we did a little bit of practice minesweeping in '42 and then we were pulled off of that to be escort with convoys. We escorted freighters down to San Juan and Trinidad and down there and back and then up to Newfoundland and back.

Q: I read some place that the Hogan was described as a high speed destroyer-minesweeper.

Sharp: That's right. That's what they were called.

Q: What was its speed?

Sharp: Oh, 30 knots.

Q: So it still could make a respectable . . .

Sharp: No, wait a minute now, let's see. Not 30 knots because we had to take out two boilers. Well, anyway, they probably made 27.

Q: But still respectable.

Sharp: Yes. And so we escorted convoys. I remember one time going into San Juan one afternoon and this doggone engineering plant was in kind of bad shape and we were supposed to go out the next day. So as I came in, I sent word that we would have to disable our engineering plant in order to make repairs on it. I got word back from the admiral there . . .

Q: I think you might repeat the order you got from the admiral.

Sharp: As we went into San Juan, I sent a message in saying I needed to put my engineering plant out of commission in order to make some repairs and got word back that all ships in San Juan were to stay ready to get underway on a short notice. So I sent word back that I needed to put it out of commission to make some repairs so they sent the same word back again to stay in service. So I got in a boat and went boiling over to the headquarters to see why they were giving me these stupid orders. I saw the Chief of Staff and I said, "Damn it. I've got to put my plant out of commission so I can get underway the next time. I've got to make some repairs." He said, "Well, that's all right. I know your problem but the admiral said to stay in commission." So I said, "Well, let me see the admiral."

So he said, "Okay. You go in and see him." So this was Admiral Hoover. And I went storming in there and I looked at this cold fish and said, "I have got to put this plant out of commission so I can get underway tomorrow."

Q: You were only asking for overnight.

Sharp: Yes. And I said, "There's no way you can fix it without putting it out of commission." So he gave me -- he reluctantly said okay. So I went back aboard the ship and we did it.

Q: Why had he . . .

Sharp: He was just a so-and-so. He has a reputation, always did have a reputation, for being a so-and-so. My boss -- the Force Commander -- was Alexander Sharp, the same fellow.

Q: Is that right.

Sharp: He was then a vice admiral. So when I got back to Norfolk I went over and said, "That stupid ass down in San Juan needs to get squared away." So Alex sent him a message telling him to stop interfering with his ships when they were down there.

Now, let's see -- after convoying in 1942, we prepared for going to Africa for the landings at Casablanca. At that landing, Hogan was going to do minesweeping duties for the first time.

Q: Was this a new type of warfare? Minesweeping?

Sharp: No, no. Not a new type of warfare. They had had mines for a long time, of course, and we used them extensively in many wars but -- this was just an extension of mine warfare. The Amphibious Force was to be preceded by these minesweepers into the anchorage area off Casablanca.

Q: But the whole concept of amphibious warfare was new, wasn't it?

Sharp: It was new, yes. So we spent quite a bit of time getting ready for this and then we were part of the convoy that escorted the ships over to Casablanca. And the night before the landing we swept ahead of the main body into the landing area. We didn't know whether we would get opposition from the French who were occupying their base there at Casablanca or not.

We were told if we were to encounter any opposition we were to come on the radio and say "Play ball," which was the code word for there is opposition which meant it was a new ballgame.

Q: How many minesweepers were there?

Sharp: I guess there probably were at least a squadron, either ten or twelve. Some of them were these converted destroyers and some of them were regular ones. Well, Hogan was up sort of up in the fore of this force and we saw a ship coming in. It was about the size of a minesweeper patrol craft. It came busting right into the formation and as it passed close to the Hogan they shot a few rounds of machinegun fire.

Q: What flag was she flying?

Sharp: Well, it was dark so we couldn't see. And I had to swing the Hogan around to avoid being rammed by the ship. We swung around and I knew that my battery was manned so I opened up on the ship with 20mm machineguns and at the same time yelled "Play ball" on the radio. Very shortly the ship was dead in the water and we left and went on sweeping in ahead of the force. But that was probably the first shots that were fired in that battle.

Q: And you put it out of commission?

Sharp: We put it out of commission, yes. Then we went on and one of the ships in the rear picked it up and boarded it.

Q: That was your first contact with the enemy.

Sharp: Yes. So we went on in and swept all the way in. We had one of the early models of radar, it actually was supposed to be an air search radar but you could get the surface picture fairly well. I can remember that the only radar repairman or operator was an ex-ham radio lad.

Q: Just happened to be there?

Sharp: Well, he was assigned.

Q: He was assigned for that purpose.

Sharp: His training had been ham radio, a ham radio operator. He was pretty good at keeping this piece of equipment going and I depended on him a lot in going in at night and it worked out very well. Anyway, we swept in and the force came in. There were no mines discovered.

Q: Can you tell when you hit a mine?

Sharp: You can usually tell.

Q: And you did not find any.

Sharp: We didn't find any. So we came in without any trouble. The next morning, of course, they started the landing and there was considerable opposition including some from the French battleship -- what was it? The Jean Bart, I think, was in there.

After we got in, then one of the things they did -- we did -- was put a mine field in. I mean the Hogan didn't do it, but we had the mine-layers there and they put down a mine field, presumably to protect our own ships from submarines. After that, all the destroyer types were detailed to patrol the area for submarines.

Q: Outside the harbor?

Sharp: Outside the harbor, yes, but it was pretty much in the open sea and we had this mine field on one side of us, you see, and we patrolled the other. German submarines got into the area and one night we lost about three or four ships from submarines. We got contact with the submarine and chased it but the submarine ran right into the mine field and got away with it. Of course, we couldn't go any farther because we would have been blown up by our own mines. So that fellow got away. We stayed there for quite a few days and then we finally went down to Safi, which was down about 1500 miles south of Casablanca.

Q: Weren't there landings made at several places? At the same time?

Sharp: Yes, landings were made at Port Lyautey and at Safi at the same time they landed at Casablanca. We were down in Safi for two or three days and then came back up to Casablanca and went into the harbor which was full of sunken ships at that time, absolutely loaded with sunken ships.

Q: Do you have any pictures of it?

Sharp: No, I didn't have a camera along. I should have then.

We used to go in there to fuel. We stayed around there for -- I don't know -- maybe a month -- and then came back to Norfolk.

Q: The French had already capitulated by that time?

Sharp: Yes.

Q: What were the commands? The commander of the task force and so on?

Sharp: Well, Admiral Hewitt was commander of the amphibious outfit and the Army commander was Patton.

Q: Oh, was he?

Sharp: Yes.

Q: Jocko Clark refers to it as 150 ship armada.

Sharp: It was a big outfit.

Q: Joined at he said at mont which was the mid-ocean area from which the group then proceeded.

Sharp: I don't remember that, those details.

Q: When you went in to this operation, how much briefing had you been given? How much did you know of what you were going for and your objective or did you just have individual ship orders that said this is what you, the Hogan, is supposed to do?

Sharp: We knew we were headed for Africa for a landing. I don't remember exactly what the orders were. My memory is not very good for that sort of thing.

Q: No, I just wondered if you had had a meeting of all of the commands together or . . .

Sharp: There had been numerous conferences for it but, of course, they didn't put out all of the dope at the conference, naturally. We knew where we were doing because we had the area we had to sweep and all that sort of thing.

So we went back and I guess it was late November or December of '42. Then I got orders to go to the West Coast and be skipper of a new destroyer that was going into commission. So we drove across the continent again and arrived in Long Beach in late December, I guess it was.

Q: Had you enjoyed your tour as commanding officer?

Sharp: Oh yes, sure. It was a lot of fun. It was a lot of fun just keeping the old crate going.

Q: Well, again your experiences as an engineering officer and engineering training probably paid off, didn't it?

Sharp: Yes. I can remember one time. We were in Norfolk Navy Yard in the middle of summer and it was hotter than the dickens and the ventilation blowers in this old ship were direct current. So a direct current motor, if its insulation gets bad, they just go slower and slower. The ventilation was terrible and there was an ammunition scuttle right in the wardroom passageway and I wanted to put a motor with a blower on it to blow air right down the passageway to keep the wardroom cool. So they said they couldn't give us the money for that sort of thing although I could see other ships that wangled it somehow. So I had a friend there that I knew when I was in BuShips. I used to come down and work with this man, this officer, and he was the ship superintendent for our ship, I guess it was. So -- no, I guess he was the planner for that type of ship. One day when it was really hot I invited him down to lunch and we normally ate lunch in our shirt sleeves because it was so darned hot. But this day we put on our blouses and we sat through the lunch and it was really hot. At the end of this thing everybody was soaking wet. But at the end of the lunch I did get a fan for the blower for the wardroom passageway.

Q: There is more than one way to get things accomplished, isn't there?

Sharp: Yes. So we go to the West Coast and visit with my mother and father there. They were then in Rosemead, California, south of Pasadena. We got ourselves a house in Long Beach and I reported as prospective commanding officer of the Boyd (DD-544) in January of '43 and the ship was commissioned, as I recall it, about March perhaps. Then we went through training and so forth. The Boyd was commissioned on the 8th of May, 1943.

After commissioning we had the usual fitting-out period and then trained under Commander Training Command, Pacific Fleet, at San Diego. With our training completed in early July, as I recall it, of '43 we proceeded to Pearl Harbor. We were in Pearl Harbor a short time when we were directed to proceed to Noumea and escort a British carrier back to Honolulu.

Q: And this was just your ship.

Sharp: Yes, just one ship. Just the Boyd.

Q: Was that usual to have just one ship doing escort duty?

Sharp: Well, they use as many ships as they have available but they were short of destroyers as they always are in a war and this wasn't considered to be a very hazardous trip. So we went down and picked up the British carrier which I think was the Victorious, if I'm not mistaken, and escorted her back to Honolulu. Actually this is a part of the darned history that I'm a little foggy on and it's not in here -- not in this book. But in any event, the first big war action that we took part in was the occupation of Baker Island which took place on the 1st of September 1943. We then proceeded and joined the task carriers as a unit of the screen and the first action with the carriers was the Wake Island raid on 5 and 6 October of 1943.

Q: What task group was this?

Sharp: This was either 58.1 or 38.1, depending on whether Admiral Halsey or Admiral Spruance was in command.

The next action after the Wake Island raid was the Gilbert Island landings from the 19th of November until the 8th of December.

Q: Can you describe these actions, that is, as to your part in them? What you thought about it? What you actually did as a participant?

Sharp: On both of these we were a unit in the screen of the carrier task force, actually carrier task group 58.1. We were shifted around a little bit but generally speaking throughout this whole period we were with 58.1 or 38.1 whichever -- they are all the same ships but depending whether the Fifth Fleet or the Third Fleet was . . .

Q: Spruance or Halsey, wasn't it?

Sharp: Yes. After the Gilbert Island landings . . .

Q: I meant though really what you personally felt. You were commanding officer of this ship. Did you have any anecdotes or items of interest that aren't part of the history books already?

Sharp: I think possibly one night would interest -- going back a little bit. When we left San Diego and were headed out to Honolulu on our first sojourn to join up with the forces out there. We had abandon ship drill one day, among other drills, and this is one of the normal drills that they hold.

After this abandon ship drill, I got the officers together and said, "Well, we had an abandon ship drill. I just want it understood that we will never need an abandon ship drill in the _Boyd_ because if we ever leave this ship it will be because she is sinking out from under us and there won't be any organized drill such as abandon ship. You'll get as many boats out as you can and get into whatever you can that floats but the main thing we will do is fight the ship until she goes down." I think that's rather important to understand what attitude was to be in that ship and it certainly was that. And everybody understood it.

Q: That was because the commanding officer felt that way, of course.

Sharp: Yes.

Q: How many people were on board?

Sharp: Let me see -- in the neighborhood of 250, I believe. Yes, in the neighborhood of 250. It varied a little bit, of course, but I think that's roughly correct.

Q: What you are indicating is that you set the tone of the ship right then and you never had occasion, I'm sure, to change it.

Sharp: That's right. After the Gilbert Island landings, we went -- the force we were with -- went by Nauru Island on the 8th of December and bombarded the island without any reply from the island. There were a lot of battleships and cruisers and destroyers and they knew there were Japanese on the island. They tried to spot shore batteries and did a lot of shooting at the island without any particular -- there was no reply so they didn't know whether they hit anything or not.

We had left the island probably two hours when word came back that a plane was down off the island, one of the planes from one of the carriers, and the carriers planes were overhead and they thought they had a man in the water, a pilot. We were ordered to go back and try to rescue the man. The first word was the plane was down about five miles off the island, as I recall, and there didn't seem to be any problem. But as we were on our way in we were in contact with the aviator and he said that the slick was about two miles off the island.

Q: This is the aviator flying overhead?

Sharp: So that brought up the possibility that we were getting pretty close in case there were any shore batteries there. The division commander that was aboard sent a message to the Task Force Commander calling attention to that and the Task Force Commander said to continue on your mission.

Q: And who was that at the time?

Sharp: I think that was Commander Battleships -- Vice Admiral Reed. Well, we went on toward Nauru at 27 or 28 knots and in the meantime we got all our boilers on the line and were ready for -- went to general quarters and we were ready for anything that would happen.

Q: Did everybody on the ship know why you were going in?

Sharp: Yes.

Q: Did you tell them on the loudspeaker?

Sharp: Yes, everybody understood it. We went charging on in about 27 or 30 knots or something like that and the plane was circling overhead and said there was an object in the water. They thought it was a man. And as we pulled up to a spot we could see what looked like a man's arm waving in the water. So as we pulled up alongside I backed down full and we had almost come to a stpo when we could see that this was a float light bobbing around in the water and we just had started up when the shore battery opened up on us and the first shots hit in the forward engine room. The others were quite close. Well, when it hit I rang up flank speed all we could make, and at that time the shore batteries really opened up on us. We started firing back but it was very hard to locate the shore battery. All we could see were the flashes of the gun and I started zig-zagging and chasing the splashes. That is, when the splashes were over on the starboard bow I would turn the ship toward the splashes and hope that the gunner would try to correct his shot and I would be over where the fall shot was last time.

This worked fairly well. We didn't get hit again although we did have some close ones. We finally chased along this way and got out of range of the guns. By this time we had found out that the forward engine was out of commission. The steam lines had been pierced by the shells and the forward engineroom was full of steam. We had been going full blast and the boilers were pouring steam into those engines because we didn't realize at first that it was out of commission.

So we right away had a big job to do. The chief engineer who was down in the forward engineroom was able to get up the hatch but apparently when he opened the hatch the steam from the engineroom went up the hatch and he inhaled so much steam that he just got up and fell on deck and died right away.

There were about twelve to fifteen people down in the engineroom and, of course, it was extremely hot down there. They apparently tried to get down in the bilges to get out of the heat but they were all killed. The engineroom was filling up with water fairly fast. The forward engineroom was the only place where we had any penetration of the hull. It finally filled up about three-quarters of the way with water and we got the lines isolated and all that and continued on at a slower speed to rejoin our task group. Meanwhile trying to pump out the engineroom and plug up the holes and we soon found we couldn't plug up the holes until we had a chance to stop and put somebody over the side.

So about -- this must have been around noon that this happened, I guess. I finally joined the Task Group about two or three o'clock in the afternoon or something like that. We went alongside the flagship and got some medical assistance. In the meantime, our doctor had been doing operations down on the wardroom table and had pretty well bandaged up all the

the people that had flesh wounds from shrapnel.

The chaplain came over from the battleship and gave the last rites on the people that we hadn't been able to get out of the engineroom. We decided to go off and have a burial at sea. The chaplain couldn't stay with the ship so we went on off and I performed the burial -- I guess it was the next morning that we did that, either that evening or the next morning -- I can't remember.

Q: Were the bodies left down there until time for it?

Sharp: We got them out as soon as we could get the engineroom pumped out. So it was the next day, I guess, when we had the burial at sea.

Q: You let men over the side to put a temporary patch on and then you were able to . . .

Sharp: Yes, while we were alongside. The first lieutenant, who was Lieutenant Anderson, went over the side and patched up, put a plug in the hole. So we had a burial at sea in which I acted as the Catholic chaplain. After that we were told to join the Denver.

Q: Before we leave the thought, a couple of questions. What do you think of having a ship with as many men on it as you had going to pick up an aviator?

Sharp: Of course, what people didn't recognize in this action was that there were shore batteries there and I think it was rather careless of the Task Force Commander to just simply say continue on your mission to the division commander when he questioned whether it was the right thing to do. The aviator on the spot should have been able to tell -- it was broad daylight after all -- whether or not there was really a survivor there. If there was no survivor, there wasn't any sense in sending this destroyer in that close to the beach.

Q: Even if that had been really just one man.

Sharp: If there had been one man, you would still have to question whether that was the right thing to do. But I would say on balance, you should probably at least send a boat in there because there is no use just leaving a man and we weren't certain that there were shore batteries that could bear on that spot.

Q: How did you feel -- I'm thinking now really of yourself as a participant. Here you are the commanding officer and you're going in and to have this damage -- Can you tell me how you felt aside from what actually happened as these various things progressed?

Sharp: Well, I was just doing the job I was being trained to do, that's all. There wasn't any particular feeling to it.

Q: You weren't mad because he gave you these orders?

Sharp: Oh, no. There wasn't any use in being concerned about the orders. When you get in a situation like that you don't worry about the orders, you worry about what you do next, not what you were told to do.

Q: And when the ship was hit though, what then was your reaction?

Sharp: The reaction then was to shoot back at what was shooting at us and get the heck out of there, because it was obvious that we were in a very dangerous position.

Q: Was this your own idea of following the splash and zigzagging out or had that been part of training?

Sharp: No, that was just -- I had heard of that being done and did it because it seemed like the best thing to do.

Q: It seemed that it was. Now, when you served as chaplain, what were your reactions?

Sharp: Oh well, of course, I was burying some very good friends and some good shipmates so it was a sad occasion.

Q: It must have been a terribly distressing situation.

Sharp: It was a distressing situation. I must say I was a little bit unhappy that the battleship couldn't spare a chaplain to participate in a service that important.

Q: I would think so. Fourteen or fifteen men, did you say?

Sharp: Yes.

Q: What did you read from a . . .

Sharp: I read from a burial service. I got him to tell me what to do.

Q: At least he told you what to read. That would have seemed to be, as I read the rest of your career, perhaps the most tragic experience that you had, as far as our own men are concerned.

Sharp: Yes. After this it was obvious that the ship was in pretty bad shape and had to get into a shipyard, because the starboard engine had been run until it froze.

Q: Is that where the hit was?

Sharp: The hit was in the starboard engine, yes. Then we ran the thing until the bearings froze just from lack of lubrication.

Q: What was the attitude on the ship then? What was the morale like? How did the men feel? Did you talk to them?

Sharp: The men were distraught, of course, about losing their shipmates but this was war and that's the way things go.

Q: I wondered it you had talked to all of them or had any occasion to?

Sharp: Oh, I walked around the decks and talked to various people and the exec was all over the ship.

Q: You were a very young man still in those days.

Sharp: Oh, I was a lieutenant commander.

Q: So then you had to go back and have some repairs.

Sharp: We returned to Espiritu Santo in the New Hebrides and got some patches put on the ship and I believe we had the starboard propeller re moved. Yes, I'm sure we did. We went into drydock and got patches -- permanent patches -- on the holes and got the prop off and got the wiring fixed up satisfactory so we could get back to San Francisco. I guess we were in Espiritu Santo for perhaps ten days or something like that. Then we went on out with the Denver. The

Denver had been in a big action and I believe that some of her machinery was out of commission, too.

So we went back. We were supposed to escort the Denver. Actually we were escorting each other pretty much.

Q: The engine wasn't removed then?

Sharp: No. They couldn't do that. Every now and then going back our steering gear would go out because of the defective wiring. At that point the ship would start running in circles. So I sent a signal to the Denver saying, "Excuse my circles. I'll be with you shortly." And we'd get together again and go on.

Q: Did you actually go in circles, complete a circle?

Sharp: Well, with only one engine and no rudder or the rudder going the wrong way, why you're bound to go in a circle. You can't steer with your engines gone.

Q: Well, how did you correct it then?

Sharp: We'd get the steering gear fixed. So we went on in to Mare Island and got in there in December of '43 and stayed there until I guess it was March of '44, getting repaired. This did give us a chance to let the men see their families.

Most of the families came up to Mare Island and we had a chance to give some people some leave and also we got some improvements in the ship, including a new combat information center.

The use of radar, of course, was really just started at the beginning of World War II and very few ships had radar in the early part of the war. As the war went on, they began to see that they had to have some kind of a center where all of the radar information came in along with all the other information and they could use that to put the ship into the most advantageous position for action. Actually, also they used the radars to control our fighter aircraft to intercept other fighters -- enemy fighters and all that sort of thing. It was obvious that they had to have some kind of a center for us so they got up this combat information center and we had one of the first makeshift combat information centers in the Boyd. It turned out that in the future it was going to be very useful to us.

We got the best radars that they had at that point. We got back to Pearl Harbor on the 23 March, 1944 and again joined Task Force 58. The first action we were in after that was the Hollandia landing on the 21st to the 24th of April. I don't remember that there was anything out of the ordinary.

Q: You were operating with the Seventh Fleet then, were you not, when you went down in Australia -- New Guinea, rather?

Sharp: Seventh Fleet? No, we were in the Fifth Fleet. Seventh Fleet was landing there but Task Force 58 was supporting it.

Q: I see. Was Mitscher the commanding officer then? I mean in charge of the carriers?

Sharp: I don't remember who was in charge of the carriers then. Mitscher, I guess. After the Hollandia landings, then, the next job was the Truk, Satawan, and Panope raid which took place 21 April to 1 May.

Q: Would you be kind enough to say those names again?

Sharp: Truk, Satawan, and Ponape. These are all islands around Truk.

Q: I knew all of them but Satawan was a new name for me.

Sharp: The next thing that came off -- I guess after those raids we probably went back to some place like Ulithi. I don't recall that now but probably we went back to Ulithi and stayed there for maybe four or five days for repairs and re-provisioning and a little bit of recreation time. Then we went off for the Saipan landings which took place from the 11th to 24th of June. Of course, during these landings we had numerous raids going on. There was a raid going on up in the Bonins and it seems to me on this one we went by -- I can't remember what islands were hit in the Bonins -- but generally speaking on this the Boyd was just out in the screen of the carriers.

Then there was the Battle of the Philippine Sea on 19 and 20 June.

Q: Are you not skipping when you sank the Japanese transport?

Sharp: When was that?

Q: The 15th of June.

Sharp: Yes. That was during the first Bonin raid then.

Q: Admiral Clark tells about that in his book.

Sharp: Did he?

Q: Yes, and I think he says that some of the fighters or torpedo airplanes, anyway, hit it, the Taksukawa Maru, and that the Charette and the Boyd then sank her.

Sharp: Went off and sank the craft, yes.

Q: Could you expand on that?

Sharp: We were just detailed to go off and get rid of her.

It was sort of a target practice. There wasn't too much to it. We were out on that side of the screen so we were just detailed to go off and sink it. We shot it up and it sank rather quickly. We went and picked up the survivors and hauled them back to a transport, I guess. I can't recall what we did with them.

Q: I think a lot of them went on the carrier.

Sharp: Maybe they went on the carrier, yes.

Q: Do you recall the rescuing of them and whether they would let themselves be rescued? One hears the story many times that the Japanese didn't want to be rescued. Did you see any experience with that?

Sharp: I don't recall it. I don't recall any of them not wanting to be rescued. There might have been. That sort of thing never impressed me very much. We just picked up as many as wanted to be picked up. I think we got them all, as I recall it.

Q: Did you interrogate any of them or your intelligence officer?

Sharp: No, we didn't have a Japanese speaker.

Q: So your job was to pick them up and take them some place. Also I think this incident of picking up Commander Price occurred. I have the date of that as the 23rd of June.

Sharp: 23rd of June.

Q: Have we gotten to that yet?

Sharp: No. The Battle of the Philippine Sea was on the 19th and 20th of June and during most of these battles we were out on radar picket duty. We would be sent out 15 or 20 miles from the carriers and use our radar to watch for enemy planes and often had a fighter CAP (Combat Air Patrol) under our control. If any enemy showed up we would direct the fighters to the intercept.

Q: How far ahead on the surface would your radar take you in advance of the twenty miles?

Sharp: Oh, another 15 miles or so.

Q: So really you were out 35 miles ahead of the task force, weren't you?

Sharp: No, we were out maybe -- I don't remember -- it could have been as far as 50 miles. It was some place in that general neighborhood. Actually, we got out far enough that you could maintain good communications with the carriers but still be out as far as useful. We liked to be out far enough to be darned sure that we weren't going to get involved in getting shot at when they started shooting the airplanes. Because sometimes if you are with six, eight or ten miles, you are apt to have shots falling on you all the time.

Q: From your own group.

Sharp: From your own group. The battle of the Philippine Sea, of course, was a big day. Quite a battle in which our people just really did the Japanese in. There were some losses, of course, including this -- no, I guess this Lieutenant Commander Price had been lost in an earlier raid. As I recall it, he was the Air Group Commander from one of the small carriers.

Q: Cowpens.

Sharp: Cowpens? Yes. Well anyway, our Task Group, I guess it was 58.1 -- this was when Admiral Clark was in command. He had been in command all the time. We devoted one whole day to searching an area that they knew the general vicinity where Price had gone in. The planes had been out all day long and just about before sundown the planes had all come back and landed and we were out on screen station. One of my look-outs reported that he saw a boat in the water or a raft. So we dashed over to this object and sure enough here was a man in one of these little rubber rafts and he was looking away from us and didn't see us until we were right alongside of him. This was Lieutenant Commander Price. He had been in the water for 11 days. We got him aboard and he was in fairly good shape.

Q: Was he able to climb up a ladder?

Sharp: Yes, people got down to help him up the ladder but he was in quite good shape. He said that he had been able to to catch a seagull and had eaten the seagull which kept him going pretty well.

Q: I'm sure you'd eat anything under those circumstances.

Sharp: The doctor looked him over and said he was in good shape and we were told to take him to come carrier. So we went over to the carrier and transferred him by high line.

So the battle of Philippine Sea was from 19 to 20 June. And the next thing we did was do another raid on the Bonins on the 24th of June. Then cruised around again there off Saipan and then went back again for a raid on the Bonins on the 3rd and 4th of July. I remember on the 4th of July we were detailed along with a couple of other destroyers to go in and bombard Iwo Jima. We went in and shot at Iwo Jima for a while. This is almost like recreation for these people when they've been around for a long time and haven't been doing any particular shooting to go in and get a little shore bombardment in. So this was lots of fun.

Q: Well, you weren't shot back at.

Sharp: No. So now we're up to the 4th of July and of course the Saipan landing had been going on there now. We went -- at one point, we went in and anchored off Saipan for a while and also steamed up and down Saipan. I remember going alongside a tanker to fuel off Saipan. The tanker would steam along in sort of a big race track pattern and the destroyer would go alongside and fuel while he was going around in this race track.

Q: Of course, that was one of the devices by which we were able to carry out into the far distances of the Pacific, wasn't it, because of these service squadrons?

Sharp: Yes, we had all the fuel and provisions and everything right along with us. I remember one time the <u>Boyd</u> was out 89 days.

Q: Goodness. Operating constantly?

Sharp: Yes. Then we would go in and stay three days and go out again for 75 days.

Q: That must have been a terrific physical drain.

Sharp: No, it wasn't any grind at all.

Q: You make it sound as though it wasn't difficult.

Sharp: Well, actually, it was fairly easy because you were out steaming around all the time but everybody knew what they were doing and the weather was pretty good and nice and warm. You just steamed around and acted as a screen for these big ships. One of the jobs the destroyers used to have was running around delivering and getting mail from some place. Or they would have mail that they wanted to have distributed around or provision or parts or anything like that. And the destroyers were always dashing around after some ship and getting the mail or something and delivering it around to 16 other ships.

Q: What would your day's activity be like?

Sharp: One of the things that some of the destroyers would be doing would be going around to one ship after the other all the time passing mail or pieces of something or other. But generally speaking, about half an hour before sunrise everybody went to general quarters and got up and went to general quarters and stayed at general quarters until well after daylight. Planes started flying just at daylight. They didn't fly at night. Then you'd go through a regular day or you'd be just screening or you'd be delivering things or you'd maybe have a gunnery shoot or practice or you might be involved in some kind of a raid.

Q: Did you ever have a recreation period?

Sharp: Oh, you just ran through the day and people who were not on watch could do whatever they wanted to. Sometimes people who weren't on watch were repairing the gear. They had to keep it repaired all the time.

Q: With that kind of operation and 90 days stretch it would seem to me that you would have constant underway repairs.

Sharp: Oh yes, there would be repairs and sometimes you'd have to get permission to put a boiler out of commission for a while to clean it and all this sort of thing. Then every second or third day you had to fuel from somebody, either a carrier or a tanker or a battleship. Then you'd get provisions every now and then.

Q: Did you ever have any personnel problems?

Sharp: No, not really. Oh, somebody would get out of hand every now and then but most of the time . . .

Q: Probably in wartime there was probably less tendency to have trouble because of the motivation.

Sharp: That's right and there wasn't any way to get into trouble unless it was, you know, getting smart with the chief petty officer or something like that might get somebody in trouble. Generally, you just didn't have any trouble that wasn't settled down at a very low level.

Q: Did you have to have mast?

Sharp: Oh yes, we had mast.

Where are we now -- we got the Saipan landings done. The next thing, I guess, was the invasion of Guam which took place on the 12th of July to the 15th of August. I remember before they invaded Guam they used to send us -- I mean Guam was being hit by the planes all the time. And every now and then they'd send us down to go around Guam and do a little shooting at various targets around the island.

Q: But you weren't shot back at.

Sharp: No, I can't remember any time. I can remember one time seeing a mount trained on us following us along but they didn't shoot. There was such overwhelming power there that if the people started shooting, why they knew they just were going to get shellacked, you see, so we had them pretty well cowed.

So the invasion of Guam goes on from 12 July to 15 August. I think during that time we went off and did another raid. There were three or four carrier task groups in the Fleet at that time and one group would stay supporting the amphibious landings, or maybe two or three. And another group would go off and do a raid. We went off for a raid on Palau, Yap and Ulithi. I guess we were going into Majuro first and then . . .

Q: Ulithi we already had at that time, didn't we?

Sharp: I thought we did, too. Anyway, Palau and Yap, I guess, we went off for a raid on the 25th to 27th of July. Then we went up again to the Bonins on the 4th and 5th of August. Then we went back down to Palau.

Q: I heard say on that operation at the Bonins that this task group destroyed an entire Japanese convoy.

Sharp: That could be. This must have been the planes. I'm hazy about the whole thing. We were just mostly . . .

Q: Well, you've done so much since then anyway.

Sharp #1 - 87

Sharp: Where were we now?

Q: Then I have that it was the destroyers who sank three Japanese craft on the 3rd of August.

Sharp: It was at this maru that we . . .?

Q: No, it would apparently have been three patrol craft -- patrol surface craft.

Sharp: I don't remember. We must not have been in it.

Q: Some of these destroyers would have been in this particular screen.

Sharp: Oh gosh, in one screen there would probably be two squadrons a piece.

Q: Sixteen?

Sharp: Sixteen to twenty. There were destroyers all over the place.

Q: You didn't ever run into each other.

Sharp: No, we were fairly . . . Oh, they did collide now and then but we never had any problem that way. We were very, very careful. We used to take great delight when we had to change orientation of the screen, why it meant the destroyers had to swing around and all. And we took great delight in swinging around as fast as we could so the other guy would have to swing around as fast as he could. But it was just a good snappy maneuver and we were always careful to not get involved in any collision situation. But by that time they had been doing this so long, it was just second nature.

Q: By that time they must have been extremely sophisticated, having worked together that long.

Sharp: Yes, we had been doing this so long that they were just a fine group of ships. Every now and then a new destroyer would join up and they'd take time to get them broken in and we finally got them broken in, too. You'd have to watch them at first.

Let's see, the next thing was the occupation of the southern Palaus, 9 to 24 September. We must have gone into port some time here and reprovisioned and so forth. But as I told you, they'd stay out for 50 or 60 days and as long as 89, which was the longest we ever stayed out. The southern Palaus 9 to 24 September -- that would have just been another raid at that time. And then they landed at Moratai on the 15th of September.

Q: In your mind did these kind of blend together because all the islands looked alike and all the raids were much the same?

Sharp: Oh, sometimes the action was fairly hot and sometimes we were just screening when the planes went in. And sometimes it was fairly hot. I was trying to recall the strikes against Okinawa on the 10th of October or it was on for most of them the 11th and 14th. The 11th and 14th of October was the time that we were sent up -- let's see, we had gone into Manus some place here for a few days and then we went up and they did a strike on Okinawa and then -- but as I recall it, the first strike was against, or the strike that we participated in was against Formosa. The Japs came out and one afternoon, as I recall it, our planes had all landed and out comes a Jap Betty (bomber) and torpedoes that -- let's see, the first one to be torpedoed was the Houston or maybe it was the Canberra. That's right, I guess the first one was the Canberra. So the Canberra was out of commission and couldn't stay with the speed so a couple of destroyers and the Canberra went off to sort of head back towards Manus or wherever they were going. The Houston went into the slot that the Canberra had left and the next night, by golly, they came out and got the Houston.

Q: Not really.

Sharp: Yes. Then we were detailed to screen the Houston and I recall that on the Houston they were pretty well banged up. They ordered a lot of people to abandon ship, apparently. They got part of the crew to abandon ship and the darned people started jumping over the side. Fortunately, it was moonlight and they had all these darned people in the water all over the place.

Q: Had someone mistakenly given the order to abandon ship?

Sharp: Well, I don't know if it was mistaken or not, but anyway they were going over the side and the ship was dead in the water and drifting. We were told to go ahead and pick up these survivors. My gosh, they were all over the place so we finally decided that since the ship was drifting, we'd just go up wind where the first people had jumped over the side and we'd stop and we'd drift down and sweep through the place. So we did that and we picked up three hundred and sixty-some people, as I recall.

Q: In boats?

Sharp: On no, we just drifted down and picked them up by putting nets over the side.

Q: Oh, nets.

Sharp: Yes.

Q: Just like you were catching fish.

Sharp: Oh no, we just put a cargo net hanging on the side.

Q: Oh, and they'd grab ahold.

Sharp: They'd grab ahold of the cargo net as the ship came on. I guess we had some swimmers out. We might have had a boat or so out, I don't know. But mostly we just swept right down through the water where they had been when they jumped off the ship and picked them up by sweeping through the same water and drifting just like the Houston, you see. We got an awful lot of people and we kept them aboard that night and the next day we delivered them to some cruiser. I can't remember the name of the cruiser now. Quite a few of them -- well, the cruiser subsequently got into a battle and some of these people were killed aboard the cruiser. Anyway, then Halsey directed the cruiser Boston and Boyd and four or five other destroyers to take these two damaged cruisers and head on back towards Manus, I guess. I can't remember where we were going. But anyway, they called us the streamlined bait group because the rest of the carriers went on south of us and we were the most northern group left and they thought that the Japanese might come out and go after us and then they would come back and get a good shot at the Japanese. But they never did. We did have a few . . .

Q: But you were also going slower.

Sharp: We were going slower, yes. We did have a few minor raids on us but they weren't anything too bad. So we finally got these craft headed back to wherever we were going. I can't remember now whether it was Ulithi or Manus. But anyway, we turned them over and then I think at that point that was about the last thing that I participated in as the skipper of the Boyd. From there we went back to Guam which by then had been occupied. I went into Guam in November. In November 1944 I was detached.

Q: While you were on the Boyd you received two silver stars for gallantry in action against the Japanese and I know that one of them was for the supposedly downed aviator off Naru. What was the second one?

Sharp: Well, let's see, what was it? I can't find it. Oh, the other silver star was for this escort of the two damaged cruisers off of Formosa in October of '44.

Q: I wish you would read what the citation says.

Sharp: I'd have to dig it out. I don't know where it is. I've probably got it around here some place. We can throw that into the thing later, can't we?

Q: Yes, I'd like to make it part of the manuscript.

Sharp #1 - 93

Sharp: So anyway, we went back to Guam. As I recall it, we went back as part of a task group and I had my relief aboard at that point.

Q: Didn't you hate to give up command of the Boyd or did you feel that you had had enough of that tour?

Sharp: Oh, I didn't like to give up command. Of course, nobody likes to give up command but I had had a fairly full cruise on the ship. It was just part of the job. I don't have strong feelings about things like that. I mean I just take them in stride.

Q: Well, I think that's part of your training.

Sharp: Yes, sure.

Q: I think it would stand in the way of your being a good naval officer if you let yourself have feelings related to things of this sort.

Sharp: Right. One interesting thing. Here I had had this doggone ship for all this time and I had probably gone alongside carriers and oilers and everything else, gosh, 300 times I suppose and never had any trouble. And here it was, I was just about to be relieved and we had a job to go alongside a carrier one night for some reason. I can't remember what it was -- to transfer something. So I asked my relief if he wouldn't like to try to bring the ship alongside and he said, "Sure." So he proceeded with me watching him very carefully. As we got right up close, why he was too damned close and I could just see that mast getting ready to get tangled up in the carrier. So I said, "I'll take it", and moved off and kept it from then on.

Q: Wouldn't that have been horrible?

Sharp: I could just see myself going into Guam with a wiped-out mast after all this time. But anyway . . .

Q: I'm just curious to get a picture of that. Which side of your ship was to what side of the carrier?

Sharp: Well, you go alongside of either side.

Q: I know, but I meant in that particular instance.

Sharp: In that particular case it was our port side.

Q: Your port side was to their starboard side? And so you had to give a hard right to stay away from it.

Sharp: Yes.

Q: Did that shake him up? Your relief?

Sharp: Oh, I don't know if it shook him up or not.

Q: Did they give court martials or inquiries on that sort of thing during the war?

Sharp: You mean for minor collisions?

Q: Collision.

Sharp: Oh no.

Q: It would have been minor even if he had touched it?

Sharp: Yes. No, they didn't pay any attention to them.

Q: I wouldn't think they could.

Sharp: Not unless you did it too many times.

Q: And then you just got relieved, I imagine.

Sharp: So that's the end of the Boyd as far as I was concerned and then I was detached in Guam and went up and caught an airplane and got back to Pearl Harbor. At that time, I knew I was going to go to Commander Destroyers Pacific, who was in Guam -- I mean in Honolulu -- as Combat Information Center and Radar Officer. I was to get a month's leave before I reported. Well, I got to Honolulu and stayed there about half a day and went right on through. I didn't even go over to see Commander Destroyers. They were a little bit upset that I had gone through without going over to see him. But they got over it.

Q: Who was that then?

Sharp: Oh, at that time it must have been Admiral Blandy, possibly. Maybe Admiral Hainsworth. I think probably he had gone by then. Well anyway, I went back and came back to San Diego. Pat was living in San Diego at that time. We spent about -- almost a month in San Diego and I went back to Honolulu and reported in there in January I guess it was, on the staff. This was January of '45. I stayed there until . . .

Q: I have July '48.

Sharp: We stayed in Honolulu though until sometime in early '46, as I recall it. Something like April of '46. We stayed there until the war was over, of course. I was out there in Honolulu when the war was over. We stayed on there for a few months until we got things pretty well organized and then the staff in a destroyer tender moved back to San Diego. We were there then until -- well, it's been there ever since.

Q: It was right outside my window.

Sharp: Outside your window?

Q: I was on the Navy pier. Not really outside my window but I could always see the   . In fact, I was there in '48.

Sharp: It seems to me I became operations officer.

Q: That was about the longest tour you had had any place up 'til now.

Sharp: Yes. During that time I shifted from CIC officer to operations. Then in . . .

Q: Can you tell me something about what those duties were? Besides the titles?

Sharp: Out in Honolulu the CIC officer and radar officer were involved in seeing to the better functioning of CIC, Combat Information Centers, and actually shortly after I got out there I was involved with the CIC Center at Camp Catlin with designing the CIC for the first picket destroyers, radar picket destroyers. Remember the DDRs? We gave them a design, gave Washington a design on how the radar should be -- the console should be set into place so that they could best do the fighter directing and all that sort of thing.

Q: They directed the guns as well as all of it. As I recall seeing them, they did all of the fighting and all of the battle information intelligence came into this line.

Sharp: Yes, it came into there. That's right.

Q: How anyone was able to read it, I've never been able to figure.

Sharp: That was the first real good design of CICs that we still have today.

Q: And you designed that?

Sharp: Oh no, I didn't design it but I was part of the team that made recommendations on the design for the radar picket destroyers.

Q: Well, again your engineering experience and training was invaluable wasn't, it?

Sharp: Yes. Well, let's see now . . .

Q: That was your main activity while you were in Pearl?

Sharp: Yes.

Q: And then when you came back to San Diego, what?

Sharp: I came back and took over as operations at some point there, I don't know just when. We were looking after the operations of all destroyers in the force and of course that was the time when we were having a big reduction in personnel and a big reduction in ships and we had ships running around with very few people on them. In fact, we'd have to strip one ship in order to send another ship out to sea. It was a pretty grim time.

Q: I was wondering if you had anything to do with the reduction of the force.

Sharp: Oh yes. We had to decide what ships we were going to use and which ones we had to tie up alongside of a pier.

Q: Which ones you were going to put into mothballs?

Sharp: Yes, we had to decide that, too. So it was busy. I

stayed there until '48, I think it was May of '48, wasn't it, I went over . . .

Q: I have July.

Sharp: July? Okay, July.

Q: Anyway the middle of the year.

Sharp: San Diego. July of '49 I was commanding officer of Sonar School which now is called the ASW School. In July of '49 I was ordered to the War College.

Q: Are you going to skip that year when you were commanding officer of the Fleet Sonar School?

Sharp: Oh, not to skip it but . . . I was a pretty routine year. We were just training sonar men.

Q: Wasn't that in the development stage at that time?

Sharp: Oh no, sonar had been -- was pretty well developed.

Q: I mean the school itself. It seems to me that it grew a lot during that period.

Sharp: The school was growing but it was a well-established school. It was a very interesting job but it was nothing out of the ordinary.

Q: You felt it was a training job?

Sharp: It was a training job, yes. It was a good thing to have in my record and very useful to me and I think I was useful to the school.

Q: There's no question about that. Were they using the consoles in training that you had helped design out in Pearl?

Sharp: No, we didn't design consoles. We were just designing the arrangement of the CICs. Now, this is a different thing. This Pearl thing didn't have to do with the sonar at all. This was chiefly radar.

Q: That was mostly radar and this when you go into ASW, of course, by its name is underwater.

Sharp: No, that was a very interesting time and very useful and being in San Diego was very pleasant. Our children were going to school.

Q: We've only spoken of one child and I know you have another.

Sharp: That's right. We didn't mention Grant, who was born in 1939 here in San Diego. By now, he was in about the seventh or eighth grade or something like that and my daughter was graduated from high school while we were there in San Diego and started going to college. She went to San Diego State College for a year and then we went to Newport to the War College and she went to Rhode Island University for a year. Then we went back to the West Coast and she enrolled in UCLA and she stayed there until she graduated.

Q: So you have the two children -- a girl and a boy.

Sharp: Yes.

Q: And your son, I know, is in the Navy now.

Sharp: Yes, he's a lieutenant commander right now.

Q: And Mrs. Sharp said that you went back for the commissioning of his new ship.

Sharp: Yes.

Q: I'm sure you got a kick out of that.

Sharp: Yes, it was very nice. Well, we've just about run out of tape.

Q: Yes, I know and we were just getting into a phase of your duties which, aside from the War College, picks up in Korea. So far, you've had battle experience off North Africa and all through the Pacific.

Sharp: Now we're getting into Korea.

Q: So shall we stop here for this time?

Sharp: Yes, I think we ought to.

Q: Thank you.

Sharp #2 - 104

Interview No. 2 with Admiral U.S. Grant Sharp
Place: At his home in San Diego
Date: 1 November 1969
Subject: Biography
By: Etta Belle Kitchen

Sharp: I was detached from duty as commanding officer of the fleet sonar school in July of '49 and proceeded to the Naval War College at Newport for a year under instruction. The year at Newport was very useful to me. It gave me a chance to get a lot of reading done and to talk to people about strategy and generally get up on basic government policy and Navy policy and joint policy, which was to be very useful to me. I graduated from the War College in June '50 . . .

Q: Were there any unusual incidents that happened other than what you might consider your usual curriculum?

Sharp: I don't think really. We had a lot of good lectures, of course, and many panel discussions and it was just a typical War College course. I think the Naval War College is an excellent institution. It was a great help to me.

Q: Were there any officers there other than U.S. Navy?

Sharp: Yes, there were Air Force officers there and Army officers, some Coast Guard officers, some Royal Navy officers, and I made quite a few friends there that I saw many times later in life.

Q: That's always helpful, too.

Adm. S.: Yes, it was.

Q: To know the people you're working with certainly gives you a different mental approach to things you hear of them, about them, or that you actually know they are saying and doing.

Adm. S.: That's right. Well, next we left the War College in June of 1950. We were traveling across the continent by automobile when we heard that South Korea had been invaded. Incidentally, I had received my orders to be a destroyer squadron commander and that's why I was en route to San Diego to relieve the destroyer squadron commander . . .

Q: Was it the same one that you did command in Korea -- Destroyer Squadron Five?

Adm. S.: Yes, it was Destroyer Squadron Five. That's right. So we got to San Diego in July of 1950, after traveling across continent, and, incidentally, en route, stopping for a short visit in Fort Benton, Montana, which was the town where I went to primary and high school and from which I went to the

Naval Academy. My only comment on that was that it just further demonstrated to me that I was very fortunate to go to the Naval Academy.

Q: Yes, I can imagine.

Adm. S.: So in July of 1950 I assumed command of Destroyer Squadron Five in San Diego, and settled our family in a rented house in La Jolla. In mid-July of 1950, we departed San Diego with one division of my squadron and sailed to the Western Pacific.

Q: Which division was it?

Adm. S.: It was Destroyer Division 51.

Q: The Rowan, the Gurke, Henderson, and the Sutherland -- are those the correct names?

Adm. S.: Yes, Rowan, Gurke, Henderson, and Sutherland. I guess that's right.

Q: Which one were you on?

Adm. S.: I was in the Rowan. We stopped in Honolulu for a couple of days, and then went on to either Yokosuka or Sasebo, I can't remember which.

Q: Were you briefed in Pearl Harbor on the situation and what to expect?

Adm. S.: We were briefed onthe war. That's right.

Q: By whom?

Adm. S.: By Commander-in-Chief, Pacific Fleet, staff.

Q: Admiral Radford?

Adm. S.: No. It was not Admiral Radford. Some of his . . .

Q: Oh, by his staff?

Adm. S.: By his staff, yes.

Q: I see. Did you know what to expect?

Adm. S.: Well, we knew there was a war going on and we were going out to get in it. So we went on out, then, to - perhaps we stopped in Yokosuka, probably did, and then sailed to Sasebo. In any event, in early August we were in Sasebo getting ready to go up and join the forces off Korea. We were about to sail - I wish I knew where it was - for and join a carrier task group off the east coast of Korea, one morning in - I guess it was mid-August when that happened, when the flag lieutenant of Commander, Seventh Fleet, wanted to see me, and this was Vice Admiral Struble. I told the flag lieutenant that I was supposed to get under way at 8:30 - it was now about 8 o'clock - and take my division up off the coast of Korea, and I thought I should go ahead and do this and not go over to the flagship. Well, the flag lieutenant said the Admiral said he wanted to see me and he wanted me to come over. So I got in a boat and went over to - held up the division from sailing - got in a boat and went over to the flagship. There I was met by Captain Bill Terrell, who was the - I guess he must have been the assistant chief of staff, plans and operations. He might even have been the chief of staff. Bill had been an instructor at the war College and I knew him quite well. We'd also been shipmates in the old Saratoga. Bill said that the Admiral wanted to talk to me, so we went in to see Admiral Struble. Admiral Struble asked me what planning experience I'd had, and I told him I was a graduate of the Naval War College, but other than that I hadn't had any planning experience. He said, after conferring with Bill Terrell for a few minutes, he said, "Turn your squadron over to your senior commanding officer and pack a bag and come over to the flagship. We need you for temporary additional duty." Well, I complained mildly that I thought I should take my squadron, but he said, "No, we need you, you just turn your squadron over to your senior skipper." So I said, "For what length of time shall I pack a bag?" He said, "We don't know, but it might be a month."

So I went over to the ship, turned the squadron over to the senior commanding officer, packed a bag, and came back over to the flagship.

Q: What grade were you then?

Adm. S.: I was a captain. We were only there a short time when we were told that we were flying to Yokosuka that afternoon - or perhaps it was Tokyo. In any event, we went over to a carrier that was in port and there got aboard a - I guess we boarded a helicopter - and went over to the airfield - no, it wasn't an aifield. I guess we got in a helicopter and flew up to Iwakuni, and there got in a plane and flew to Atsugi. From Atsugi we went to Tokyo, as I recall. Yes, we went to Tokyo. I think it was Tokyo, might have been Yokosuka. In any event, on the way up in the plane, Admiral Struble said that we were - the Commander, Seventh Fleet, had been directed to make a complete plan for the Inchon foray - operation, he didn't tell me what it was at that time - make a complete plan for an operation that was coming off. In the party in the airplane was Commander V. G. Lambert, who was also pulled off of his permanent duty station. He was operations officer for a carrier division commander. Admiral Struble told us that I was to be the fleet planning officer for this job, and Lambert was to be my assistant. We then asked what assistance we'd get from the Seventh Fleet staff and we found that the Seventh Fleet staff had a lieutenant commander in the plans division and that was about it. So it became obvious that we were the planning department - the two of us.

Well, we went up to ComNavFe's headquarters, Vice Admiral Turner Joy, and there received our first briefing on what the operations was, this was to be the invasion on Inchon, which was scheduled to take place on the 15th of September. One thing that became obvious immediately was that we had very little time in which to draw a complete plan. Fortunately, the amphibious forces had been planning on this operation for some time. Rear Admiral J. H. Doyle was to be the amphibious force commander. He had his plan practically finished and we, of course, had access to that. However, the Seventh Fleet commander had just been inserted into this chain a few days before, so the Seventh Fleet had no plan whatsoever. We got briefed up on the plan and stayed in Tokyo at ComNavForces, Far East, headquarters for a few days. By that time the Seventh Fleet flagship, the Rochester, had left Sasebo and come in to - it was either Yokosuka or Yokohama, I'm not quite sure which. The reason the location isn't very clear is that for the next two weeks we were buried in the ship writing plans and we had no time to go ashore at all.

Q: It didn't make any difference to you where you were because you didn't see it anyway?

Adm. S.: It didn't make a bit of difference where we were. The thing I remember most about the planning operation was that we took over the ship's library to use as a planning office because there was no other space available . . .

Q: And what ship were you on?

Adm. S.: This was the Rochester.

Q: You were on the flagship?

Adm. S.: Oh the flagship, right. Well, this was late August - middle to late August - and it was terrifically hot in Japan. The ship's library had inadequate ventilation, so that we were frequently working in temperatures of 110 . . .

Q: Oh, come on . . .

Adm. S.: . . . and it wasn't exactly the most pleasant place to work.

Q: I don't know how you could keep your mind on what you were doing in that temperature.

Adm. S.: It wasn't easy. Lambert and I immediately started writing the fleet plan. Commander, Seventh Fleet's task in this operation was to coordinate the operation of the amphibious forces, the carriers, and supporting ships.

Q: You had, in other words, to write the over-all plan.

Adm. S.: So we were really writing the over-all plan, right. And, for this operation, Commander Seventh Fleet, was subordinate to Commander, Naval Forces, Far East. General MacArthur, of course, was in over-all command of the whole operation. Well, we very soon had a plan roughed up...

Q: What do you work from in making a plan like that?

Adm. S.: We worked to some degree from the amphibious plan, but we just had - we didn't have anything to work from.

Q: From your own knowledge of what should be done?

Adm. S.: We worked from our own knowledge. That's right. And we had a lot of conferences with the area task force staff that was to be in the operation and with the amphibious force staff.

Q: Who was the carrier commander?

Adm. S.: It seems to me it was Rear Admiral Ewen. As I recall, it was probably about the 20th to the 25th of August that we got our first rough draft plan. Maybe it was about the 20th. The procedure we went through then - we met with Admiral Struble about 5 or 6 in the afternoon and went over the plan

with him and he had with him his chief of staff. Admiral
Struble made comments and criticisms of the plan and then
we went back into our planning office . . .

Q: Hot box!

Adm. S.: Hot box - after two or three hours with him, and
started re-writing it. As I recall, we'd gone through this
procedure for 12 days before we finally got a plan that everybody thought was useful, so we had 12 rough drafts of this
plan before it finally turned out to be the finished product.

Q: When you say "everyone," did you have to take into consideration the amphibious group and the carrier people and . . . ?

Adm. S.: We had to confer with the amphibious people to see
what comments they had on it. That's right.

Q: And the carrier group as well?

Adm. S.: To some degree. It was chiefly - Admiral Struble,
of course, was in touch with all these people and he spent
his day talking to people and getting - he talked to General
MacArthur - and getting new ideas and all that sort of thing -
to Admiral Joy. Admiral Arleigh Burke was - I don't know
that he was there at that time - yes, he was, on Admiral
Joy's staff.

Q: So he actually got the top comments and somehow related them to you and you put them in so that then they would be acceptable.

Adm. S.: That's right. So after we'd gone through, as I say, I think it was 12 rough drafts of this plan, we finally got it into shape and...

Q: How many yeomen did you get?

Adm. S.: Not very many. I think we got two. In any event, we got the plan out some time around the first few days in September. As I recall, it was about the 3rd. We then prepared to go up off the coast. Commander, Seventh Fleet, was going to go into Inchon Harbor...

Q: Before we get to that, excuse me and if I did start to spoil your chain of thought, invite me out, but can you tell me what the plan was, or is that too complicated?

Adm. S.: Oh, it was just a plan that coordinated gunfire support, air support, the timing of the amphibious landing, when ships would come into the harbor, and all that sort of thing. It was an over-all coordinating plan.

Q: And there are, of course, official copies of that in the records.

Adm. S.: Oh yes. I used to have one myself, but I don't know what I did with it. I probably had to burn it.

Q: Probably. How many pages did it come out?

Adm. S.: Oh, I would say, off hand, it was probably - it wasn't much more than an inch thick. It wasn't a great big tome.

Q: Then each of the other commanders had to get out their individual operations orders supporting the plan?

Adm. S.: That's correct. Well, I can't remember exactly when we sailed, but we probably sailed around the 5th or 6th of September, I guess, and went around to Sasebo, then went on up to the coast of Korea . . .

Q: Still in the Rochester?

Adm. S.: Still in the Rochester, that's right. We stayed off the coast for - we probably got there about the 10th, I guess . . .

Q: West coast?

Adm. S.: The west coast of Korea, that's right. We probably got up there around the 9th or the 10th. By that time, the carriers were making strikes to soften up the defenses and on the 12th, as I recall - could have been the 11th, but it was probably on the 12th of September, we went in to Inchon Harbor and Commander, Seventh Fleet, sort of supervised the entrance of the force into Inchon Harbor. There were probably two squadrons of destroyers, maybe a half squadron, I guess it was, of destroyers that went into the harbor and anchored along the river to act as gunfire support ships, and then there were, I think may be, two other cruisers beside the Rochester. I remember, I believe it was the Toledo that came in, and we had told her to anchor just to the left of the channel as you go up the harbor. Fortunately, she came in on a falling tide, and of course, the rise and fall of tide there is about 30 feet, it's a tremendous rise and fall. As a matter of fact, it was so heavy that the amphibious force commander had grave doubts as to whether he could really make the landing successfully.

Well, this day - and it might have been the 12th or the 13th - the Toledo was coming in, she started toward the anchorage and she saw a mine ahead on the surface - it was a moored mine that was on the surface - and she stopped to sink the mine with rifle fire. It took some minutes to sink the mine, and by that time, they saw another mine on the surface, the tide was falling quite rapidly. Before they got through, they had sunk by rifle fire, probably, as I recall it, six or eight mines. There was a mine field there that we didn't know about and fortunately, at low tide, the mines were on the surface so we could see them . . .

Q: That was providential for the next day's operations, wasn't it?

Adm. S.: Yes, it was. So we got those mines sunk and then detailed some ships to search for mines and sink them with rifle fire, and I guess we had a minesweeper, but I don't remember. I'm sure we did. Well, we got the destroyers anchored in there and then, and the destroyers were getting quite a little action from the island of Walmi Do, which was a key island up close to where the landing was to take place.

As a matter of fact, one of the landings was to take place on Walmi Do. Some of the ships got hit. We had more or less continuous air strikes flying in there in the daytime, and then ships took over bombardment of night. The Rochester also was participating in the bombardment. This went on on the 12th, 13th, and 14th . . .

Q: One of the ships in your Squadron Five was hit, I think.

Adm. S.: That's right. The Gurke was hit during the time, and one other ship was hit, too. I can't remember the name of the ship.

Q: And the Henderson, I believe.

Adm. S.: No, the Henderson might have been hit, but there was another squadron in there, too, that had a couple of casualties. So, then, on the 15th, the landing took place, and the landing went off very well. There weren't too many casualties, and the troops got ashore quite rapidly in spite of the large rise and fall of the tide. The evening of the 15th there was still quite a little fighting along the beach close to the landing, but the troops were well ashore. Admiral Struble that evening had proposed to General MacArthur that they get in a boat and go along the landing area and inspect the state of the landing in the boat. Well, he asked me to go along and, as I remember it, the flag lieutenant was the boat officer and was supposed to be taking care of the boat. Well, General MacArthur and Admiral Struble were sitting in the stern of the boat talking and every now and then they indicated they wanted to get in closer . . .

Q: Was it dark?

Adm. S.: Yes, it was dark, it was pitch dark. And the flag lieutenant was having trouble with the navigation, so Admiral Struble told me to go up and take over, which was, since I hadn't really looked at the shallow water and all of a sudden I was tossed this job on a pitch black night.

Q: What was the tide doing at that point, in or out?

Adm. S.: As I recall it, the tide was probably, at that time, was starting to flood again, but I can't recall. Anyway, we were feeling along - going along the sea wall . . .

Q: Oh, you were clear up to the sea wall?

Adm. S.: We were close to the sea wall. We were probably 50 or 100 feet off the sea wall, and we could see personnel carriers or tanks going along, and the Admiral and General MacArthur were looking over the situation with great interest, when somebody on the sea wall yelled at us, "Get the hell out of there. We're going to blow up this causeway in a few minutes." So, here we were close to this causeway that they were going to blow . . .

Q: Was that the one going to the island, from the town to the island?

Adm. S.: No. This was not that causeway. This was some other spot that I don't remember.

Q: They, of course, didn't know who you were?

Adm. S.: No, they didn't know who we were.

Q: It's a wonder they didn't think you were enemy.

Adm. S.: They just knew that we were - that all the boats in the harbor were friendly. There were lots of boats floating around, but we were too close to the beach. So, with that, we - General MacArthur's and Admiral Struble's curiosity got abated a little bit and we headed back out, much to my relief.

Q: I'm sure of that. Were there any lights in the town?

Adm. S.: Well, there was a lot of shooting going on.

Q: The city itself, was it in darkness?

Adm. S.: It was dark. Well, we went on back to the ship and we stayed on there in Inchon for - oh, I can't remember how long. Quite a long time. Maybe a week or ten days after the landing, at least. One day we decided, or I guess maybe Admiral Struble suggested that we might like to go over and get off the ship and look around the beach. We thought that was a good idea, so the skipper of the Rochester, who was Captain Eddie Woodyard of the class of '24, and Lambert and someone else, whose name I can't recall, and I went over on the beach, went over to Inchon, there was lots of activity at Inchon at that time.

They were just getting ready to cross the Han River that night and go on up to Seoul, so there was an awful lot of activity on the roads. We stopped a truck that was empty and told them we'd like to go up to Kimpo Air Base, and he said he'd be happy to take us. So we got in the back of this 2½ ton truck, I guess, with an Army driver, and went dashing up the road. After a few minutes, we noticed that soldiers were going along on each side of the road with their guns ready, acting as though they were looking for snipers, and this made us wonder if we were really on the road to Kimpo. Then we passed some howitzers that were firing over a hill, sort of parallel to the road, and finally we said to the driver, "How many times have you been to Kimpo?" He said, well, this was his first trip. So we said, "Okay, let's stop and ask somebody where we are, whether we're on the right road." So we finally saw a noncom or an officer along this road, and stopped and asked him if we were on the right road to Kimpo, and he said, "No, you're on the road to Seoul, you're just about to pass over into the enemy lines." So we turned around and went back and finally ended up at Kimpo, looked that over, and then went back to the ship.

Q: When you go ashore on a day like that, what was your uniform?

Adm. S.: Oh, we were in khakis.

Q: Were you wearing a garrison cap or your cap with . . .?

Adm. S.: I don't remember what we were wearing. Probably . . .

Q: What was the weather like by that time?

Adm. S.: It was quite warm.

Q: Who decided - I forget if I know the answer - to land at downtown Inchon? Was that MacArthur?

Adm. S.: MacArthur was the one that made the broad decision to land at Inchon, and after that, why, the troop commanders and the amphibious commander got together and decided where to land.

Q: There's a falling tide in all the pictures one sees, they show the exposed mudflats. I don't think I've ever seen a picture of Inchon without the flats being exposed.

Adm. S.: Yes, well, this is more newsworthy - the mudflats.

Q: I guess. The story they tell of this man - is it Price or Clark - who went ashore several days ahead and lived on one of these small islands to bring intelligence back. Do you know that story?

Adm. S.: No, I don't.

Q: It's quite interesting and I wondered if you might have ever known him or known of him.

Sharp #2 - 123

Adm. S.: What's his name?

Q: I think it's Price.

Adm. S.: No, I don't know him.

Q: He was a young naval officer.

Adm. S.: Was he?

Q: Yes, and he went ashore and was disguised as a - I don't know whether he was disguised or not - but he made many friends on the island and also had a group of youngsters, like teenagers, who would go into the city and get information for him and come back - if it's true, it's quite . . .

Adm. S.: Yes. I don't remember it.

Q: . . . interesting.

Adm. S.: After the landing was pretty well along, I started agitating to get back to my destroyer squadron, but . . .

Q: Did Admiral Struble ever congratulate you on the plan?

Adm. S.: Oh, yes. Anyway, I tried to get moved back to my destroyer squadron, but with difficulty. Admiral Struble didn't want us to leave until everything was pretty well buttoned up. So we stayed there in Inchon - I guess we must have stayed ten days at least after the 15th, and - I don't recall where we went then, maybe back to Sasebo.

Q: And where was your destroyer squadron all this time?

Adm. S.: The destroyer squadron had been at Inchon, then I believe they finally went around to the other coast, the east coast. I can't recall - it must have been - they must have been attached to the Seventh Fleet for well over a month. Here are some dates that revise some of the dates that went before. I was in transit from the War College and on leave from the 16th of June 1950 to the 17th of July 1950. So apparently on the 17th of July I reported in to the - reported in as Commander, Destroyer Squadron Five. I then had command of Destroyer Squadron Five until about the 20th of August - as a matter of fact, it says here the 25th of August. No, I think it must have been earlier than that. This must be off. Then I was with temporary additional duty with Commander, Seventh Fleet, from about the 20th of August to the 30th of September.

Q: That's remarkable, that you could make that plan in that short a time for that size of operation, just so few of you.

Adm. S.: Yes. Well, then, apparently - in fact it may be

that I was longer than the 30th of September. In any event, the next time that I can tell from these papers, during the months of November and December of 1950, I was operating as a unit of Task Force 77, in Task Group 77.2. 77.2 being the screen for Task Force 77.

Q: You never went back to your destroyer squadron?

Adm. S.: Yes. I was in my destroyer squadron then.

Q: Oh, that's what this was. I see.

Adm. S.: Yes. So it looks as though some time after the 30th of September I rejoined my squadron.

Q: And that became then 77 . . . ?

Adm. S.: And was attached to Task Force 77.

Q: What was its number then?

Adm. S.: 77, just 77.

Q: You had two divisions in that squadron?

Adm. S.: No. Let's see, my other division, I guess - I guess by that time I had the other division out there. No, I don't think I did. I think there was still just the one division. In any event, after I left Seventh Fleet staff and went back to my squadron, or my division, we did some independent duty on the west coast of Korea - we were getting ready then to invade Wonsan.

Q: On the west coast, did you say?

Adm. S.: Oh the west coast, yes. No, no, on the east coast.

Q: Yes, I thought.

Adm. S.: No, no, on the east coast. And I remember when we were preparing for that invasion, we were assigned to escort the battleship Missouri. At that time, I think Admiral Struble had moved into the Missouri. In any event, I remember going alongside the Missouri one time to transfer Rear Admiral Smith - Hoke Smith - we were taking him from some ship to the Missouri. I recall telling the skipper, before we went alongside the Missouri, that one problem of going alongside a battleship, the battleship's underwater body was quite broad and there was a distinct sweep at the stern from the beam in toward the ship - toward the stern, so that you had to be very careful that you didn't get caught in that current and get swept against the stern of the ship, of the battleship. Well, Admiral Smith and I were out on the wing of the bridge watching the Rowan being brought in alongside the Missouri, and the skipper got in too close, despite the warning I'd given him, and it was pretty obvious that he was going to wipe off some stanchions. Admiral Smith got excited and said, "What are you going to do about this? What're you going to do about it? I said, "I'm not going to do a thing. I warned the skipper how to do it and running the ship is his business, and he's got to go ahead and do it." Well, sure enough, he came alongside and caught the current just like I told him he would, and we knocked off a couple of stanchions, off of the Missouri's lifelines . . .

Q: Did you touch?

Adm. S.: Yes.

Q: You got close enough to actually touch?

Adm. S.: Oh, yes. The anchor of the Rowan knocked off a few stanchions. But he finally got squared away. But having been a skipper of a flagship before, I was allergic to unit commanders that would interfere with a one-ship operation.

Q: Well, when you were relieved from the Boyd, didn't you have almost the same situation? You relief was . . .

Adm. S.: Yes. My relief got in too close.

Q: Except you were still in command of it, and you took it away from him.

Adm. S.: Yes. Well, that was a minor incident, but it was kind of interesting. So, then, in the months of November and December we were up off the east coast of Korea. It was getting pretty cold then. As a matter of fact, it seems to me that at that point the ground forces were way up in the northern part of - getting pretty well up in the northern part of North Korea, and this was just about the time that the Chinese came in and . . .

Q: Wouldn't that have been December of '50?

Adm. S.: Yes. December of '50 the Chinese came in, I think. We had to pull out of there and drop back to the Chosen Reservoir - had to drop back and they were getting ready to evacuate the people from Hungnam. I remember being up off Hungnam and acting as screen for the carriers. And I guess it was early December, I got my orders to - it must have been operations officer for Commander, Second Fleet . . .

Q: Are you leaving Korea, then?

Adm. S.: Getting ready to, yes.

Q: I just wondered if there were any interesting incidents when you were operating as a screen. That was almost like the duty you had done, in a slightly different capacity, in World War II, wasn't it?

Adm. S.: Yes. Well, yes, it was kind of an interesting operation. It was a big screen and every - I don't know, there must have been three carriers in there - in the group - at least, and every evening one of the carriers would drop out and go back to refuel and provision and take on more ammo. Then, of course, some of the destroyers would drop out at dusk and go back to fuel, so there was a constant milling around in the screen, and it was a fairly interesting operation for the screen makers. It was a great big screen and always somebody going in and out, rotating around, and it was a very interesting period.

We're now up off the east coast of Korea and acting as part of a screen for the Task Force 77. One evening, just after dark, the task force picked up on its radars some ships that were moving at about 30 knots and they were coming down the coast of Korea, and it looked as though they were coming - yes, they were coming off the coast of North Korea out toward the task force - and it looked as though they might be PT boats - they were making about the right speed. So I was directed to take five ships and intercept these boats - intercept these pips, whatever they were. Well, the five ships that I got were, let's see, there was a British destroyer, an Australian destroyer, a Canadian destroyer, one other U.S. destroyer, and the Rowan. So we really had a mixed bag.

Q: It was made up just for that purpose?

Adm. S.: Yes. As a matter of fact, it may be that I had this outfit as a task group for some particular reason. I can't remember what it was, but anyway, we headed out toward these pips and before we had gone too far, they changed course and flew more or less north, so then we thought they really could be PT boats that had picked up our ships on the radar and were turning and running, so we chased after them at high speed for about 30 minutes, but the radar contacts didn't quite make sense, although they were pretty good contacts and they were in line as a group of boats might be. But we decided after analyzing them for a while that it was a flock of geese that were flying along.

Q: Really? That's a pretty good speed.

Adm. S.: Yes. I guess 30 or 35 knots would be about what they would fly. So we finally turned around and came back. I do recall that the officer on the radar, on the radio telephone on the British destroyer got a very thick British accent and as time went on I think they must have had their ration of liquor, because his accent got quite thick. So we've just about covered the duty with the carrier task force.

Q: Did you participate in the evacuation at Hungnam?

Adm. S.: No. Well, we were in the general area, but we were still with the carrier task force, as I recall it. Yes, I think we were. Then, as I said, I got my orders to be relieved and report back to Commander, Second Fleet, staff. My relief was a captain of the class of '25, and for the life of me I can't think of his name now, came out aboard a carrier that had come in from Sasebo, and on the 26th of December 1950, I think it was, he came aboard - went alongside this carrier and he came aboard by high line. He came aboard and instead of the carrier putting him in a chair like they normally did, he came aboard in a cargo bag.

Q: That must have been comfortable!

Adm. S.: And the carrier in lifting him off the deck, the carrier crew that was handling the line sort of botched the job, and this cargo bag with my relief in it banged against the waterway of the carrier, so when he came aboard he was limping.

Q: I should think pretty much shook up.

Adm. S.: Apparently, he had hit his knee pretty hard on this waterway. I think this was on Christmas Day, as I recall. So we went aboard and he went down to the cabin and turned in rather shortly because he was limping so badly, and the next day his knee was all swollen up and he really didn't look as though he was ready to do anything but stay in bed for a while. Well, I said, "Do you want me to hang on to this job, or what would you like to do?" And he said, "No. I'm ready to relieve you and I'll be able to get around all right." So, then, I was relieved the next day. There was some sense of urgency in my orders. So I was relieved the next day and went back to Sasebo in a tanker, then flew on back to the United States and went to La Jolla where my family was, and we moved out of the house that we'd rented and drove across the continent, took the southern route because it was the middle of winter, and arrived in Norfolk and reported to Commander, Second Fleet, in July of '51 - I mean in January of '51.

Q: As operations officer?

Adm. S.: As operations and plans officer. So I was operations and plans officer. I relieved John Sylvester of the class of '26, and he became the chief of staff. I had relieved John once before in CruDesPac's staff, so we'd been on two staffs together. Then I became operations and plans officer and, according to this thing - I must have been operations and plans from January '51 until 25 August, I guess.

Q: I had October '51.

Adm. S.: Oh, wait a minute. No, I'm wrong. Until October '51, when I became chief of staff. Is that it? This thing's not too clear here. Okay, that's probably right. Something like that.

Q: In any case, you served on that same staff from January of '51 clear up until August '53.

Adm. S.: Right. Yes.

Q: So that was a long stay in one place for a change.

Adm. S.: Yes. That's right. That sure is right. Admiral Gardner was Commander, Second Fleet, when I arrived, and he was relieved by Vice Admiral Felix Stump.

Q: That was interesting, wasn't it?

Adm. S.: Yes. He was relieved by Vice Admiral Felix Stump I think in about March or April of '51. I guess it was March of '51, probably. Yes, that's right. In March '51 Admiral Gardner was detached, and I believe relieved by Admiral Stump. Then in October of '51 I became chief of staff.

Q: And aide?

Adm. S.: And aide, right. Well, this was a very interesting period in the Second Fleet. We did one big fleet exercise, did a lot of NATO planning, and made a trip to England, as I recall it, with Admiral Stump.

Q: What was the exercise?

Adm. S.: As I recall it, it was naval exercise Mariner. I think it was. Yes, naval exercise Mariner.

Q: Where was that?

Adm. S.: That was off the coast of Norway.

Q: Oh, that's interesting, wasn't it? Can you expand on that somewhat?

Adm. S.: Oh, I don't think it's worth expanding on. I was chief of staff during that exercise.

Q: How many countries participated?

Adm. S.: There must have been - I think it was mostly British and U.S.. I guess the Norwegians were in there with a few small craft and we used their bases in Norway, and there might have been a French and Canadian ship or two. I don't recall. We went through a period in which there was quite a little planning involved and I met a lot of people from the other navies, and, as far as my career is concerned, having served with Admiral Stump was a very fortuitous . . .

Q: I wanted to ask you about him and your experience with him.

Adm. S.: Well, he and I got along very well. He was a pretty gruff individual. He was especially gruff with his contemporaries or his close contemporaries in aviation, and I can remember a good many times him getting a rear admiral aviator in there and really giving him a pretty tough time, and they were pretty apprehensive of the old boy, but I always got along with him. A very fine gentleman, I thought.

Q: Maybe he demanded a very high level of performance.

Adm. S.: He demanded performance and when he told people he wanted something done, why, he wanted it done and you'd better go ahead and do it.

Q: Of course, I like that, don't you?

Adm. S.: I do, too, I think it's wonderful.

Q: You know where you stand. It's always easy to say I have to do this first because he told you to.

Adm. S.: Yes. Well, I must say it was very pleasant duty, actually.

Q: It must have been very illuminating also.

Adm. S.: Yes, it was. It was excellent training for me. It just gave me a chance to see a complete staff in operation and participate in it. It was excellent training. I couldn't have gotten into a better job, really.

Q: As you look back, perhaps, and would expect that you can see every step that something was taught you for your subsequent job. How large was the Second Fleet at that time?

Adm. S.: Well, Second Fleet is a planning outfit, really, and its ships were attached to it for exercises, and the Second Fleet commander had a responsibility for over-all fleet readiness. The ships would be attached normally to the type commanders until they were attached to the fleet for . . .

Q: For a particular exercise?

Adm. S.: For a particular exercise. That's right. During that period, we bought a house in Norfolk and were fortunate enough to live in that house for almost three years. It was the longest time we'd been in one place for quite a long time.

Q: Actually, it was the longest tour you'd had.

Adm. S.: I guess it was.

Q: Ashore, at all.

Adm. S.: Yes. So, it was very pleasant duty.

Q: Your family was developing at this time?

Adm. S.: Yes. Our daughter at that time was going to UCLA, I guess. Yes. She'd been with us in Newport and went to Rhode Island State University for a year, and then when we went out to La Jolla she started going to UCLA, and when we went back - I guess when we went back to Norfolk, she continued to go to UCLA. Yes, I think that's right. Our son was with us in Norfolk, and also my mother lived with us in Norfolk.

So we were now with the Second Fleet and in October of '51 I became chief of staff, and I stayed in the Second Fleet as chief of staff up until August of '53, at which time I became commanding officer of the Macon, a heavy cruiser in the Atlantic. Admiral Stump before, just before I left Second Fleet staff, knew that he was going to be CinCPac and CinCPacFlt - the two jobs were together at that time - and he told me that after I had had my year as - in command of a cruiser, he wanted me to come out to Honolulu and be a member of his staff. So then - and this was also an important step in my career because it brought me into a planning job that turned out to be very useful for the rest of my career.

Q: You mean the one with Second Fleet?

Adm. S.: No, when I went out to Honolulu. Anyway, I took command of the Macon in August of '53, and we cruised up and down the East Coast to a certain degree, went down to Guantanamo.

Just had a more or less normal year there, operating out of Norfolk. We did go off - took the midshipmen on a midshipmen's cruise in June of '54. Oh, let me see, I guess I should go back and say that Admiral Burke was the cruiser division commander of the Macon's division.

Q: This was Arleigh Burke?

Adm. S.: Arleigh Burke, yes, that's right. And part of the time the Macon was his flagship. As I recall it, Macon was his flagship on this midshipmen's cruise. This, again, was a fortunate thing for me because I became known to Admiral Burke and I must say he thought very favorably of me, and this had a great influence on my career also. In any event, we did have a good midshipmen's cruise and went to the - picked up the midshipmen at Annapolis, went over to the Mediterranean, and in to, I guess it was Rotterdam, and some place in England, I can't remember where, then brought them on home. I was due to be - I had my orders, knew that I was going to be detached at the end of this midshipmen's cruise to go back out to Honolulu.

Q: So you knew all the time what your next duty would be?

Adm. S.: Yes, I knew all the time what my next duty was going to be. I knew it was going to be on CinCPacFlt staff. I didn't k exactly what, but I knew I was going to be in the planning business somehow. I was relieved from command of the Macon in August of 1954, and we packed up and drove across the continent again.

Q: You were coming to know that route pretty well, weren't you?

Adm. S.: Well, we - actually we tried to take a different route every time, so we had crossed the United States on most every transcontinental route. It was a lot of fun, great experience for us, and a great experience for the children. At this time, our daughter was - let's see - she was just graduating, I guess it was, from UCLA. She was preparing to be a laboratory technician, which was a very nice thing, and she had, I guess, she graduated, I guess, in June of '54, and announced that she was going to get married in August. So we sort of arranged for our part of the wedding by remote control from Norfolk, and they had their wedding scheduled so that we could participate in the wedding on our way out to Honolulu. So we drove across the continent, stopped in San Diego and visited friends for a few days, I guess for a couple of days, then went on up to Los Angeles, met our future son-in-law - and I must say that we thought very highly of our daughter's choice . . .

Q: That was nice.

Adm. S.: . . . and participated in this wedding, which was about 20 August, or in that general neighborhood. I remember that my orders to - gave me a delay in reporting until about the 1st of September, as I recall. I sent a message to Admiral Stump - I guess I was supposed to get in with less delay than that, and I sent a message to Admiral Stump telling him that I - our daughter was going to get married and so I needed some additional time and I wanted to take some leave on the West Coast. I got a message back from him saying, "Very fine. Glad to have you stay until your daughter is married and I will see you on (a date which was about three days after the wedding)", which just barely gave us time to get out there. So our leave was a little shorter than we really thought we would like to have had. But anyway, the wedding went off very well and we had a big reception, I think it was at the Biltmore Hotel, and we had two or three days in Los Angeles, then we drove up to San Francisco and turned our car in and we were going to fly out from San Francisco aboard one of the old Mars seaplanes, which took off from Alameda.

I remember our daughter and her new husband were in San Francisco on their honeymoon and we met them and they drove over to the airport to see us off. Which brings up a certain interesting little situation. I had always kidded our children about the size of mosquitoes in Montana. I told them that mosquitoes had a wingspread like an eagle and all that sort of thing, and they were always saying, "Oh, Dad, don't exaggerate," so it was kind of a family joke. Well, we got in this taxicab to go from San Francisco over to Alameda and I happened to ask the taxidriver where he was from, and he said he was from Montana, and I said, "Oh, I'm from Montana, too. Up there in the good old mosquito country." And he said, "Yes, those mosquitoes are as big as eagles." Which gave the kids a big kick. Well, anyway, Pat and I and my mother and our son got aboard the Mars seaplane and flew out to Honolulu.

Q: They never look like they can fly.

Adm. S.: It was very comfortable, as a matter of fact. It had bunks. And we arrived in Honolulu on, it must have been the 28th of August 1955 - no, 1954, and I reported in to Admiral Stump to be on the staff of Commander-in-Chief, Pacific Fleet. They had reorganized the staff to some degree, and I was the first one to get deputy chief of staff for plans, operations, and intelligence. They combined those functions under a deputy.

Q: That was the first time you'd gotten into intelligence, isn't it?

Adm. S.: Yes. Actually, the intelligence pretty well ran itself and I was more concerned with plans and operations than anything else. So I was then deputy chief of staff to the CinCPacFlt until - when?

Q: I think July '56.

Adm. S.: Until some time in '56. I was attached to the staff of CinCPacFlt until July of '56. I guess we probably ought to comment a little bit on the CinCPacFlt job.

Q: I would think so. I'm sure it was interesting and expansive.

Adm. S.: Well, this was a really top-notch staff. In my particular part of the staff - the plans, operations, and intelligence bailiwick - Captain Horatio Riviero was - many members of the staff were destined to be very high ranking officers in the Navy. When I first arrived, Captain David McDonald was the plans officer. He was relieved two or three months after I arrived. Captain Riviero, who was later to get four stars, was the operations officer, I guess it was. Captain Shinn was the air operations officer. Captain Hyland was in the operations division. Captain Bowen - Hal Bowen - was in the ordnance part of the staff.

Q: Did you use the name Rivet?

Adm. S.: Rivets Riviero, yes. Let me see. I've missed somebody. Another officer we had that became an admiral was Commander Ralph Weymouth. I probably have missed one or two because that staff was just loaded with talent, really an outstanding group.

Q: It must have been exciting to work with people of that caliber.

Adm. S.: It was a lot of fun to work with them, and it was - let's see, Rear Admiral Hopwood was the chief of staff at first. No, I guess he was a vice admiral at that time. And then Vice Admiral Germany Kurtz was chief of staff. Admiral Stump, of course, was CinCPacFlt the whole two years I was there. They were just getting ready to separate CinCPac and CinCPacFlt, and actually right at the end of my tour Admiral Kurtz was promoted to four stars to be the deputy of CinCPacFlt. Well, I mentioned that toward the latter part of my duty on CinCPacFlt staff, Admiral Kurtz - Vice Admiral Kurtz, he was the chief of staff - became a full admiral and had additional duty as deputy CinCPacFlt. This was the first step in separating CinCPac and CinCPacFlt assignments.

Q: What was the thinking behind separating them?

Adm. S.: Well, they needed to be separated because the unified command job was getting to be too big a job to be done in addition to the CinCPacFlt job. It just required two people to handle the job.

Q: Each with a separate staff?

Adm. S.: Separate staffs. When I was there, the staffs were fairly well separated. Admiral Stump had a chief of staff for

CinCPacFlt duties. Then Admiral Kurtz became CinCPacFlt.

Q: It was during this time that you became admiral, was it not? Rear admiral?

Adm. S.: Yes. I was selected in 1955, and from mid-1955 on I was a rear admiral.

Q: Did you ever have any problems with your promotion?

Adm. S.: Any problems?

Q: Yes. Were you ever not selected when you thought you would be?

Adm. S.: No. Some of my class were selected a year ahead of me. As a matter of fact, I believe there were one or two that were selected two years ahead of me. I'm not sure. But I made admiral at the time I would normally expect to. The two years duty there on the CinCPacFlt staff gave me a chance to work on a major staff, commander-in-chief's staff, with, as I've said before, outstanding officers working with me and for me. It gave me experience in the Pacific in a job which I would come back to.

Q: It would have been awfully difficult for future jobs not having had this as a background, would it not?

Adm. S.: Oh, no. It isn't that. It's just a great advantage to have had this duty pattern that I was working myself into. And I must say that I was working myself into it as much by luck as anything. For example, I think it was very fortunate for me that I worked for Admiral Stump when he was commander Second Fleet. It was fortunate for me that I'd known John Sylvester on numerous occasions, because I'm sure he was instrumental in bringing me to the Second Fleet staff, and, likewise, I was fortunate to have a cruiser in Admiral Burke's cruiser division. So I just had a whole lot of luck, which I managed to make the best of.

Q: That's the important thing. Other people could have had the same assignments.

Adm. S.: Other people could have had the same - that's right.

Q: They could have had the same assignments without taking advantage of them.

Adm. S.: That's very true. Well, during my tour on CinC-PacFlt's staff, I had an opportunity to make a couple of trips in the Western Pacific and familiarize myself with that area. One of the trips I made was with Admiral Burke. He was then a rear admiral, who had just been selected to be CNO, and he came on a trip to the Pacific and took me with him on his trip. We had a very useful, hard-working trip.

Q: How did you travel, by air, I presume?

Adm. S.: We traveled by air.

Q: Did you see parts of the Pacific you hadn't seen before?

Adm. S.: Yes. We got to Thailand. It was the first time I'd been in Thailand. We went to Cambodia, the first and only time I was ever in Cambodia.

Q: What was the purpose at that time of going to those countries?

Adm. S.: Well, Admiral Burke was just getting familiar with the area, and we were, too.

Q: Did we have military advisers in that year? That was in '54, I guess.

Adm. S.: There was somebody in Cambodia. I can't remember who now.

Q: I meant - I was thinking of Vietnam, we had military advisers there.

Adm. S.: Yes, there were military advisers there.

Q: And did you go to Vietnam on that trip?

Adm. S.: We did. Yes. And went to Bangkok. So, although there wasn't any major event during that time. Yes, there was, too. It was during the year 1954 and 1955 that we had the big shift of people in Vietnam.

Q: Yes. '54 was the Geneva partition.

Adm. S.: The Geneva treaty was 1954, and then, as a result of that treaty, of course, the Vietnams were divided and people in North Vietnam that wanted to go to South Vietnam were given permission to do so, and from South Vietnam to North Vietnam, and the United States Navy transported all these people, and CinCPacFlt was involved in sort of directing that operation.

Q: Were you involved in any of the planning on that?

Adm. S.: Yes, we were involved in the planning. That's right. From the Commander-in-Chief's level.

Q: Did you foresee trouble then?

Adm. S.: Oh, no. I don't think we were - well, no one liked the way the thing turned out, of course, but under the circumstances it was about as much as you could expect. The French, in effect, bugged out of Vietnam and left the field to the Communists and I think, under those circumstances, the result was about what you'd expect. But anyway, that was the time when a lot of people from the north came south, and some of them undoubtedly were sympathizers of Ho Chi Minh's who came down under Ho Chi Minh's directions to start the attempt to regain South Vietnam. And many of those people that went down south were recruited by Ho Chi Minh at a later time and used as guerrillas. Also, many of the southerners that went north were turned around and sent down into South Vietnam at a later time as guerrillas.

Q: I don't think I knew that.

Adm. S.: Yes. That's where they got some of the knowledge of the territory, you see. They had people that were from the south, and they sent them back down into South Vietnam. So we did stop in Saigon and, at that time, Iron Mike O'Daniel was the commander of the Military Assistance Command out there. We saw him.

Q: That was the only Navy? We had no Navy there at all, as far as any . . .

Adm. S.: No. A couple of advisers with the Vietnamese Navy - didn't amount to anything. So those two years were busy and, other than that Vietnam deal, I don't remember anything of great historical importance that went on. So now we come to July of 1956, when I was detached from the staff of Commander-in-Chief, Pacific Fleet, and the same day took command of

Cruiser Division Three, which was in Honolulu on its way to the West Coast. I had change of command at the naval base in Pearl Harbor and left the next day for Long Beach.

Q: What were the cruisers in your division?

Adm. S.: The Columbus, the Helena, and the Worcester. Wait a minute, that's not right. Columbus, Helena, and - I don't remember. There were three of them. What the other one was, I don't remember.

Q: Which was your flagship?

Adm. S.: The Columbus was the flagship. The Columbus was the flagship part of the time, and the Helena was the flagship part of the time. Well, again, I'm having a hard time jogging my memory.

Q: But you returned to Long Beach?

Adm. S.: We returned to Long Beach. As Commander, Cruiser Division Three, my three cruisers operated out of the port of Long Beach. We participated in various exercises along the Pacific coast. I had a period of time when I was involved in - aboard the Helena evaluating the Regulus I missile. This consisted of taking the ship up off the city of Monterey, California, and preparing the Regulus missiles on board for firing, and then firing the missile at San Nicolas Island. We conducted numerous firings over a two or three month period in an evaluation exercise with the Regulus, and the missile firings, in general, were quite successful. We did have a cruise to the Western Pacific, and I joined the Seventh Fleet in the Western Pacific, and, as I recall it, we were out there for a period of about four months, and then came back to Long Beach. And not too long after our return to Long Beach I was detached in, I guess it must have been, September 1957, and in October I reported to Washington, D.C. to be Assistant Director of the Strategic Plans Division in the office of the Chief of Naval Operations. I was Assistant Director until November of 1958, when I became Director of the Strategic Plans Division. During this period, I was - served under Admiral Libby, who was Op-06, and then he was relieved by Admiral Austin. Admiral Burke was CNO during all this period. This was a period of very intense activity, long hours keeping up with Admiral Burke. It was sort of the usual thing to be in your office until 7:30 or 8 o'clock every evening.

Q: He was there that late?

Adm. S.: Admiral Burke was there that late.

Q: And expected everybody else to be?

Adm. S.: Well, he didn't say so, but yes.

Q: Was there enough work to keep that . . . ?

Adm. S.: There certainly was.

Q: What were you doing? Can you describe what happened in Strategic Plans?

Adm. S.: We were working on - in the JCS Strategic Plans Division - and were involved in Joint Chiefs of Staff matters, and what we were doing, actually . . .

Q: Worldwide?

Adm. S.: Yes. What we were involved in was preparing the Chief of Naval Operations and the Deputy Chief for Plans for their appearances in the JCS, and the Strategic Plans Division was the chief division involved in JCS matters.

Q: Can you give me any for instances, or is that classified material?

Adm. S.: Well, what we did was just prepare all of the strategic papers for the CNO for his use in the JCS. And we briefed the CNO for each meeting that he went to. That was the general idea.

Q: Before Congress, as well as before the JCS?

Adm. S.: No. This was for the JCS and for meetings with the Secretary of Defense and that sort of thing. So this was a very busy two years and a very eventful two years, and very useful to me in my career, too. And, again, this was a stepping stone, which I think my career followed by happenstance, possibly, followed an ideal pattern for the job that I finally ended up with.

Q: How did this relate to the Vietnamese?

Adm. S.: Well, this related, not to the Vietnamese war so much, but it related to the whole joint operation. We were involved in discussions and in planning with people of all the other services, so that I got to know people in the other services that I subsequently was involved with on many occasions. The head of the Strategic Plans Division was involved in planners' meetings as a member of the Joint Strategic Plans Committee. There was an Army, Air Force, and Marine member, we met on matters within our cognizance before they got up to the JCS. It was sort of, if you will, a junior, junior JCS, because there were also the operations deputies, and that was the DCNO for plans. The deputy for plans and ops of the Army and the same thing in the Air Force, and the Marines.

Q: In other words, you were meeting with your opposite numbers?

Adm. S.: We were meeting with our opposite numbers and I got to know many people in those days that I worked with many times later. I knew and worked with General Wheeler and General Martin in the Air Force, General Woolnough in the Army, and many other people of that time that I worked with many times later on. So it was a good training period and I made many contacts that were useful later on and I learned a lot about how things run in Washington.

Q: I was going to say. The last time I was going to it probably was useful to know how Washington operates. This had been your first tour in Washington, as I recall.

Adm. S.: No, I was in Washington before World War II in the Bureau of Ships, but this was my first time in the office of the Chief of Naval Operations.

Q: You were in BuShips in May '40?

Adm. S.: Yes.

Q: It's quite a revelation, isn't it, to see how things do or don't work at that . . .

Adm. S.: Yes, it's - it was a very eventful period. Now. We're, I guess, through with that period as much as needs to be said about it.

Q: Excuse me, when you made these plans, were they like - I

used to know about during World War II - that there were plans for every possible exigency that could occur, or were they plans for things that were presently occurring?

Adm. S.: These were - some of them were contingency plans, some of them were such things as the Joint Strategic Objective Plan. These were the basic JCS-level plans for everything.

Q: For our nation?

Adm. S.: For our nation, yes.

Q: That must have been awfully interesting.

Adm. S.: It was. Now I guess we get on to February 1959 when I was detached from OpNav and reported to San Diego and relieved Admiral Smedberg as Commander, Cruiser/Destroyer Force, U.S. Pacific Fleet. I now was returning to a command where I had been for three years a member of the staff, and I had served a lot of time in destroyers, so this was like coming home in more ways than one. Coming home to San Diego where we'd spent a lot of time and where my wife lived before I married her, and also it was coming home to a force that I'd worked with for a long time.

Q: So you felt very comfortable, I'm sure.

Adm. S.: That's right. I did. We - this also was a very interesting and busy year spent managing the destroyer force, inspecting destroyers, and doing all the other things that a type commander does. We were based in San Diego the whole time. I did make one or two trips to the Western Pacific to see the destroyers that were deployed and to visit around the area.

Q: You refer to destroyers, but not to the cruisers.

Adm. S.: Destroyers and cruisers, yes. Of course, part of the force was based in Long Beach, so we made numerous trips back and forth. And there was a large amount of activity in the San Diego area with the civilians in this area. San Diego is very - is a very pro-Navy town. Naval officers are taken in by the people of San Diego traditionally, and we had very many friends here from living here for so many years, and had a very pleasant time. I was out on a trip to the Western Pacific in, this must have been, early 1960, round in there, February 1960, perhaps. We'd stopped in Guam for a layover and to see the base facilities there. I was out on the golf course playing golf one day, when a chief petty officer came up and - driving up in a golf cart - and handed me a message, which was a message from Admiral Burke telling me that I had been selected for vice admiral and was to assume command of the First Fleet for a short time before I would report back to Washington as Deputy Chief of Naval Operations for Plans.

Q: How did that make you feel?

Adm. S.: Well, it made me feel pretty good, because not only did I - was I surprised to get the news, which I hadn't known about ahead of time, but also that day I had a 79 and it was the first time I'd broken 80. Well, I guess it was the first time I ever broke 80, so it was a very successful day.

Q: It sure was.

Adm. S.: Then in April - I guess it was on the 30th of April - 1960 - well, two or three days before I was relieved as Commander, Cruiser/Destroyer Force, and on the 30th of April I relieved Admiral R. E. Libby as Commander, First Fleet, and was promoted to vice admiral on that day.

Q: Was there a ceremony for that?

Adm. S.: Oh, yes. There was a ceremony here in San Diego aboard a carrier, and I had the First Fleet for just about four months, until July of 1960. Then I was relieved as First Fleet commander . . .

Q: Did you enjoy that, even though it was a very short time?

Adm. S.: Oh, yes. It was an interesting job. There wasn't an awful lot going on at that time. As a matter of fact, I remember at that time I really wasn't too busy with this job. I knew I wasn't going to be in it very long and there wasn't too much going on at that particular period. I remember that my wife said one day, "You know, you really are not completely occupied, and when you're not completely occupied, you're a bother around the house," because I'd come home and tell her things that she ought to be doing.

Q: That was what she meant today, I guess, when she said she was glad you were on active duty . . .

Adm. S.: That's exactly right. That's the only time, I think, that I've had a job where I really wasn't completely occupied and Pat didn't think much of it.

Q: Did you go into quarters?

Adm. S.: No. The First Fleet didn't have quarters in those days. Actually, my relief went into quarters and that was the first time the First Fleet had ever been in quarters.

Q: Oh, so you just stayed in your own . . .?

Adm. S.: We just stayed in the house we lived in in Coronado.

Q: But it was very prestigous even though for a very short time?

Adm. S.: Oh, yes. It was a fine job. Well, so now, where are we?

Q: Now you went back to Washington.

Adm. S.: Now we're going back to Washington.

Q: Have you ever plotted your career or your travels on a map to show all of your back and forths?

Adm. S.: No. Of course, that map up there tells where I went when I was CinCPac, but it's . . .

Q: Is that just for that purpose?

Adm. S.: Yes.

Q: It's fascinating.

Adm. S.: All right. So now we're in July or August 1960, I guess, and I think I reported to Washington in August.

Q: I had July was when you went, but that doesn't mean that you didn't report a little later on. My information says that you commanded the First Fleet until July '60.

Adm. S.: Yes.

Q: So probably it was in August when you went to D. C. and Plans and Policy.

Adm. S.: Okay, so we'll say it was probably August of 1960 when I reported to OpNav to relieve Vice Admiral Austin as Deputy Chief of Naval Operations for Plans and Policy.

Q: Had you requested any of these jobs? You said it was a matter of luck, and I just . . .

Adm. S.: No, I didn't request any of them. The pattern of my career was, as I told you, I was very fortunate to fall into jobs like the planner on Seventh Fleet staff for that month and a half that gave me a reputation as a planner . . .

Q: As a planner?

Adm. S.: Yes. And then I went to First Fleet and I met Admiral Stump, and had a reputation as a planner and was his planner, and he brought me out to CinCPacFlt staff as a plans and operations, and then I got the cruiser division, and then I went to CNO's startegic plans, and then I went off on cruisers/destroyers, and then First Fleet, and I went back as, a logical way to go, Deputy Chief for Planning.

Q: But it's so wonderful that you had something on which to build everything.

Adm. S.: It was a combination of luck and satisfying my superiors . . .

Q: Well, yes.

Adm. S.: It plotted out as an ideal career pattern to go to the top, which was very fortunate for me.

Q: Every job I had in the Navy, at the end of it I thought it was always in something entirely new. I never had had any background for any job I went to, and always at the time I left I felt if I could only go on in this, or if I'd known when I came what I know now. Of course, WAVES were a new entity in the Navy because you couldn't plan a career that way, but I can appreciate how enviable . . .

Adm. S.: Oh, yes. My career gets down into the most wonderful pattern you can imagine. All right, so now I'm Deputy Chief for Plans and Policy.

Q: Whom did you say you relieved?

Adm. S.: I relieved Vice Admiral Austin, and we moved into his quarters . . .

Q: Was that on 26th and . . .?

Adm. S.: No. On Nebraska and Massachusetts, out there at the Security Station.

Q: I've never seen that place.

Adm. S.: Oh, they're nice quarters. That was our first experience in the Navy in quarters.

Q: Isn't that funny after quite a few years you'd been in? Who was CNO then?

Adm. S.: Admiral Burke.

Q: So again you were working with someone who you'd had experience with.

Adm. S.: That's right, and I'd worked for him a good many times before, of course. So this is three years of extremely busy time. Of course, we got there at the end of the Eisenhower regime, and President Kennedy came in in January of '61, wasn't it?

Q: Yes. I remember that bad snowstorm the day he was . . .

Adm. S.: Yes. That horrible snowstorm. Yes, I remember that day - of course Secretary Gates was leaving as Secretary of Defense. He was being relieved the next day by Secretary

MacNamara. I went in to say goodbye to Secretary Gates, it must have been - oh, I don't know, 5 o'clock in the afternoon, the evening before inauguration, and it was a horrible snowstorm was going on, and while I was in there, the District Commissioner called up and told him that he had to have some help from the Army, because he had to have some equipment and men to help clear the streets because otherwise they just couldn't pull off the inauguration, and he asked for equipment and men from Fort Belvoir, and Secretary Gates gave him this permission. At any rate, the next day Pennsylvania Avenue was completely clear of snow.

Q: I remember very definitely because I was then at Bainbridge and we went down a group of WAVES. It was the first time WAVES had ever marched in the inaugural parade.

Adm. S.: It was cold that day.

Q: Terribly cold.

Adm. S.: I also remember going home that night after talking to Secretary Gates, and I had a Volkswagen and fortunately had snow tires on the Volkswagen. I took off for home, it must have been 6 o'clock, I guess, maybe later, and I got home in about an hour, but an awful lot of people didn't get home till after midnight.

Q: Cars were stuck all over town.

Adm. S.: Cars were stuck all over town. As a matter of fact, in the Volkswagen the main problem was getting around the cars that were stalled.

Q: I'll bet it was.

Adm. S.: Well, let's see. So I was in the process -- Deputy Chief for Plans - you sit with the CNO in the JCS meetings, and also participate in separate meetings, which are called the meetings of the operations deputies, and they sort of act as a junior JCS, meeting with the director of the joint staff, running the meetings, and they act on JCS matters that they can resolve satisfactorily and if they work on them, why, then the Chiefs don't have to work on them. So it was a very interesting job and in it I met many of the people that I'd met before when I was in Op-60, met a lot of new people that I would work with again. But most of all I got to know everybody in the joint arena and the people in the Secretary of Defense's office.

Q: Was your office then in the Pentagon?

Adm. S.: Yes. And we went through some crises there. First, the Kennedy administration wasn't in very long before we had the Cuban missile crisis, and that was a very interesting time where we were working day and night for quite a spell.

Q: Yes, I wish you would expand on that because in the information I have about you it said that you were deeply involved in the planning for naval operations, including those during the Cuban crisis in 1962, and when I asked you about that briefly one day, you said, "I didn't have much to do with planning that fiasco."

Adm. S.: Well, as far as the Cuban missile crisis goes, when they discovered that the Russians were putting missiles in Cuba, we had a very intense series of meetings with the SecDef and the JCS and agreed on a plan and it involved, of course, the trailing of Russian ships and searching for every ship that was coming in. So we were much involved in getting the Navy lined up to do that job. The Bay of Pigs landing, of course, we were somewhat involved there, too, although the President didn't choose to do that thing the way the Chiefs would have liked to have seen it done and a lot of that was handled right in the White House. And that's about all I'll say about that. I mean I'd have to sort of dredge up in my memory just exactly how that went.

Q: I would think that would be interesting.

Adm. S.: Well, it would be if I could dredge it up, but I don't have a darned thing to refresh my memory, you see. That's the problem.

Q: I could understand the Bay of Pigs being referred to as a fiasco, but I hadn't thought the Cuban missile crisis was.

Adm. S.: Well, I didn't mean to say it was a fiasco, it went fine as far as it went. I mean it was a good, strong stand that the United States took in the first place that made Khrushchev back down and get his missiles out of there, but whether we shouldn't have gone right on after that and polished off Castro, that's open to argument.

Q: Did the Navy want to do it?

Adm. S.: Oh, I think, generally speaking, the Joint Chiefs of Staff would have preferred to have dealt with Castro at the time. Of course, you also have to look at it from the President's point of view and he made a , probably made a, commitment that if Khrushchev would get his missiles out of there, why, we'd leave Cuba alone. I would say that that isn't the way we'd like to have seen them go.

Q: Well, when one is in a certain position, you do as much as you can, then somebody else has to make the final decisions.

Adm. S.: That's right.

Q: But you were awarded the Distinguished Service Medal for your - for the way you performed your duties in that job.

Adm. S.: Oh, yes. The Distinguished Service Medal at the end of a thing like that is sort of a - like a Vice Admiral's Good Conduct medal.

Q: Not that casual, is it?

Adm. S.: Well, it's not quite that casual.

Q: I had wished that it was quoted here, but I don't have if for quotation -

Adm. S.: Oh, I've got it quoted some place.

Q: I'd like to put it in the record.

Adm. S.: I'll have to dig it out. It is around some place.

Q: I want to read the citation of the President of the United States takes pleasure in presenting the Distinguished Service Medal to Admiral Ulysses S. Grant Sharp, Jr., United States Navy, sets forth the following:

> "For exceptionally meritorious service to the government of the United States in a duty of great responsibility as Deputy Chief of Naval Operations, Plans and Policy, from August 1960 through August 1963, exercising outstanding professional competence and dedication in an assignment which involved a thorough knowledge of

all aspects of national power, Admiral, then Vice Admiral, Sharp made a signficant contribution to the security of the United States during a period of continuing international tension. As the principal adviser to the Chief of Naval Operations on matters under consideration by the Joint Chiefs of Staff and as the principal adviser to the Secretary of Navy and the Chief of Naval Operations on international political military affairs, he served with unique distinction, participating directly in the formulation of strategic concepts and plans for the defense of the United States and in the establishment of security policy designed to strengthen and preserve peace throughout the world. Through his vision and wide knowledge of the role of naval forces as a component of total national strength, he engendered the admiration and respect of all with whom he served. His comprehensive grasp and understanding of military power enhanced his brilliant contribution in support of national objectives, as typified during the Cuban crisis in October 1962. Admiral Sharp's distinguished service throughout this period reflects great credit upon himself and the United States naval service. For the President, Paul H. Nitze, Secretary of the Navy."

Adm. S.: During this period, one of the interesting events was Mr. McNamara's first meeting with the JCS, a meeting in which he seemed most anxious to get the JCS views and was most attentive and asked many questions about the subject matter under discussion. It was a different McNamara that attended JCS meetings during the last year of my tour as D/CNO Plans.

Q: How do you account for that?

Adm. S.: At that time, he was not willing to listen to discussions with the same degree of accommodation that he was at first.

Q: This in a three-year period?

Adm. S.: Yes.

Q: How do you account for his change?

Adm. S.: He was getting rather arrogant. He was impatient to a considerable degree. He would often cut the meeting short before the Chiefs had had a chance to have the discussion with him that they desired to have.

Q: What made him be that way?

Adm. S.: Well, he was just getting to the point where he was relying on his own staff and not relying as much on the Chiefs.

Q: His civilian staff?

Adm. S.: Yes. He had started the great centralization of authority in the office of the Secretary of Defense and he was cutting the Chiefs out of the pattern of decision-making to a considerable extent. As I say, he frequently didn't attend JCS meetings at all.

Q: That must have been extremely frustrating.

Adm. S.: Well, it was an interesting pattern. Got even worse as time went on. Anyway, the point is that I attended the first meeting of the JCS that McNamara attended, and I watched him over a six-year period, and it was a very interesting change in this way.

Q: During the three years that you were in D/CNO Plans and Policy, what were the developments in the Vietnamese picture?

Adm. S.: There were, of course, many developments. At first I guess I should say that during the period of, starting, perhaps, in 1958, it became quite clear that the Viet Cong were being reinforced by cadres sent in from North Vietnam. Many of these people were people that had left South Vietnam during the 1954 period, when our Navy was moving people from South Vietnam to North Vietnam and from North Vietnam to South Vietnam. So some of these people who had left South

Vietnam in 1954 were beginning to come back to South Vietnam, having been trained in North Vietnam in the Communist ideology and were trained as guerrillas and were now coming back.

Q: And I presume that because of their contacts in the South and their training in the North, that actually put them in leadership jobs?

Adm. S.: That's right. After they'd had intensive training in both military and political fields, these people - and they were called Regroupees, were infiltrated back into South Vietnam to go into positions of leadership in guerilla forces. And, of course, during the period '59 and '60, assassinations and kidnapings of people opposed to the Viet Cong were increasing, and then during 1968, the infiltration of Regroupees from the North was even higher . . .

Q: I think you mean 1960.

Adm. S.: Yes. 1960, that's right . . . were even higher and there were many Communists from North Vietnam coming down into South Vietnam. And, again, the North Vietnamese were using the people that had regrouped from South Vietnam, because they needed this familiarity with the countryside in South Vietnam in order to make good guerrilla fighters.

Q: And when you were in Washington, the JCS, of course, were well aware of what was going on?

Adm. S.: Well, the JCS, of course, were very interested in the happenings out there and kept close track of what was going on. In September of 1960, there was a meeting of the Lao Dong Party in Hanoi, and that Party set the liberation of South Vietnam as one of its primary tasks. This congress called upon the people of the South to form a united front and to struggle against what they called the United States-Diem clique in order to - what they said, "Unify the fatherland." So at that point it became clear that Hanoi was going to attempt to take over South Vietnam by one means or another.

Q: Did the JCS have any plan for subverting that, or for stopping it, or what was their approach to it?

Adm. S.: The JCS were keeping track of the situation. They knew that things weren't going the way we'd like to see them go, and it amounted mostly to sending in more advisers to help out without really getting into combat.

Q: And all we could do was to support the President's policy at that point?

Adm. S.: Well, that's what we're supposed to do. Yes, that's right.

Q: Whether you like it or not!

Adm. S.: Well, I think the Chiefs were in accord with the way the United States was handling the situation. Then in January of 1961, Radio Hanoi announced that there was being created a National Liberation Front in South Vietnam, and that's the first time we'd heard of the National Liberation Front called the NLF, and we heard it for years after, and still do. At the same time, the guerrilla forces in South Vietnam were growing quite rapidly and, I think, at the end of the year 1961 there were something like 26,000 local and main force units in South Vietnam, which was five times as many as there were at the beginning of the year. So the Chiefs were very concerned about how things were going, and there were increasingly large attacks on units in South Vietnam and on cities and hamlets. Then, on the 13th of May 1961, Vice President Lyndon Johnson and President Diem issued a joint communique which announced that United States Defense and Economic Development programs for Vietnam would be expanded because of the worsening situation. Toward the end of 1961, President Kennedy decided to enlarge U.S. support for the South Vietnamese. The United States agreed at that time that the South Vietnamese regular forces should be increased to 200,000 and they would give support to such a size armed forces. Then there were also increases in the regional forces and the popular forces.

Q: You used two phrases there - the regional forces and the popular forces. What was the difference there?

Adm. S.: Well, regional forces are organized forces that move around the country, but generally stay in the province in which they live and act as sort of a civil guard. The popular forces are - were also called self-defense forces, and they're essentially people recruited from a village or hamlet that act in defense of their own village.

Q: Are they part of the Army?

Adm. S.: No, they're not part of the Army.

Q: Are they paid?

Adm. S.: They're paid a very small amount, but they're given arms - at first they didn't even have uniforms, but finally they gave them uniforms. Continuing on with the - with how things developed in South Vietnam, because I think this is important . . .

Q: But I wonder - did we increase at that time our military advisers when we supported their increase of the South Vietnamese Army, did we agree to increase our personnel there, too?

Adm. S.: Yes, at that point I think we agreed that military advisers would work with operational Vietnamese units in the field, and this was the first time this had happened. Then in December of 1961 it was decided to deploy two U.S. Army helicopter companies to South Vietnam to provide support for the South Vietnamese Army, and also to help train Vietnamese helicopter units.

Q: How many does that mean - two U.S. - when you say two U.S. Army helicopter companies, how many helicopters are we talking about?

Adm. S.: I think, as I recall it, an Army helicopter company has roughly 20 to 25 helicopters.

Q: Oh, so that was a goodly number -

Adm. S.: Quite a few, yes.

Q: And, of course, all our personnel went with them?

Adm. S.: Yes, that's right. So I think, then at the end of '61, there were probably around 3,000 American military in Vietnam. In 1962, I think the first thing we did was install a tactical air control system in Vietnam, and then we sent in some logistic support aircraft, the C-123 aircraft, and these were used for airlift and they were very useful aircraft because they could take off from a fairly short field. Now, in 1962, the North Vietnamese continued to infiltrate and they were building up their forces in the South by recruiting South Vietnamese and kidnaping them if they couldn't recruit them, and the situation got steadily worse. In February of 1962, they set up the United States Military Assistance Command in Vietnam and Made General Paul Harkins the commander of that unit.

Q: Was he an Army general?

Adm. S.: He was an Army general, right. Well, I think - during '62 they sent in some more C-123s and I think there were a few more Army helicopters sent in, so that in that year I think we had four helicopter companies in Vietnam.

Q: Helicopters have really come into their own. I meant to ask you when we were talking about Korea - actually started being an integral part of the military forces in Korea, did they not?

Adm. S.: Yes. They were used in Korea.

Q: Not much in World War II, were they?

Adm. S.: No, they weren't used at all . . .

Q: Not at all.

Adm. S.: But by the time the Korean War came along, helicopters were far enough advanced that they were used at first to pick up pilots from fallen aircraft and do things like that, then they got to be used more and more, of course, in the Korean War. Then, of course, by the time the Vietnamese War came along, why, they were pretty well developed.

Q: It's interesting that that was the first military assistance we actually gave them.

Adm. S.: Yes. Right. Well, in that country where you have poor roads and the Viet Cong were able to intercept convoys on the roads all the time the helicopter gets to be a very important way of moving people and freight around. I guess in '62, of course, there was a lot more guerrilla activity and a lot of attacks on towns and all that sort of thing and the terrorists were getting worse and worse. By the end of 1962, we had about 11,000 U.S. military in South Vietnam. We put Special Forces detachment into Vietnam during 1962 and set up a U.S. Army Special Forces Command.

Q: What was that for?

Adm. S.: They were there to assist the South Vietnamese, to train the South Vietnamese, and to counter the - as counter guerrilla forces, really.

Q: But I was trying to think what they did as opposed to the advisory people.

Adm. S.: Well, you know, they were advisers to units of Vietnamese - Vietnamese Special Forces kind of guerilla fighters, anti-guerilla fighters, you'd call them.

Q: Oh, the Special Forces were anti-guerilla fighters?

Adm. S.: That's right. I think it's important to recognize that there was a steady buildup of American forces for very good reasons. They were trying to help this country stay free and the country was having a tough time, and our assistance increased as the North Vietnamese aggression increased. So people that say that we - it was a mistake to get into this war, why, you'd have to say, yes, it was a mistake to get into it if you are willing to have the United States back out of the Western Pacific, out of Asia, and not help our friends. But if we're willing to help our friends, why, then it was pretty important for us to increase our commitment.

So we go on into '63. We began to have problems in 1963. Our helicopters were getting shot at. We lost some helicopters in 1963, and we sent in more helicopters. It was during this year that we began to have Buddhist monks burn themselves to death. That got to be a big problem.

Q: I kind of felt that if they wanted to burn themselves to death, go ahead.

Adm. S.: It was a painful, sad thing, and you notice that they've gotten over that now. They don't burn themselves anymore. So, if we get up as far as September of '63, we're now into the area where I'm being detached from duty in D/CNO for Plans. So after three years in Washington as D/CNO, Plans and Policy, I was detached in August of '63 and reported to - August of '63, it was either August or early September, I can't remember which.

Q: I have you reported as Admiral and Commanderin-Chief, Pacific Fleet, on September 30. Is that the date you have?

Adm. S.: Yes, that's right. I can't remember how much leave I took in between the two duty stations. Probably not very much. Anyway on September 27th, 1963 I was promoted to Admiral . . .

Q: How did you get that word?

Adm. S.: Well, of course, I was in Washington when I was told I was going out there to be CinCPacFlt and I don't remember how that happened.

Q: They told you at the same time that you'll go out and you knew then that you would be admiral by getting that job?

Adm. S.: Yes. Then, on the 30th of September I relieved Admiral Sides as CinCPacFlt.

Q: Can I ask a personal question? Why were you selected for that job?

Adm. S.: Oh, I guess - well, again, of course, my career pattern was ideally set up for me to be CinCPacFlt. I'd had duty on CinCPacFlt's staff. I'd had duty on First Fleet, I'd have a type command. I'd been in OpNav in planning jobs, and I was just - couldn't have had a better career pattern. And I'd been fortunate in working with the people that were making the decisions, and I also had enough time left before I retired to be eligible to be CinCPac when Admiral Felt retired, you see. And I was known by all the services and by the SecDef and all the people in that line, so . . .

Q: Well, of course, they selected you because you were the best man for the job, really, but I wanted your comment.

Adm. S.: Well, whether I was the best man for the job or not - maybe I was, but - what I'm saying is I was pretty lucky in having an ideal career pattern for it. Okay, I think that's enough, isn't it, for today?

Interview No. 3 with Admiral U.S. Grant Sharp
Place: San Diego, California
Date: 13 December 1969
Subject: Biography
By: Etta Belle Kitchen

Adm. S.: I arrived in Honolulu on September the 27th, 1963 with my wife and my mother to take command of the Pacific Fleet, relieving Admiral John H. Sides. We had the turnover ceremony on 30 September 1963 aboard the USS Topeka (CLG-8) at the Naval Station, Pearl Harbor, Hawaii. After the change of command there was the usual reception on the grounds of the Officers' Club in the shipyard at Pearl Harbor.

The Pacific Fleet - or I should say as CinCPacFlt, I headed the world's largest naval command. There were more than 400 ships, 3,000 aircraft, and 250,000 men, sailors and Marines, under my command. The area of responsibility was about 80 million square miles, or more than 40% of the earth's surface. It extends from the West Coast to the middle of the Indian Ocean, and from the North to the South Pole. On the afternoon that I took over, I was informed that there had been a number of men injured in a beachhead assault on the island of Molokai. This was part of a training exercise under the command of Rear Admiral John S. Coye, Commander of Amphibious Group Three. No, Coye was going to investigate the incident. I don't have the name of the officer in charge of the landing. In any event, about fifteen landing craft were damaged in varying degrees in the heavy surf while they were attempting a landing. I ordered a helicopter that afternoon and flew to the scene of the landing with two or three members of my staff.

Q: That was the day you took over?

Adm. S.: Yes. The conditions were unusual and, apparently, unexpected.

In any event, my tour as CinCPacFlt started out in high gear. When I returned from the scene of the landing, I ordered an investigation to determine just what had happened, and also issued a message praising the courage of the crews involved in the mishap. On the 2nd of October I started my routine calls by calling on Admiral H. D. Felt, U.S. Navy, Commander-in-Chief, Pacific, at his headquarters at Camp Smith. On the 7th of October, Vice Admiral Sir Wilfred Hastings-Harrington, Chief of the Naval Staff of the Royal Australian Navy, visited me at my headquarters. On of 9th of October I called on General Jacob E. Smart, U.S. Air Force, Commander-in-Chief, Pacific Air Forces, at Hickham Air Force Base. That week I also called on General James F. Collins, U.S. Army, Commander-in-Chief, U.S. Army, Pacific, at his headquarters. On the 28th of October I departed on my first tour of the Western Pacific and the seventh Fleet as Commander-in-Chief, Pacific Fleet. On this tour I visited Guam, the Philippines, the Seventh Fleet, Taiwan, Hong Kong, Okinawa, Korea, and Japan. On the 30th of October I called on the Governor of Guam,

Manuel F. L. Guerrero. Then I went on to Manila and called on President Macapagal of the Republic of the Philippines on the 31st of October. That day, accompanied by Rear Admiral J. P. Monroe, Commander Naval Forces, Philippines, I also called on the Honorable Makerio Peralta, the Secretary of National Defense of the Philippines. From Manila, we proceeded to Baguio for the Seventh Fleet scheduling conference which is attended by Commander, Seventh Fleet, and most of his flag and general officers. I should correct my last statement: we did go to Baguio for a short visit and a game of golf with Rear Admiral Walter Price, Rear Admiral Bill Irvin, all of us of the class of 1927 at the Naval Academy. After the golf game, we returned to Subic Bay where the Seventh Fleet scheduling conference was held. Do you think we ought to go into the people that were present at this conference, the flag officers? I don't know whether it's necessary.

Q: I think if there were any particular interesting items, but other than that, I would not think . . .

Adm. S.: I'll just say that this scheduling conference was held quarterly by Commander, Seventh Fleet, and is held for the purpose of coordinating the fleet schedule for the coming quarters. At this particular conference, Vice Admiral T. H. Moorer was Commander, Seventh Fleet, and was in attendance and running the meeting. Vice Admiral Taylor Keith, who was Commander, First Fleet, was in attendance, also Rear Admiral W. D. Irvin, Commander, Service Force, Rear Admiral Jack

Monroe, Commander Naval Forces, Philippines, Rear Admiral Marshall E. Dornin, Commander, Cruiser/Destroyer Force, Pacific Fleet, Rear Admiral E. M. Metzger, Supply Corps and the Force Supply Officer for Commander Service Force, Rear Admiral E. S. Miller, Rear Admiral James R. Davis, Civil Engineer Corps, Rear Admiral John M. Lee, Rear Admiral Harry Richtor, Rear Admiral Robert A. McPherson, Rear Admiral Francis E. Boyle, Rear Admiral C. A. Karaberis, Rear Admiral Russell Kafauver, Rear Admiral Walter H. Price, and Rear Admiral Frederick L. Ashworth.

Q: How many stars did that make?

Adm. S.: Quite a few -- 44, it says here.

The Marine generals in attendance were Major General James M. Masters, Commanding, 3rd Marine Division, and Major General Frank C. Tharin, Commander of the 1st Marine Air Wing. Along with the flag and general officers there were four captains, eight commanders, five lieutenant commanders, one lieutenant, and a lieutenant, junior grade.

Q: How did he get in there? That really was a schedule to plan the whole . . .

Adm. S.: That was the plan for Seventh Fleet employment and to tie it in with the First Fleet.

Q: Was Vietnam a subject of the meeting, or do you recall?

Adm. S.: Yes, it was, and it was a very important part of the meeting because while we were there we received word that Diem had been - that there was a coup in Vietnam and that Diem had been thrown out.

Q: That would have been in November '63, then, wouldn't it?

Adm. S.: That's right. 1 November '63. So we immediately had a conference considering the changed situation.

Q: Did it affect the scheduling?

Adm. S.: It did not affect the scheduling at that time. Admiral H. D. Felt, the Pacific Commander-in-Chief, was in Hong Kong on that day, and Rear Admiral - I mean, and General Jacob B. Smart, the Pacific Air Forces Commander, was in Japan. It was just a coincidence, of course, that we three senior officers of the Pacific command were in the Western Pacific at that time. As a result of the coup in Saigan, I had to change my schedule to eliminate a planned trip to South Vietnam.

Q: Why was that?

Adm. S.: Because of the unsettled conditions in Saigon. So, instead of going to Saigon, I spent several days observing Seventh Fleet operations. On the 4th of November I arrived in Taipeh and was met by Vice Admiral Charles L. Melson,

Commander, Taiwan Defense Command, and Admiral Ni-U-Si, Commander-in-Chief, Chinese Navy. This was the first of many visits to Taiwan in the next four and a half years, and was the first of a warm acquaintanceship with Admiral and Mrs. Ni. On arrival, I had a press conference with the local press and then had lunch with Admiral Jerauld Wright, United States Ambassador to the Government of the Republic of China - a luncheon that was hosted by Admiral Melson. Included in my visit was a call on Admiral Ni at his headquarters, and also a call on the Minister of National Defense, Minister Yu-Ta-Wei.

We next visited Okinawa and called on Major General Masters, Commander of the Third Marine Division, and Rear Admiral McPherson, Commander, Taiwan Patrol Force. Included in the visit was a combat review of the Second Battalion, Ninth Marines, at Camp Hanson in Central Okinawa.

We then went on to Seoul, Korea, where we were met by Rear Admiral J. M. Alford, Commander, U.S. Naval Forces, Korea, and Vice Admiral Lee Maeng Kee, who was the Chief of Naval Operations, Republic of Korean Navy, and his wife. This was our first acquaintance with the Lee Maeng Kees that was to go on for several years. They are a most pleasant couple. I called on Admiral Lee and on Lieutenant General Kim, the Commandant of the Korean Marine Corps, then to a luncheon hosted by Vice Admiral Lee Maeng Kee, followed by a call on Korean Prime Minister Kim

Our last stop was in Japan where I called on Rear Admiral Walter Price, Commander, U.S. Naval Forces, Japan, and also on General Hiyashi, Chairman of the Joint Staff Council of the Japan Defense Agency. On this call I was accompanied by General - Lieutenant General M. A. Preston, U.S. Air Force, Commander of U.S. Forces in Japan. Following this call, we called on Admiral Ichizo Sugie, Chief of the Maritime Staff. Here, again, I made the acquaintance of a very delightful - some very delightful friends in Japan. General Hiyashi and Admiral Sugie. Mrs. Sharp accompanied me on this trip, as she did on almost all of the trips that I made to the Western Pacific, and she made some delightful and lasting friendships in all these countries.

Q: I'm sure she did. I'm sure she added a great deal.

Adm. S.: I should add that in each of these countries, I called on the ambassador, the United States Ambassador and made friendships which were to be very useful to me when I became Commander-in-Chief, Pacific. In Japan, at that time, the ambassador was Edwin Reischauer. On the 20th of November, 1963, Secretary of Defense Robert S. MacNamara and General Maxwell D. Taylor, Chairman of the Joint Chiefs of Staff, arrived at Hickham Air Force base for a conference at Pacific Command Headquarters. Along with the other CinCPac component commanders, I met Mr. MacNamara and General Taylor at the airfield, and subsequently attended their conference at Camp Smith, where Admiral Felt presided.

Q: What was the purpose of their visit?

Adm. S.: The purpose of their visit, as I recall it, was an assessment of the situation in Vietnam.

Q: Did you attend?

Adm. S.: I did attend, that's right.

Q: Do you remember any major decision, if any, that were made then?

Adm. S.: No, I really don't. On the 22nd of November 1963 Vice Admiral Siri, Commander-in-Chief of the Royal Thai Navy, arrived at start a week-long orientation visit in Hawaii. I recall that on that morning, having met Vice Admiral Siri, I escorted him to the Macalapa BOQ, where he was to stay.

As we arrived at the BOQ, we heard a radio announcing that President Kennedy had been assassinated. This happened as the conference at Camp Smith was just terminating, and changed the plans of many of the participants in the conference, for all of theWashington contingent proceeded to Washington immediately.

Q: Do you recall MacNamara's attitude toward the military at the time of this conference?

Adm. S.: No, it wasn't anything out of the ordinary. His attitude toward the military wasn't too bad. I also recall on that day, after dropping Admiral Siri off at the BOQ, I returned to my headquarters, told my flight lieutenant that the BOQ was - the suite that Admiral Siri was in was not suitable, and for him to get the CinCPacFlt guesthouse ready for Admiral Siri. This involved a change in plans because Admiral Claud Ricketts, Vice Chief of Naval Operations, was to stay in the guesthouse part of the week that Admiral Siri was there. Nevertheless, I was apprehensive that the - that Admiral Siri would be offended at the inadequate quarters in the BOQ at Macalapa, so I put in a hurried telephone call to Washington to Admiral Ricketts and explained the situation to him and said that Admiral Felt would put him up in his guesthouse. It turned out that this was a very prophetic move, because when the flag lieutenant went back to inform Admiral Siri that he was to be moved into the fleet guesthouse. Admiral Siri was on the phone to the Royal Hawaiian Hotel. He was moving into a hotel because the quarters were so bad. So we averted losing a good friend to the United States.

Q: Yes. Did you even have any relationships with him subsequent to that time?

Adm. S.: Oh, yes, I knew Admiral Siri for a good many years after that. A very fine gentleman. Admiral Ricketts arrived in Hawaii for a day on the 25th of November. He was on his way to - for a one-month tour of the Pacific.

My next trip was one to the West Coast on 16 December 1963 to join Navy Secretary Nitze in a visit to the Pacific

Fleet and West Coast naval establishments. This involved a visit to the recruit depot at San Diego and the Marine base at Camp Pendleton, and aboard various ships. At the conclusion of this visit, we returned to Honolulu. During this visit we also visited the Naval Air Station at Lemoore, and were aboard the First Fleet for a two-day operational-readiness demonstration.

Back in Honolulu for the holidays and a large reception for our many friends in Honolulu and for the military of all services on duty on Oahu. I've forgotton just what day that was held. I guess it was held probably on the 30th of December. Also on the 30th of December we had the pleasure of greeting His Eminence Francis Cardinal Spellman who had completed his Christmas trip to Antarctica. Cardinal Spellman was the Roman Catholic vicar of the armed forces of the United States.

The next trip to the continental United States was made in early January 1964 - or mid-January 1964 - to address the Naval War College at Newport, Rhode Island. On the 25th of January we were in Los Angeles where I was the guest of honor at the 1964 Navy Ball. Chairman of the Ball was Mr. Hugh Evans.

Q: Was that Navy-League-sponsored?

Adm. S.: No. This was sponsored by the people of Los Angeles. It's a very nice Ball and we attended a number of times. Commander-in-Chief, Pacific Fleet, is normally the guest of honor, so after I became Commander-in-Chief, Pacific, I was no longer - actually, I wasn't invited to it because I was a unified commander then.

Back in Honolulu on the 28th of January I talked to the Annual Typhoon Conference held by military and civilian weather men. About this time there began to be rumors about who would relieve Admiral Felt as the Commander-in-Chief, Pacific.

Q: Who all was mentioned?

Adm. S.: A news item in the Star Bulletin of 27 January 1964 said, "A pair of the favorites to succeed Felt are General Jacob B. Smart, Pacific Air Forces commander, and Admiral U. S. Grant Sharp, Pacific Fleet commander. Other men in the running include General Hamilton Howze, U.S. Army, then in command in Korea, and Admiral Claud V. Ricketts, Deputy Chief of Naval Operations."

Q: Who actually makes the selection?

Adm. S.: The selection was made by McNamara. Well, in consultation with the President, of course.

Q: Had that been part of the reason for his coming out, do you suppose?

Adm. S.: No.

Q: But he did meet all the people involved at that time, didn't he?

Adm. S.: Yes, everybody was there, but Admiral Ricketts wasn't there. On the 9th of February, I think it was, I left for a trip to Vietnam, which was to be my first visit to Saigon. On the 11th of February I arrived at Ton Son Nhut airport and was met by General Paul D. Harkins, Chief of the Military Assistance Command, Vietnam, and General Nguyen Van Cao, Director of the Combat Development and Test Center, also met by Captain Chung Tang Kang. On the 26th of February, Vice Admiral G.A.F.D. Bush, Royal Navy, Commander of the British Navy Staff and Naval Attache in Washington, D.C., visited me in Honolulu . . .

Q: Excuse me, at Saigon, you only visited in the Saigon area? Did you visit other places in Vietnam?

Adm. S.: As I recall, I was just in Saigon. And he was joined in Honolulu by Vice Admiral D. P. Dryer, Flag Officer and Commander-in-Chief, Far East Fleet. We had a good visit with these outstanding British naval officers and I saw them many times after that. On the 28th of February, Washington announced that I had been named by President Johnson to succeed Admiral Felt as Commander-in-Chief, Pacific.

Q: Is that the way you received the news?

Adm. S.: I think I got it a little ahead of time by somebody telephoning. Not very much ahead of time because everybody was scared to death that it would leak out before the President announced it because he wouldn't like that.

Q: What was your reaction when you got the word?

Adm. S.: Well, I knew I had a pretty good chance to get it, so I wasn't exactly surprised.

Q: You were pleased, of course?

Adm. S.: Oh, sure. Naturally. I immediately received congratulations from my good friend Jake Smart, who I'm certain was disappointed at not getting the job, but took it like the wonderful person that he is.

Q: Was it unusual that one Navy man should replace another Navy man?

Adm. S.: No. CinCPac has always been Navy.

On the 2nd of March 1964, Lieutenant General Victor H. Krulak, U.S. Marine Corps, assumed command of the Fleet Marine Force, Pacific. "Brute" Krulak, an old friend, was a welcome addition to the Pacific Fleet. He and I conferred almost daily from the time of his arrival until he left - retired - in May of 1968. He was one of my closest and most valued advisers.

On the 3rd of March, we had a visit from Dr. Thomas W. McNew, Vice Chairman of the Board of Trustees of the National

Geographic Society, and Mrs. McNew, old friends whom we had known in Washington.

Also on the 4th, I guess it was, of March, Vice Admiral E. P. Holmes, U.S. Navy, Commander, First Fleet, arrived in his flagship the USS St. Paul for a visit to Honolulu.

On the 6th of March, Secretary of Defense Robert S. McNamara and General Maxwell D. Taylor arrived in Honolulu to discuss the serious situation in South Vietnam with Admiral Felt, Commander-in-Chief, Pacific, and with CinCPac's component commanders. Secretary McNamara said at a press conference, "the situation is serious. As you know, we've had three governments in three months. The Viet Cong has sought to take advantage of the changes and has greatly increased the rate of their attacks, their acts of terror and harassment." The Secretary and General Taylor left at midnight for Saigon after conferences throughout the day at Camp Smith. Traveling with McNamara, in addition to General Taylor, was David E. Bell, administrator of the Agency for International Development, AID, Arthur Sylvester, Assistant Secretary of Defense for Information, and John T. McNaughton, Assistant Secretary for International Security Affairs. Also William P. Bundy, Assistant Secretary of State, and William Sullivan, Chairman of the new Vietnam Coordinating Committee.

On the 11th of March we departed Honolulu and arrived at the Naval Air Station - no, I guess we departed Honolulu on the 10th, and arrived at the Naval Air Station, San Diego, on the 11th and hosted a reception at the Naval Air Station that day. From there we flew to various shipyards on the

West Coast, including the Long Beach Naval Shipyard, the San Francisco Naval Shipyard, Mare Island Naval Shipyard, and Puget Sound.

Q: Were you the inspecting officer?

Adm. S.: Oh, I was just looking the places over. It wasn't an inspection trip.

Q: You weren't accompanying anyone like did you Nitze before?

Adm. S.: No. I had Rear Admiral Irvin, who was my Commander, Service Force, along on this trip.

Back in Honolulu on the 20th of March, Secretary Nitze arrived for a visit, was given briefings, honors, and we had a reception for him. I should have mentioned that on the 11th and 12th of March I hosted the Fourth Annual Pacific Fleet Flag Officers' Conference at North Island.

I am now going back to summarize the situation in Vietnam chronologically in 1963.

Since the introduction of American helicopters to provide added mobility to the ARVN, Viet Cong units had generally refused to stand and fight when South Vietnamese forces were airlifted into close proximity, but in January of 1963, at Ap Back, in the Delta, a Viet Cong force engaged a superior ARVN force, attempting to surround it by using helo-borne assault tactics in conjunction with conventional ground movements. Five American helicopters were destroyed and nine damaged. The VC inflicted heavy casualties and later withdrew. The ARVN forces did not close the trap they had set and failed to take aggressive advantage of their superiority. The results of this battle increased the Viet Cong's confidence in their ability to fight successfully against government forces with superior equipment.

In April 1963, President Diem proclaimed a sweeping chou hoi, or open-arms, campaign promising clemency, financial aid, and family reunions to guerillas who stopped fighting and returned to live under government authority. In 1963 the new UH-1B helicopters were used for the first time in ARVN operations with considerable success. The first operation was in June. The increased speed and maneuverability of these aircraft compared to the CH-21s were a welcome improvement. Growing tension between South Vietnam's various factions led to a riot in Hue early in May. Tensions increased and martial law was imposed in Hue in June.

Also in June a Buddhist monk, Thick Quang Duc, committed suicide by burning himself in public. Within several days riots broke out in Saigon and were forcibly put down by South Vietnamese troops. As the Buddhist crisis persisted, martial law was extended throughout the entire nation in August. However, intermittent rioting continued.

On 18 August the show place strategic hamlet of Ben Tuong, the first built of all strategic hamlets in Operation Sunrise, was overrun by the Viet Cong. Also in August armed government police and troops raided the Buddhist Xa Loi pagoda in Saigon. Incidents such as these caused periodic self-immolation by Buddhist monks and resignations from the South Vietnamese government, and kept feelings at a high pitch.

On 24 October, in response to an earlier invitation from President Diem, the United States fact-finding mission arrived in Saigon to investigate charges that the government was oppressing Buddhists. The fact-finding mission reported to the United Nations 24 hours before Diem was assassinated that the charges were unfounded.

The following day another monk burned himself to death in public, the seventh such suicide in four months. On 1 November a military coup organized by key forces of the armed forces deposed President Diem and his brother, Ngo Dinh Nhu, and both of them were later killed. A provisional military government was established under the leadership of Major General Duong Van Minh, also known as Big Minh. By year's end, it was clear that the November coup had proven costly in the countryside. Many strategic hamlets were overrun or revealed to be Communist-controlled. Weapon losses to the Viet Cong increased sharply. Many local paramilitary units simply melted away into the population. It was unclear at this time whether the new government would be able to heal the internal wounds and provide leadership required to reverse the course of the struggle.

By the end of 1963, the Communists were rapidly taking over the country. The number of VC-initiated incidents had risen precipitously to 188 per week. During the year some

2,000 assassinations and 7,000 kidnapings were perpetrated. Crisis was at hand. The cautious optimism that had prevailed in 1962 was a thing of the past.

On 29 March 1964 in Honolulu, I was visited by Vice Admiral Lee Maeng Kee, who I had visited earlier in Korea. Vice Admiral Lee called at my headquarters for a conference and we had a dinner party for Vice Admiral and Mrs. Lee in our quarters.

On 7 April General John K. Waters, U.S. Army, the new Commander-in-Chief, U.S. Army, Pacific, called at my headquarters. In late April '64, I visited Mare Island Naval Shipyard to make the principal address at the commissioning of the USS Daniel Boone.

On the 14th of May 1964 I was in Los Angeles where I gave the Armed Forces Day address to the Los Angeles Junior Chamber of Commerce.

On 22 June 1964 Vice Admiral Thomas H. Moorer relieved me as Commander-in-Chief of the U.S. Pacific Fleet.

Now, to relate the situation in the first six months of 1964 to the Vietnam situation, I will summarize chronologically the major events of the first six months of 1964.

On the 2nd of January 1964 a Vietnamese army force in the Delta region seized a large cache of Communist-Chinese manufactured equipment, including mortars, 300,000 rounds of small arms ammunition, and recoilles rifle ammunition.

On 18 January 115 helicopters, the largest airlift of the war, carried 1,100 Vietnamese troops into the critical War Zone D region, north of Bien Hoa. Despite the magnitude of this action, no enemy contact was made and the operation produced no significant tactical results.

On 27 January Lieutenant General Westmoreland assumed duties as Deputy Commander, United States Military Assistance Command, Vietnam.

In late January there were persistent rumors of impending political upheaval. These reports turned out to be true when on 30 January General Khanh ousted the government of General Minh. The modest tactical successes achieved in January were offset by a wave of Viet Cong terrorism and victories in February. Violence first erupted in the vicinity of Kontum City on 3 February when enemy forces attacked the compound of the U.S. Military Assistance Advisory Group. During the period 3-6 February, Viet Cong forces launched a major offensive in Tay Ninh province and in the Mekong Delta. In both areas government forces suffered heavy casualties. On 7 February the enemy initiated a series of bombing attacks in Saigon. Three U.S. personnel were killed and 50 wounded by Viet Cong bomb explosions in a theatre at a time when it was occupied primarily by American personnel and their dependents. Continuing his reorganization of the government, General Khanh assumed control of the nation by naming himself Premier and appointing General Minh as Chief of State on 10 February.

On 2 and 4 March, Vietnamese forces achieved an encouraging victory. Vietnamese airborne and mechanized troops operated on the Plain of Reeds along the Cambodian border, killing over

100 and capturing 300 of the enemy. In the course of this action, Vietnamese units inadvertently intruded into Cambodia and precipitated a sharp exchange of diplomatic notes with Cambodia. In an effort to consolidate his political control, General Khanh on 6 March replaced three of the incumbent South Vietnamese Army corps commanders and five of the nine division commanders. This purge of the military high command was followed by wholesale replacement of province and district chiefs over the next several months. Due to the weakness of the central government, these corps commanders had enjoyed autonomy approaching that of the traditional war lords. They were not only responsible for military operations within their corps areas, but also had been assigned the additional role of so-called government delegates, which embraced civil and administrative powers. Each time the command structure of the Vietnamese army was altered by the power struggle in Saigon, mass changes in provincial and district leadership occurred automatically. As much as any other factor, this turbulence in the administrative structure of the nation contributed to the deterioration of the government's credibility and concurrently increased the prestige and power of the enemy's position among the people. And, of course, these rapid changes also made the administration of the government more inefficient - even more inefficient than it was before. In contradiction to the chaotic state of the nation's political affairs, the Vietnamese army in the Plain of Reeds provided a second gratifying victory over the enemy on 22 March, trapping a

Viet Cong battalion in a fortified village and killing 120 of them. Although the general morale and efficiency of the Vietnamese armed forces was poor, there were isolated examples of great valor and aggressiveness on the parts of some commanders. By and large, the airborne and Marine troops, some Army units, and some of the Ranger battalions acquitted themselves well. These examples were enough to confirm my conviction that a major problem within the armed forces was poor leadership. This leadership problem started with the central government and permeated the entire civil and military system. The growing aggressiveness of the enemy around the capital city and indications of a possible counter-coup prompted General Khanh on 7 April to create a special military zone around Saigon. Less than a week later, the district capital Kien Long, in the southern tip of the Mekong Delta, was overrun by the enemy. Apart from the general concern which resulted from the loss of a major political center, the Vietnamese Army suffered over 300 killed and 200 civilians also were killed or wounded.

On 2 May a Viet Cong underwater demolition team sank the helicopter-carrying USNS *Card* while it was at berth in the port of Saigon. The *Card* was a MSTS ship used to transfer airplanes, both fixed and rotary-wing, from the United States to various places in the Western Pacific. Meanwhile, in Saigon . . .

Q: Apparently our government made no actual response to that, did they?

Adm. S.: No. Terrorism continued unabated, including an abortive Viet Cong attempt to mine a bridge along Secretary of Defense Robert S. MacNamara's route into Saigon on the 10th of May. A major re-organization of the U.S. command took place on 15 May. The Military Assistance Advisory Group was abolished and its functions integrated with the MACV structure, facilitating and simplifying coordination.

Q: Would you say that MACV structure again? What was that?

Adm. S.: Military Assistance Command, Vietnam. Eliminating duplication of effort and achieving a significant economy in U.S. personnel.

On 20 June General Harkins departed Vietnam and General Westmoreland assumed command as Commander of U.S. Military Assistance Command, Vietnam. Also in June, Ambassador Lodge resigned and was replaced by General Maxwell D. Taylor early in July. Mr. U. Alexis Johnson was appointed as Deputy Ambassador. Two successful Vietnamese operations were conducted on the 24th and 25th of June. In the first, Vietnamese forces again scored a victory over the enemy on the Plain of Reeds, killing 99 of the Viet Cong. A day later the Vietnamese army attacked a Viet Cong training camp in Quang Ninh province and killed 50 of the enemy. June also marked the beginning of a growing tide of Free World assistance to the Republic of Vietnam. On 29 June a New Zealand army engineer detachment arrived to assist government officials in developing priority civic action projects.

On the 30th of June, I relieved Admiral Felt as Commander-in-Chief, Pacific, aboard the USS Ranger.

The Pacific Command had headquarters at Camp H. M. Smith on the island of Oahu. It is the largest of U.S. unified commands. It had at that time 940,000 military personnel of the Army, Navy, and Marine Corps, and Air Force in the command, in addition to more than 7,500 operational aircraft, and 560 major ships. The Pacific Command area extends on the West - from the West Coast of the Americas - some 8,000 miles across the Pacific into the Indian Ocean, and from the Aleutian Islands down to the area of the South Pole, an area encompassing 85,000,000 square miles. As commander of all U.S. armed forces in the Pacific, CinCPac is responsible directly to the Joint Chiefs of Staff. He is also the U.S. military advisor to the South East Asia Treaty Organization - SEATO, he is the U.S. military representative to the Philippine-United States Defense Council, and the representative to the Australian-New Zealand-United States Council, called ANZUS, and also a military adviser and member of the United States-Japanese security consultative committee.

Q: The command structure is actually pretty well spread out, is it not, in the command structure chart which I want to attach.

Adm. S.: Yes. That's a good thing to attach to it.

Q: Did it ever frighten you or astonish you to have that much authority, command over that . . .

Adm. S.: I can't say that I gave it much thought.

On the 30th of June the State Department rejected a Soviet proposal to reconvene the Geneva conference in Laos, and also on that day, in Vietnam, a U.S. helicopter was shot down by VC ground fire, killing two Americans.

Q: This would be an Army helicopter?

Adm. S.: Yes, I guess it was. Then on the 1st of July we lost a second U.S. helicopter, in which the pilot was killed and three others were hurt.

On the 1st of July in Honolulu I had calls from General Waters, CinC U.S. Army, Pacific, General Smart, Commander-in-Chief, Pacific Air Forces, and Admiral Moorer, who had relieved me at CinCPacFlt. On the 2nd of July, New Zealand's Prime Minister, Holyoake, came through Honolulu. I met him at the airport and we talked at some length on the international situation. This was the first of many meetings with Prime Minister Holyoake.

Q: Excuse me for interrupting, but would it be fair or true to say that for the major portion - or for all of the time that you were CinCPac - was the major concern, were your major efforts toward the war in Vietnam? And related problems?

Adm. S.: Yes. The Vietnam war took up the major part of my time.

Q: So, if we cover your relationships to the whole military's thing in Vietnam, we've really covered the job? There were no extraneous matters really . . .

Adm. S.: Oh, sure, there were things going on in Korea. The Japanese wanted Okinawa back.

Q: And those things we will discuss?

Adm. S.: Yes, sure.

Q: So there's a lot more than just the Vietnamese war that is involved in this job?

Adm. S.: Yes, but the Vietnamese war, naturally, kind of holds the center of the stage, since it was the major thing going on.
The military personnel strength in the Pacific Command was 439,190 on the 1st of January 1964, and 455,689 at the close of the year. That is a correction to the something like 970,000 . . .

Q: You used 940,000 but that included all the various . . .

Adm. S.: Well, it all depends on when that biography was written, see. The personnel strength went up each year, and I guess we'll have to put that in as it goes along.

One of the problems that came up in July of 1964 was Indonesia's claim to territorial sea areas. Indonesia announced her intention in December of 1957 to depart from the three-mile breadth of her territorial sea and claim a 12-mile breadth, measured from straight base lines connecting the outermost points of the islands of Indonesia, and also claimed the waters inside these base lines as national waters. The United States strongly protested this action as being contrary to established international law. However, subsequent to that time, the U.S. on more than one occasion offered to accept a six-mile breadth of territorial waters with an additional belt for exclusive fishing control. In 1960 President Sukarno signed a government regulation officially constituting the 12-mile claim and Indonesia, on several occasions, took positive action to assert her alleged rights in the waters she had claimed as internal. The Indonesian claim had serious strategic implications if allowed to stand. In a July meeting of my staff, I directed that a study be undertaken regarding the maritime and air space of the Indonesian area. I stipulated that the purpose of the study would be to determine the Pacific Command position relating to the serious effects upon the Free World, should the Indonesians restrict maritime and air traffic over and through the Celebes and Java seas. This study was completed on 1 September and constituted a thorough history of the law of the seas concerning territorial waters, including Indonesia's claims, and an analysis of the U.S. position regarding the Indonesian claims.

Q: What was our position . . . ?

Adm. S.: I will not go into the position on the study because it would take too much time. While the stated policy of the U.S. had consistently been to recognize nothing more than a three-mile limit, its actual policy had been one of providing prior notification to Indonesia of intended transits through the area in question. The United States in 1964 informed Indonesia in advance when the Concord Squadron was scheduled to transit the Moluccan Straits.

In May of 1964, upon completion of the annual Coral Sea celebration in Australia, ComSeventhFlt proposed that the destroyer *Gridley* transit the Indonesian internal sea in making its passage from Perth, Australia, to Subic Bay, Philippines. The American Embassy in Djakarta took the position that the U.S. should inform the Indonesians of *Gridley*'s route, or otherwise there was grave danger that such passage would create further difficulties in the already strained U.S.-Indonesian relations. As in the instance of the Concord Squadron, the U.S. gave prior notification to the Indonesians. The U.S. thus had not actually executed its stated policy in the matter. Instead, through fear of exacerbating U.S.-Indonesian relations, the U.S. was, in fact, complying with the Indonesian internal sea and territorial waters edict.

On 2 December the U.S. Ambassador in Djakarta advised that Indonesian officials were taking a belligerent attitude as a result of the recent passage of a British warship through the Sunda Strait. In this instance, notification had not been given to the Indonesians' satisfaction, and they had threatened retaliatory action should the British attempt to pass through the Sunda Strait again. The Ambassador stated that the British probably intended to re-transit the Sunda Strait on the return voyage to Singapore about 12 September. CinCPac immediately recommended to the JCS that they contact the State Department to urge unstinting U.S. support of the United Kingdom position, and that close coordination be initiated between the U.S., United Kingdom, Australia, and other friendly governments to exercise rights of freedom of access to international seas and straits. The JCS concurred with CinCPac's recommendation, but the United Kingdom subsequently gave advance notification to the Indonesians and returned the warship to Singapore by the Lombac Straits, in order to preclude provocative action.

In October CinCPac recommended that the actual practice of the U.S. be modified to the end that the U.S. exercise its historic right to the free use of those waters of the Indonesian archipelago and to claim waters of all other countries which it considered to be high seas, by the frequent and unannounced operation of warships and aircraft therein. And then that the U.S. come out loud and clear in opposition to the illegal Indonesian claim. By the execution within the time frame of the next two months, and at frequent intervals thereafter, of operations within the waters in question to include transits of the Sunda and/or Lombac Straits with appropriate naval forces on an unannounced basis.

The JCS then asked CinCPac to make recommendations for specific cruises, and CinCPac did recommend two cruises.

On the 4th of July the VC launched attacks against U.S. Special Forces training camps in the central provinces.

On the 5th of July General Maxwell Taylor, who had been Chairman of the Joint Chiefs of Staff and was now the newly appointed U.S. Ambassador to South Vietnam, came through Honolulu on his way to Saigon, and I had a chance to talk at some length with him in my office.

On the 6th of July the Nam Dong Special Forces camp in Vietnam was hit and there were 58 friendly casualties, including two U.S. and one Australian, so that the Viet Cong action was staying up. Ambassador Taylor arrived in Saigon on the 7th of July.

On the 8th of July United Nations Secretary General U Thant warned that military methods would not bring about peace in South Vietnam and proposes the re-convening of the 1954 Geneva Conference. This was the first of a series of unhelpful recommendations by U. Thant. It was obvious that it would do little good to re-convene the 1954 Geneva Conference. We'd had a more recent conference on Laos in 1962. At that conference, agreement was reached to withdraw military forces from Laos. The Western nations withdrew their forces, and the North Vietnamese left their forces in. So there was a history of complete disregard for any agreement by the Communists.

Q: What was U Thant's motivation?

Adm. S.: I really don't know. He was motivated, I'm sure, to try to get peace in the area, but his way of doing it would have resulted in caving in to the Communists, that was the unfortunate thing.

On the 9th of July Defense Secretary McNamara's testimony before the Senate Foreign Relations Committee was made public, in which MacNamara stated that the U.S. effort in South Vietnam carried the risk of escalating to military actions outside the border of South Vietnam, and on the same day Communist China warned that it would defend North Vietnam against U.S. attacks.

That day, in Honolulu, Mr. William McMahon, the Minister of Labor and National Service for Australia, came through and called on me at my headquarters and we gave him a briefing on the situation in Vietnam. This was the start of a friendship that has lasted ever since and has resulted in visits by Mr. McMahon on several occasions.

On the 12th of July South Vietnam Premier Khanh reported that North Vietnamese troops were taking an increased part in Viet Cong attacks.

On the 14th of July the U.S. announced that it was sending 600 more military advisers to South Vietnam. This would make the U.S. military mission in Vietnam total about 16,000.

On the 14th of July Ambassador William Blair, our ambassador to the Philippines, called and was briefed in our command center.

On the 15th of July I departed on my first trip as CinCPac, this time to Washington, D.C. to attend an ANZUS Council meeting - that is, Australia, New Zealand, and the U.S..

On the 15th of July Secretary McNamara stated that there is no evidence that organized units of North Vietnamese troops are moving into South Vietnam.

Q: Do you mind if I interject a comment from a report that is was during July that the first tentative report of participation by North Vietnamese Army in the Viet Cong operations occurred.

Adm. S.: Yes. I don't remember the exact situation, but it was well established by the end of the year that North Vietnamese were infiltrating. This gives a sort of an indication of what goes on. I think Secretary McNamara was trying to make the war go the way he thinks it ought to be, whether it is or not.

While I was in Washington I met with the CNO, the SecNav, the Secretary of Defense on the 16th of July. And on the 17th of July I attended the ANZUS session at the State Department, and of course I was the military - U.S. military adviser - to ANZUS. Then in the afternoon I met with the JCS and attended a dinner hosted by the Secretary of State for the ANZUS Council.

On the 18th of July I attended another ANZUS Council

meeting. The communique that was issued at the end of the meeting noted with grave concern the continuing threat to peace in Southeast Asia and the Pacific region posed by the North Vietnamese and Communist regimes, and it agreed that defeat of this aggression was necessary.

On the 19th of July I returned to Honolulu. On the 20th of July the Viet Cong attacked South Vietnamese troops at Cai Be, 55 miles west of Saigon, killing 30 children and ten women. On the 21st of July Prime Minister Holyoake of New Zealand came through Honolulu again and I had another talk with him. These talks with Prime Minister Holyoake were very valuable since he almost always came up and got briefed and we were able to keep him up with our thinking on the Vietnam war, and he turned out to be a strong supporter of the United States in everything that we did.

Q: Had Australia entered the war at this point?

Adm. S.: It was New Zealand.

Q: I meant New Zealand.

Adm. S.: At this point, I don't think they had anybody in there. On the 19th of July Lieutenant General Khanh had addressed a mass meeting in which he shouted "Bac Tien," which means "to the north," and I guess it was sort of an attempt to get his people exercised about what was going on.

On the 23rd of July, Ambassador Taylor met with Lieutenant General Khanh and disagreed with Khanh's call to go north, so this was the first incident of Ambassador Taylor putting a squeeze on the South Vietnamese and how they acted.

On the 23rd of July Malaysian Prime Minister Tengku Abdul Rahman, on a state visit to Washington, D.C., stated that he sees no chance of Malaysia making peace with Indonesia, pointing up a continuing problem in that area.

On the 26th of July 1964 I departed on my first WesPac trip as CinCPac. The itinerary included Saigon, Bangkok, and Udon in Thailand.

On the 27th, the United States announced that it was sending an additional 5,000 men to South Vietnam. This would bring the military mission in South Vietnam up to a total of 21,000.

Q: But still of an advisory nature?

Adm. S.: Still of an advisory nature. At that point they were not participating in military action. On the 28th of July, I met with General Westmoreland in Saigon and got briefed on the situation as he saw it. General Westmoreland and I called on Ambassador Taylor, talked over the situation. We then called on Lieutenant General Khanh and Major General Thieu. Lieutenant General Khanh, of course, was the Premier, and Major General Thieu . . .

Q: Is that the one who's now . . . ?

Adm. S.: Yes, the one who's now President. On the 29th of July General Westmoreland stated that the Viet Cong now have 28,000 to 34,000 full-time and 60,000 to 80,000 part-time intruders in South Vietnam.

On the first of August the VC attacked an outpost at Vinh Loc, which is only four miles west of Saigon. On the 1st of August I was over in Thailand, met with Ambassador Unger at Udorn. On the 2nd of August we had the first Tonkin Gulf attacks. The USS Maddox was attacked by three North Vietnamese patrol boats in the Gulf of Tonkin. I was airborne at the time and just about to land at Wake Island. When I returned to Honolulu, of course, I was asked by the press what was going on, and I said, "our ships are always going to go where they need to be, and if they shoot at us, we're going to shoot back."

Q: At that point you had had no particular briefing other than just the . . .

Adm. S.: Oh, yes, I got messages aboard my airplane that indicated what was going on. I knew as much as they knew in Honolulu.

Q: Do you have copies of all the messages?

Adm. S.: I don't know whether I do or not. I may. I'll have to do a little digging and see if I can find out.

Interview No. 4 with Admiral U.S. Grant Sharp
Place: San Diego, California
Date: 10 January 1970
Subject: Biography
By: Etta Belle Kitchen

Adm. S.: At the conclusion of our last interview we had come up to the Gulf of Tonkin incident. In discussing that incident, we need to go back a little bit to a proposal that I made on the 10th of July 1964, wherein I proposed that an intelligence-gathering patrol be made in the Gulf of Tonkin to investigate coastal activity in North Vietnam.

Q: Was that one of your first recommendations concerning the participation of the Navy in the Vietnamese war?

Adm. S.: No, I don't think so. That's not important.

Q: To whom did you make the recommendation, to the JCS?

Adm. S.: To the JCS. And on the 22nd July the Joint Chiefs approved of this patrol and said that it should start not later than the 31st of July.

Q: Why did you think it was necessary?

Adm. S.: That will divert me. This required getting a ship equipped with the necessary special equipment to record the intelligence and the special crews and interpreters that were necessary for this assignment. The destroyer Maddox was assigned this duty and picked up the equipment and was ready to go about the 31st of July, as I recall it. Another factor in the situation was the fact that there were South Vietnamese patrol craft operating at night against the North Vietnamese coast. This was called Operation 34A, or 34 Alpha. The craft concerned were fast patrol boats manned by Vietnamese crews.

On the 30th of July - the operation actually took place on the 31st of July - an operation by these boats against the island of Hon Me and also Hon Ngu. On the 31st of July the Maddox reported to Yankee Station and refueled. I should say that the intelligence-collecting activity had, of course, gone on in many areas. The ships were always directed to operate in international waters, and off the coast of North Vietnam they were directed to observe the junk traffic and naval activity, collect hydrographic data, and also to collect intelligence concerning North Vietnamese electronic installations. The idea of these patrols was to update our intelligence in case we had to operate against North Vietnam.

Now the Maddox started her patrol late in the - or in the afternoon of the 31st of July, and she proceeded through the evening of 31 July and 1st of August up the coast of North Vietnam. The Maddox was directed to stay 15 miles off the Chinese coast, or eight nautical miles off the North Vietnamese coast. The difference here is that as we understood the North Vietnamese territorial waters, they were, at that time five miles, as I recall it.

Q: In any case, clearly in international waters.

Adm. S.: Yes. The idea was to be always sure that the ship was in international waters which, of course, is three miles as far as the United States recognizes. But on these patrols the ships were directed to stay outside of the countries stated national waters, whatever it was.

Well, now, on the 1st of August the Maddox was in the Gulf of Tonkin. She was directed to not approach islands in the Gulf closer than four miles, thus keeping outside of our territorial recognized waters. That day she steamed by the island of Hon Me, and then she was directed at night to stay away from the coast, as I recall. On the 2nd of August, sometime in the early morning, Maddox reported that she had intelligence information indicating possible action from North Vietnam, on the morning of the 2nd she was several miles off the coast. The Maddox indicated that she believed continuation of the patrol was an unacceptable risk. She was directed to resume the patrol by CinCPacFlt and ComSeventhFlt after a decision was made . . .

Q: Were you at Pearl then?

Adm. S.: With my staff. No, I should say that I wasn't at Pearl Harbor. I think I was at Bangkok, if I'm not mistaken.

Q: I wondered if you made the personal decision, or if members of your staff, your operations . . .

Adm. S.: No, as I recall it, we were informed of the decision on the situation at Bangkok and concurred with what the staff proposed. That's very hazy memory and I'm not quite sure that that was the case. That would be the normal way that we would work it. So, the Maddox continued the patrol then and she reported, as I recall, observing a lot of junks near her patrol area, and then she picked up some patrol craft that generally paralleled her course and stayed out of range. Finally, that afternoon, the afternoon of the 2nd of August - now we're talking about Tonkin Gulf time - she was approached by these craft at high speed and took them under fire when they approached in a threatening manner, and then . . .

Q: This was visual sighting?

Adm. S.: Yes. And then they shot at the patrol craft for several minutes and, as I recall it, they sank one or two of them - I can't remember right now exactly. She was attacked by three boats in the Tonkin Gulf 38 nautical miles from the coast of North Vietnam, and I guess the report that we got was that all the boats were destroyed or damaged by Maddox' fire and by gunfire by aircraft from the Ticonderoga. The Ticonderoga was in the area and knew about the Maddox' patrol. As a matter of fact, Rear Admiral R. B. Moore, the carrier division commander, was responsible for the Maddox' patrol, as I recall it, being the senior naval officer present afloat in the area, and he supplied air support when the Maddox requested it, and the planes did strafe the PT boats and reported that they had damaged them.

I got this information of the action when I got to Wake Island for a re-fueling stop on my way back to Honolulu.

Q: Were you surprised?

Adm. S.: Oh, sure.

Q: I mean, what was your reaction to it? Did you think this means we're going to be more involved, or did it . . . ?

Adm. S.: My chief reaction to it was that we would, at the very least, continue the patrol. The thing we couldn't do was to pull the patrol out of the Gulf and not go back in, because that would indicate to the Communists that they had been able to back us down, and we can't have that happen. So I remember when we got back to Honolulu, of course, newsmen were waiting to see me and I told them our ships are always going to go where they need to be - where they need to go - and if they shoot us, we're going to shoot back. It caused, of course, a great many exchanges of messages not only between the Maddox and her commander and Captain Herrick, who was, I guess, the destroyer division commander and ComSeventhFlt and CinCPacFlt and CinCPac and the Pentagon, so there was a great deal of activity.

One thing we might want to analyze in the Tonkin Gulf incident is what influence did the attacks by the South

Vietnamese patrol craft have on the Maddox incident. The first thing you have to remember is that the Maddox went up the coast in daylight, she was easily seen from the beach, she was tracked by radar from the time she went north to the DMZ, constantly, throughout her patrol, as long as she was within radar range of the coast. So that the North Vietnamese knew very well where the Maddox was, that she was in international waters and that she wasn't tied in with these patrol craft operations. The Maddox had been told to keep clear of these operations and her schedule was arranged so that they would not interfere. On the other hand, the North Vietnamese, having had some of their radar stations shelled in a very recent period by the patrol craft, naturally would be sensitive and alert, and, of course, when they are sensitive and alert, their electronic equipment is on at the maximum amount and that's a fine time to pick up intelligence on what they have and how it operates.

Q: Did they imply that they thought the Maddox was a part of the South's patrol?

Adm. S.: Oh, I don't know. I never paid any attention to Hanoi's broadcasts, really, because they broadcast all the time and it was 90 percent propaganda. So I . . .

Q: You couldn't expect to believe them, anyway.

Adm. S.: I just couldn't be worried about it.

Going back now to the Maddox. There were a number of messages exchanged between the Maddox and the task force commander and Commander, Seventh Fleet. Captain Herrick was a little bit reluctant to continue with his mission when he intercepted some information that indicated that there might be - that patrol craft might be directed to attack, and we didn't - I should say the Seventh Fleet Commander gave him some flexibility in what he did, but did let him know that he was expected to continue his patrol until it got to the point that he considered - Herrick - considered that there was an unacceptable risk. In other words, Herrick was being prodded to stay with the job that he had been directed to do.

Q: It's surprising that he would need to be, isn't it?

Adm. S.: No. He was being prudent and, I think a little overcautious but he was being prudent.

Q: How much damage could those patrol boats have done? Did they carry . . . ?

Adm. S.: They had torpedoes, so they could have sunk the destroyer if they'd hit her.

Now, let's see, we get through this 2nd of August attack.

Q: There are really two parts to the attack.

Adm. S.: We get through the 2nd of August attack and after the engagement was broken off, Herrick was told by Admiral Moore, Rear Admiral Moore, Commander of Task Force 77, not to pursue the boats, but to proceed to the southeast and await further instructions.

One important thing that I don't think I mentioned about the Maddox incident is that when these patrol craft approached her, the first thing she did was fire three warning shots, and then when they continued to approach her she opened up with destructive fire, and I think the total results were that one boat was disabled but managed to launch torpedoes which missed the Maddox by a couple of hundred yards. Another boat was hit and turned around to the north and then was dead in the water. Then a third boat, which was hit once or twice, passed astern of the Maddox and fired a machine gun at her - that's a 12.7-mm. machine gun - and hit the Maddox with one shell. As I recall, it went into the magazine but did no damage.

So, that is a summation of the action, and then the Maddox retired from the area.

When I got back to Honolulu, I immediately had a conference with Admiral Moorer, Commander-in-Chief of the Pacific Fleet. We decided to order the Constellation out of Hong Kong - she was in Hong Kong on a recreation visit. We ordered her out of there immediately and to get south to join the Ticonderoga in the Gulf of Tonkin. And also the ASW carrier Kearsarge was ordered to proceed to the Gulf of

Tonkin with her ASW task force. There were other actions involving Air Force aircraft, and there was a general alert throughout the area, and much activity, including, of course, the recommendation that the patrol be continued. We received authority to conduct a similar patrol, using two destroyers instead of one. So the Turner Joy was directed to join the Maddox, report to Captain Herrick, and they were directed to prepare for patrol, which was to be on the 3rd of August, it seems to me. Yes, it was to be on the 3rd August. The Maddox and Turner Joy on the 3rd of August proceeded north up the coast from the DMZ, and they were on a course similar to the Maddox' course. However, they were directed to retire at night, as soon as it got dark, at high speed, to decrease the possibility of surprise attack on them.

There was an exchange of messages - there were various exchanges of messages on the evening of the 3rd of August, Tonkin Gulf time. I think, again, Captain Herrick was disturbed at the possibility at the possibility that his ship was going to be attacked. Admiral Moorer and I conferred numerous times during the period and we both agreed that the patrol should be continued. We thought that we had given him the necessary leeway and that, certainly, two destroyers could take on any number of patrol craft in daylight, and we directed them to turn out into the center of the Tonkin Gulf at night to keep them separated from the coast and the boats so that the boats would have to expose themselves for quite a long time if they wanted to attack the destroyers at night. So we thought this gave the destroyers plenty of protection and we were determined to demonstrate to North Vietnam that United States ships could go wherever they needed to go so long as they remained in international waters. This was in line with a protest that the United States Government made on the 3rd August, wherein the United States said that U.S. ships will continue to operate freely in international waters and take necessary measures for their defense, and warned North Vietnam that another attack might lead to grave consequences.

Q: Was that made by you or by . . . ?

Adm. S.: No, no. That was made by the United States Government.

Q: All the decisions were based on your recommendations, though, were they not? Made in Washington?

Adm. S.: Yes. Yes, that's right. This is not to say that we weren't on the telephone with Washington and everything like that, because we were. I talked frequently to General Wheeler, the Chairman of the Joint Chiefs, and it was a team effort. I wasn't sitting out there just throwing out dictates right and left. It was a team effort. Admiral Moorer and I were in conference together all the time.

Q: Did you ever talk directly to the President?

Adm. S.: No, I talked to McNamara, but not the President. So, we told Captain Herrick to stay on his patrol, that was the early evening of August 3rd. Then, in the early morning of August 4th, Tonkin Gulf time, the <u>Maddox</u> and <u>Turner Joy</u> had the second Tonkin Gulf encounter and this was rather confusing action because, like most night actions, it's very difficult to track exactly what's going on, even when ships are well trained and veterans of night actions, but when a ship is in its first or second night action and with a crew that had not had this experience, why, naturally, you have many reports and contacts and sonar contacts and radar contacts and sightings and all that sort of thing, and it's very difficult to sift it all out. So, one of our jobs as the great flow of reports came in was to try to sift out fact from fiction and evaluate exactly what happened. I don't have a detailed paper available to me. A great deal of detail has been written into a book by Joseph C. Goulden, the name of the book being <u>Truth is the First Casualty</u>. This man has done a lot of research and has a tremendous amount of information as to the messages that were exchanged and so forth. I don't know where he managed to get all this information, but he certainly has compiled a lot of it. I must say his conclusions and his evaluations of some of the actions are way off the mark, especially where he starts interpreting what I was thinking. However, he does seem to have a great deal of information as to messages exchanged and so forth.

Q: Will you amplify that later?

Adm. S.: Will I amplify it? How much do you want me to amplify it?

Q: Well, when you say that he was way off the mark in his conclusions . . .

Adm. S.: Well, do you think we ought to go through this book and . . . ?

Q: No. But I meant just generally, as it relates to the title.

Adm. S.: *Truth is the First Casualty*. I'm not going to get into that.

Q: Does he think that there was not a second attack?

Adm. S.: He concludes that there wasn't a second attack and generally just claims that we sort of dreamed up the information on the second attack, which of course isn't true. The important point to make, I think, is that he does have a lot of facts in his book as to what went on in the way of exchanges of messages and all that sort of thing. He interviewed a lot of people and has more information than I do, as a matter of fact. However, we'll continue on now . . .

Q: I do hate to interrupt, but why does he attribute it to you . . .

Adm. S.: Let's not get off. My idea right now is to go through this Gulf of Tonkin thing, getting in there as much dope as I can recall.

I said that Captain Herrick was concerned about how the North Vietnamese were reacting and thought that it would be better not to take the two destroyers into the Gulf on the second Desoto patrol, and his suggestion that we terminate the patrol got back to Honolulu. Of course, part of his concern was that the 34A raids were going on and he was concerned about them. So, in reply to his request, I said, first, that termination of the Desoto patrol after two days of patrol operations subsequent to the Maddox incident does not, in my view, adequately demonstrate United States resolve to assert our legitimate rights in these international waters. And so accordingly recommend that adjustments in the remainder of the patrol schedule in order to accommodate a request from ComUSMacV that the patrol ships remain north of latitude 19.10 until a certain time in order to avoid interference with 34A Ops. So we told the 4th August patrol, from Point Delta to Charley, to remain north of 19.10 north, and we went on to tell them that the above patrol would clearly demonstrate our determination to continue these operations, possibly draw North Vietnamese PGMs northward, away from the area of the 34A ops, and, of course, moving northward would also eliminate the

Desoto patrol interference with the 34A ops. I noticed that in the Senate, when Mr. McNamara testified, Senator Morse said that this cable said one thing quite clearly to him and suggested another. He said that Sharp was disappointed with the results of the renewed mission and although the Maddox had returned to the area of its first fight, the United States had yet to demonstrate its resolve. Well, he was absolutely incorrect on that. That wasn't the problem at all. I wasn't disappointed with the results. I just wanted to make certain that we exerted - that we put in our appearance to let the other side know that they couldn't bluff us out.

Now we get to the 3 August-4 August patrol. On the 3rd, of course, the Maddox and Turner Joy entered the Gulf of Tonkin. On the evening of the 4th - they went in on the 3rd and they spent the night of the 3rd and 4th, I think was essentially uneventful. Then during the day of the 4th, they continued their patrol and on the evening of the 4th the two destroyers were proceeding on an easterly course at a speed of about 20 knots. Shortly after dark, the task group commander, who was Captain Herrick aboard the Maddox, observed on the surface-search radar, according to his report, at least five contacts about 36 miles distant, and he evaluated these contacts as probably torpedo boats. The Maddox and the Turner Joy then changed course and increased speed to avoid what appeared to be an attack. About an hour later both ships' radars held contacts approximately 14 miles to the eastward. At that time the two ships were approximately 60 miles from the North Vietnamese coast. When it became evident from the maneuvers of the approaching enemy craft that they were pressing in for an attack position, both Maddox and Turner Joy opened fire. At this time they reported the enemy boats were at a range of about 6,000 yards from the Maddox. Then their radar tracking indicated that the contact turned away. They then heard torpedo noises on the Maddox' sonar. The Maddox passed this word to the Turner Joy, and both ships took evasive action. Personnel aboard the Turner Joy reported they sighted a torpedo wake passing abeam of the Turner Joy about 300 feet to port. One target was taken under fire by the Turner Joy and numerous hits were observed and they then said it disappeared from all radars. The commanding officer and other Turner Joy personnel said they observed a thick column of black smoke from this target. Turner Joy also, slightly after this, observed a searchlight which swung in an arc toward the Turner Joy and then was extinguished because aircraft from the combat air patrol approached the vicinity. They also said they saw the silhouette of an attacking boat, when the boat came between the ship and flares dropped by an aircraft. At approximately midnight the action ended when radar contact was lost on the last enemy boat, and the best estimates, according to their reports, were that at least two of the enemy craft were sunk, and possibly two more damaged. Neither of the destroyers received any damage. Both Maddox and Turner Joy reported that torpedoes had been fired at them. Turner Joy reported that at one point in the engagement she was turning to ram -

she was planning to ram one of the North Vietnamese boats,' which of course would indicate that the boat was quite close aboard.

All this was being received in Honolulu, and after the ships had reported that the attack was terminated, CinCPac recommended to the JCS that authority be granted for immediate punitive air strikes against North Vietnam. Two hours later we received a message from the Joint Chiefs of Staff which alerted us to plan strikes for the first light the following day.

Q: The message traffic must have been enormous at that point.

Adm. S.: Yes, the message traffic was very heavy, and of course one of the problems was we were trying to figure out just exactly what happened, and we got a report from Captain Herrick who said that, while the Turner Joy claimed to have positively sunk three boats, the entire action leaves many doubts except for the apparent attempt to ambush at the beginning, and he suggested thorough reconnaissance in daylight by aircraft. So he suggested complete evaluation before any further action.

Well, I was on the phone both with General Wheeler and with Secretary McNamara. McNamara was trying to confirm in his own mind that an attack occurred. Of course, that's exactly what we were trying to do also. My staff was working to try to correlate all the reports that would come in and CinCPacFlt staff was doing the same thing. Admiral Moorer, CinCPacFlt, and I decided that there was enough information available to indicate that an attack had occurred. I told Secretary McNamara that, but we also asked the Maddox to confirm absolutely that the ships were attacked and told them to get word to us as quickly as possible. We got a report from the ships which neither absolutely confirmed or denied that they'd been under attack, but the weight of evidence still was that an attack had occurred, so I told Mr. McNamara that. We also had had some radio intercept intelligence which tended to confirm the attack. So we had various conversations back and forth with Admiral Moorer and I in Honolulu and General Wheeler in Washington, Secretary McNamara in Washington and finally we received an order to attack the next day, attack North Vietnamese patrol craft bases. In the meantime we were still receiving amplifying messages from the Maddox, Turner Joy, and Captain Herrick. Generally speaking, they seemed to still indicate that the attack had occurred. Turner Joy said that crew members saw torpedoes and that a target burned when hit, and her men saw black smoke. So while we were getting the planes ready aboard the Ticonderoga and the Constellation, we were still going back and forth about the attack in the Tonkin Gulf. That covers that one.

Q: There certainly would have been no objective on your part in saying there had been an attack if you didn't believe there had been.

Adm. S.: No, that's right.

Q: There's been conversation in the press implying that there' was some motive on the part of the government trying to make the people believe there might have been when there wasn't an attack.

Adm. S.: There wasn't any motive like that. Well, what do we do next?

On the 5th of August Task Force 77 launched an attack on the various PT boat bases in North Vietnam. We were told to conduct a one-time attack against Port Waloup, Hon Gay, Phuc Loi, Quang Khe, and the Lach Chao estuary, and also against boats and POL at Vinh, and to do all of this on the 5th of August. We passed the word on out to the PacFlt and he passed it to Task Force 77. In the meantime, all these various exchanges were going on trying to get a firm determination that the 4 August attack had actually taken place, and actually we were still getting comments when the attacks were launched - when the air attacks were launched. We got word from both task groups that they had launched on schedule, and we got reports back during the day that fuel oil was burning profusely at Vinh and that PTs had been attacked in various ports and some destroyed and some damaged.

As I recall it, we had a re-strike on the Vinh POL to be sure that it was polished off, and they did re-strike the same day. We had a couple of planes lost at Hon Gay, I believe it was an A-1 and an A-4. We also had one other plane damaged so that it had to land at Da Nang. So, generally speaking, the attacks on the 5th of August were very successful. The Navy did a good job on short notice. They supposedly destroyed eight and damaged 21 boats, and they estimated that about 90 percent of the Vinh POL was destroyed.

The next thing that happened here was that we had various increases in our force posture out in the Western Pacific. On the 5th of August the SecDef announced the reinforcement of Pacific forces. He announced we were sending interceptor and fighter bomber aircraft to South Vietnam, to Thailand, and to other places in the Pacific, and that we were sending an attack carrier group to the Western Pacific, and an ASW force to the South China Sea, and further, he was alerting all Army and Marine forces in the Pacific area. Then, of course, on the 7th of August, the Congress passed the Tonkin Resolution assuring President Johnson full support for all necessary measures he might have to take to protect U.S. armed forces in Southeast Asia and giving prior sanction for all necessary steps, including the use of armed force to assist any member of SEATO that might request help. On the 8th of August I held a press conference in Pearl Harbor in which I stated that an attack carrier group was on its way from the U.S. coast, would touch at Pearl Harbor, and would leave immediately for the Western Pacific. I also mentioned a buildup of U.S. Air Force strength in the Western Pacific. Someone asked me about U.S. retaliation against the Tonkin attacks and I told them that I was happy with the way things went. Our people did a good job and the strike went off well.

In the next few days we had various movements of forces throughout the Pacific, kept us very busy. We got the Marine Expeditionary Battalion in shipping and sailed it to the South China Sea, and told the Marines to be prepared to move a Marine air group to Da Nang. We got the amphibious ready group out of the Subic area and we got authority from Thailand to put aircraft - Air Force aircraft - at Karat and Takii. JCS also directed CinCStrike to deploy two C-130 squadrons to the Western Pacific. So we immediately had a considerable increase in force posture in the Western Pacific. There were two squadrons of B-57s at Bien Hoa.

Subsequent to the Gulf of Tonkin incident and the retaliatory attacks, of course, there was much discussion of strategy, and there were several messages back and forth from the Embassy at Saigon to SecState Info, Defense and CinCPac, and also messages from the JCS and from CinCPac to the JCS. In general, about that time, I told the JCS that I thought that our action against North Vietnam demonstrated our intent to move toward our objectives, and also the augmentation of forces in the Western Pacific should indicate to the Communists that we were not fooling, that we were going to proceed to assist the South Vietnamese and they had better reconsider what they were doing. I also said that what we had not done was to make plain to Hanoi the cost of pursuing their current objectives, because pursuing their current objectives, of course, was going to impede what we were going to insist on doing. So I said we must proceed with increasing our readiness posture, deploy troops, ships, aircraft, and logistic resources in the manner in which gives us maximum freedom of action, so that we will have flexibility to do what we desire to do. Then I told them that I thought we should get on with further action against North Vietnam and that the 34A action should be increased, we should continue with the Desoto patrols, and all these things should be pursued with vigor and determination. I also pointed out that now that we are moving aircraft squadrons into South Vietnam we'd got to consider how the security of these forces was going to be assured, that we couldn't depend on the Vietnamese to give our forces ground security. Therefore, I was suggesting that we had better deploy our own combat forces to protect our own people.

There was also a suggestion that we should put the Vietnamese into jet aircraft, and I resisted that because I pointed out that we were converting the Vietnamese to A1-Hs, which of course was the old Douglas propeller attack plane that had been the mainstay of the Navy for so long. I said this was an ideal plane for counter-insurgency war and there wasn't any reason why we should divert - diffuse - our efforts by training them for jet aircraft at this point.

Q: Did they take your recommendations?

Adm. S.: Yes, they did because they didn't shift the South Vietnamese to jets until three or four years later. And I also recommended we have another Desoto patrol in the Gulf of Tonkin.

Q: Had those stopped after the second incident?

Adm. S.: Yes, they had and I recommended they start them up again.

Q: Did they take that advice?

Adm. S.: Essentially, yes. About this time MACV, General Westmoreland, requested troops for defense of the air bases where we had aircraft and for our radar and communication sites, and I supported the recommendation. In other words, I recommended that we put troops in to protect our own people and to acknowledge that we had a commitment -- more than just an advisory effort. Also this would give the Communists the information that an overt attack on South Vietnam would be a threat to U.S. forces there. The recommendation was that we establish and occupy a U.S. base in the Da Nang area, and further I told them that our action of August 5th - that's the strike on PT boat bases - had created a momentum which we should maintain.

In Vietnam during this period the situation was not good. The government was weak, the South Vietnamese just had more than they could handle between the Viet Cong and the North Vietnamese. By late summer it was evident that the Viet Cong posed an immediate threat to Saigon. They were active in critical provinces around the capital city and it became evident that one of our major problems was to keep the Saigon environs secure. General Westmoreland recommended that the Saigon government start a pacification effort radiating outward from Saigon, and they set up a combined U.S.-Vietnamese group planning this operation, which was called Hop Tac. This operation was launched in September. Hop Tac, while it probably saved Saigon, still wasn't very successful. It just didn't have enough horsepower to overcome the Viet Cong.

During this period also we found the Viet Cong becoming very well armed. They were getting the Soviet AK-47 assault rifle, and also were getting mortars and good machine guns, to the point that the Viet Cong were much better armed than were the Vietnamese. The Vietnamese airborne and the Vietnamese Marines were the best forces in the country at this time, and were forces that were used to plug the gap whenever a big emergency occurred. These airborne and Marines were traveling around the country holding the Vietnamese Army together. In August General Khanh removed General Minh as chief of state, thus further destabilizing the country. In September General Khanh became premier and they made General Minh chairman of the Leadership Committee. During this time there was also a problem with the Montagnard irregulars up in the highlands. They had an uprising and they got out of hand. And they had further trouble in Saigon on the religious side. Then on the 24th of October, Mr. Phan Khac Suu was chosen to be chief of state and he designated Tran Van Suong to be premier. So this was another change of government, and in December they had further problems with the government, so it was a very difficult year in Vietnam.

In early September I proposed a five-day Desoto patrol in the Gulf of Tonkin and suggested that it maintain 20 miles from the mainland of North Vietnam and 12 miles from islands. I got a fairly fast approval of a Desoto patrol and the Morton and the Edwards were the ships that were designated for this patrol. On the 17th of September the Morton and Edwards were steaming at night in the Gulf of Tonkin and they picked up fast-closing surface contacts on their radar and took them under fire. By radar they said it was indicated that several targets were hit. Next day the JCS directed me to plan substantial air attacks on North Vietnam in reprisal for this 17 September attack. So we issued an order - a planning order - although the attack was not executed because Navy could not find positive evidence that the 17 September attack had occurred.

On the 18th of August I left Hawaii on a visit to the Philippines, Hong Kong, Republic of China, Okinawa, Japan, Korea. In the Philippines I met with Ambassador Blair and together we visited President Macapagal and discussed the general situation in the Pacific. On the 23rd there were serious riots in Saigon by Student and Buddhist demonstrators.

While in Taipeh I visited the ambassador and also attended a dinner hosted by President Chiang-Kai Chek in my honor. In Tokyo I called on Prime Minister Ikeda and Foreign Minister Shiina and attended a dinner hosted by U.S. Ambassador Reischauer. While I was in Japan we had the fifth meeting of the Japan-U.S. Consultative Committee on Security, and this was a primary reason for this trip to the Western Pacific. We went on from Japan to Korea, where I met with Ambassador Brown, Minister of Defense Kim Song Hun, and we called on President Park and Prime Minister Chung Kwan. From there I returned to Hawaii.

On the 6th of September Ambassador Maxwell D. Taylor stopped briefly in Hawaii en route to Washington, and we had a get-together at Hickham Air Force Base and discussed the situation in Vietnam. I left for Washington on the 6th of September and on the 8th met with SecNav, CNO, and the Joint Chiefs of Staff. On the 9th I met with Secretary of Defense, Mr. McNamara, and on the 10th returned to Hawaii. And on the 11th of September Ambassador Taylor came back through on his way to Vietnam and we had a conference in the CinCPac command center.

On the 4th of October, 1964, I departed for another visit to the Western Pacific. This visit was to New Zealand, Australia, Thailand, and Vietnam. In Wellington I visited with Prime Minister Holyoake, Minister of Defense Eyre, and the Defense Committee. In Australia I met the Secretary of Defense Hicks and Minister of Defense Paltridge. Went on from there to Bangkok where we held our semi-annual SEATO conference. This was the conference of the military advisers. The acting military adviser from Australia was Major General Haskett. He was there in the place of Air Chief Marshal Scherger, the military adviser who was unable to attend. New Zealand's military adviser was Sir Peter Phipps. Pakistan's Air Marshal Asghar Khan. The Philippines' was General Santos. The British Admiral Varyl Begg. Thailand, Air Chief Marshal Dawee, and France's Vice Admiral Bernin de Roziers was there as an observer. On the 16th of October, after the SEATO meetings, I went to Vietnam and met with General Westmoreland, and on the 18th of October returned to Honolulu.

Q: When you went in to Saigon, did you ever go out in the field?

Adm. S.: Yes, I usually did. I don't know whether I did this time or not.

On the 3rd of November, of course, President Johnson was elected President. They were still having demonstrations in Vietnam during this period - a very unstable situation.

Then on the 25th of November I departed on another WestPac trip. This was to attend - or to host, rather - a shipboard air power demonstration aboard the USS Constellation. We were aboard the Constellation for three days, and then stopped in Okinawa for two days to continue the weapons demonstration.

Then on the 4th of December I returned to Honolulu. On the 6th of December the new ambassador to Laos, William H. Sullivan, stopped in Honolulu and we gave him a briefing.

On the 10th of December Thai Foreign Minister Thanat Khoman made a significant announcement with which I agreed. He said that a U.S. withdrawal from South Vietnam would mean that Laos would be lost, Cambodia would become a Communist satellite, Thailand and Burma would be in danger, and Malaysia and Indonesia would in time be lost.

On the 16th of December General Westmoreland conferred with me in Honolulu. Then on the 22nd of December General Westmoreland and I got together again. General Westmoreland was returning to South Vietnam after attending his father's funeral in the United States. On the 24th December the VC exploded a bomb at a U.S. officers billet in Saigon, killing two Americans and injuring 63. Two days later, the South Vietnamese government extended martial law for another month.

On Christmas Eve 1964 the Communists exploded a large demolition charge in the Brink bachelors officers' quarters in Saigon, as I pointed out previously. At this time a second aircraft carrier was ordered to the Gulf of Tonkin and retaliatory strikes were readied but were not executed. Throughout the latter half of 1964, we made a number of plans for strikes against North Vietnam which would be triggered by action against our Desoto patrols. These strikes were of varying intensity and generally were pretty strong actions. However, none of these strikes were ever executed. The only Desoto patrol that seemingly got into an action was the one on 17 September, and then it was so indefinite that strikes were not ordered. There were other actions, of course, in South Vietnam that would seem to have indicated the possibility of using our air power, but this air power was not used.

Q: Do you think that is indicative that when the North Vietnamese and the Communists know you've got something and you can use it that they back down?

Adm. S.: They don't back down unless you indicate that you're going to use it.

Q: Do you think they knew that you would use it . . . ?

Adm. S.: No, I don't think they did.

So, the latter half of 1964 was in general rather a frustrating year. The government of South Vietnam was so unstable that it was pretty obvious that we had to have a more stable government before anything we could do would reverse the deterioration of the situation. We were using our air power to assist the Vietnamese and also made some air strikes on the infiltration trails in Laos, but none of these things were going to change anything for the better until we had a stable government in Vietnam. While we could see that action needed to be taken sooner or later, we still weren't willing to commit U.S. forces while we had an unstable government in Vietnam.

At the end of October there was a destructive attack on Bien Hoa airfield and a number of United States aircraft were lost. In response to this attack we were ordered to move the Marine Expeditionary Force - no, the Special Landing Force, which was a battalion of Marines, into position off Da Nang, and put two Marine battalions on alert in Okinawa to move in to Vietnam. At that time I recommended that the Marines be landed in Vietnam and they be landed at Da Nang, that if we were going to put U.S. troops in the Saigon area it be the 25th Division. I recommended that the Marines and the 173rd Airborne, which was then at Okinawa, should not be used for security duty since they represent strike forces with special capabilities and have special equipment.

Q: Isn't your recommendation enough to have it done that way?

Adm. S.: Not necessarily, no. They decided it in Washington for political reasons. However, none of these moves ever took place. There was also some thought to move dependents out of Saigon, but they decided not to do that.

In late November there was further discussion of the strategy in Southeast Asia. One of the points I made was that we still had not made it clear to Hanoi that the cost of pursuing their apparent objectives would become prohibitive. Our action on the 5th of August caused some apprehension in

North Vietnam, but I pointed out that there had been no activity since that time. Thus, the North Vietnamese could feel at the moment that they can continue their present aggression, or even raise the level of action, with impunity. And I said what is needed is a campaign of dramatically increased military pressures against North Vietnam conducted in coordination with diplomatic and psychological programs.

Q: What was the reaction to that?

Adm. S.: I'm getting to that. I recommended that we might have initial air strikes on infiltration routes, then move to infiltration-associated targets, and then expand into other important targets. I suggested that the air strikes might start in the panhandle of North Vietnam and move northward, but the pattern should be progressive attacks of ever-increasing intensity and severity.

Q: I was wondering - did you get a bad reaction when you recommend something when you're out in the field and you know it's the thing to do and then nobody follows your advice?

Adm. S.: Oh, no.

Q: You don't feel frustrated?

Adm. S.: No. You just go right on recommending it. That's

what you believe.

One of the perennial problems in the Pacific has been that of command relations. There is always a certain amount of pulling and hauling going on to change that command setup. The Department of Defense Reorganization Act and its various amendments which was in effect in 1964 and is still in effect today gives the unified commander certain firm, definite responsibilites and sets up the command relationships quite clearly. Nevertheless, throughout my term as CinCPac there were continued attempts to tamper with this arrangement, and, indeed, it was tampered with considerably. The first evidence of this came in early July 1964 when retired General Maxwell D. Taylor was appointed ambassador to South Vietnam. He carried a letter from the President which told him that he had over-all responsibility, including the whole military effort in South Vietnam, and authorized him to exert the degree of command and control that he considered appropriate. General Taylor informed me of this letter on his visit in Honolulu on his way to Saigon, and told me that he did not see at the moment that there would ever be any major bypassing of the current chain of command. The next time command and control came up or command arrangements came up - was a short month later when I set forth the command and control arrangements for air strikes against North Vietnam. I said that the normal way would be for Air Force forces to be controlled through CinCPacAF. I said I had devoted much thought to this problem and had decided that control of Air Forces will be exercised through my Air Force component commander who commanded Thirteenth Air Force and was commander, Second Air Division. And, of course, control of naval air would be exercised through CinCPacFlt to the Seventh Fleet. I indicated that this made use of the large and expert staffs of CinCPacAF and CinCPacFlt in doing this important complicated planning, and that coordination between CinCPacFlt and CinCPacAF and my own staff would be facilitated, since we were all based in Honolulu. I told ComUSMacV and CinCPacAF coordination should be easily effected. I told ComUSMacV that this would permit him to continue to concentrate on emergency matters and at the same time he could closely monitor the air strikes through the Commander, Second Air Division. This is the manner that air power was controlled throughout the war. It does not mean, however, that everybody was satisfied with this arrangement and that no more problems were raised. The problems were more or less continuous and we at periodic intervals had to re-issue our command arrangements for control of air power. They stayed essentially the same throughout the war because it became obvious as the war went on that this was the most efficient way to control air power, and further I got good backing from the Joint Chiefs of Staff on this arrangement. It would probably be fair to say that I got good backing from the Chief of Naval Operations and from the Chief of Staff of the Air Force, and less enthusiastic backing from the Chief of Staff of the Army.

Q: Did you ever have any trouble with Maxwell Taylor?

Adm. S.: Some, but he wasn't too bad. He bypassed me to a certain degree when things went on in the country. I didn't have much trouble with him on the air war.

Another problem that came up originally in the Vietnam war was how helicopters and fixed-wing aircraft were to be coordinated in giving air support to ground troops. Of course, this was the first time helicopters were used for supporting ground troops and there was a slight tug-of-war between the Army and the Air Force to decide who would control what. All of this did work out as time went on and a method evolved that was quite satisfactory, with the rotary-wing aircraft being controlled by the Army and the fixed-wing aircraft by the Air Force with appropriate coordination.

And another command relations problem which came up rather frequently in '64, '65, and '66 and then fell by the wayside after that was the idea of making ComUSMacV a unified commander reporting directly to the Joint Chiefs of Staff, coming out from under CinCPac's control. There were numerous attempts to set up this sort of arrangement and we wrote many messages pointing out the reasons why such an arrangement was not a good idea, and finally the ideas more or less died out. Probably as much as any, for the reason that General Westmoreland and I were able to work things on a cooperative, coordinated basis, which was quite satisfactory to everyone.

Throughout the war, also, there was a continual buildup in the MACV staff and attempts by many people to give the staff a more balanced service manning, since it was predominantly an Army staff. There were some changes made to increase other service representation on the staff and much talk about it, but generally speaking, it remained predominantly an Army staff and I think that was a good thing, all in all, for having a predominantly Army staff he was oriented toward the ground situation in Vietnam, which was enough work for one staff. And the fact that it was a predominantly Army staff made any attempt to make it a unified staff - make it a separate unified command - less sensible than if it had been a perfectly balanced staff such as the CinCPac staff always was.

In 1964 when I assumed command, a headquarters support activity run by the Navy in Saigon was the logistic agency for the United States in Vietnam. It became apparent very soon that if there was to be any appreciable force buildup of Army troops, this headquarters support activity could not satisfy the requirements of the logistic agency. Therefore, my Army assistant chief of staff for logistics, Brigadier General Frank White, recommended that an Army logistics command be set up in Vietnam. This proposal met with an unenthusiastic response from U.S. Army forces, Pacific, and to some degree by ComUSMacV. They liked the arrangement of the Navy supplying the logistic support, since it eliminated an Army organization and corresponding expense. However, after many conferences, everyone was convinced that we should, indeed, have a logistic command. The recommendation was made to the Joint Chiefs of Staff and was finally approved, and the command started to be set up just in the nick of time. By the time the logistic command had taken over from the headquarters support activity, the logistic situation was getting to be fairly acute, and if we had waited a few months longer the situation would have been chaotic.

Interview No. 5 with Admiral U. S. Grant Sharp
Place: His office at the Naval Training Center in San Diego
Date: 7 February 1970
Subject: Biography
By: Etta Belle Kitchen

Adm. S.: As we start 1965, I think it would be of interest to review the strength of the various services in the Pacific as of 1 January 1965. On that date the Army had 107,940 men, the Navy 206,712, the Marine Corps 69,860, the Air Force 71,177. On 31 December 1965, the Army had increased to 213,911, the Navy to 255,999, the Marine Corps to 74,210, and the Air Force to 97,705.

Q: Before we start on 1965, I would like to have your comments on Senator Fulbright's remarks on a television program last night, which was answering President Johnson's discussion of the Tonkin Gulf incident, and Senator Fulbright said if the Foreign Relations Committee had had available to them one particular message from the commanding officer of the Maddox, which hadn't been made available to the Committee, they would not have passed the Tonkin Gulf Resolution so expeditiously but would have held long and careful hearings on the subject, and now he knows that the information they had was based on false, erroneous information, not only was there not an unprovoked attack, there was no attack at all.

Adm. S.: Well, I think - you know our discussion of the Tonkin Gulf incident in the last interview, we covered the story pretty well. Just basically, of course, the second Tonkin Gulf incident, especially, was a night engagement in which things were fairly confused, very difficult to evaluate. You can evaluate it one way or another. CinCPacFlt, ComSeventh Fleet, and I, all gave the JCS the best evaluation we could, and since we were responsible for the operation in the Pacific, that was the evaluation that was accepted and upon which subsequent actions took place. I don't know what message Senator Fulbright refers to from the Maddox, but certainly the skipper of the Maddox, while he was on the spot and should have a pretty good idea of what was going on, he didn't necessarily have all the information, and what we did in Honolulu was to take the best information we had at the time and make an evaluation on it, and that's the way things happen in any war we've ever been in or ever will be in, and you can always second-guess a situation if you pick out one particular aspect or one particular thought, you'll probably find that he disagrees. I don't know what the thing was, what the message was. Nevertheless, the responsible people gave Washington an evaluation and it was accepted. As a matter of fact, the people in Washington had all of the messages that we had out in Honolulu and the JCS - the members of the JCS, and the Secretary of Defense had all those messages available. The President had them available. They could evaluate with practically the same amount of information that we had, so I would say offhand that Senator Fulbright is just off on a strike again and trying to make an excuse for something that happened which now he doesn't believe in.

Q: Thanks very much for your comment.

Adm. S.: Throughout the latter part of 1964 and on into '65, and, as a matter of fact, from then on, there was always a difference of opinion between CinCPac and JCS on the one hand, and the Secretary of Defense on the other, as to what action we needed to take to achieve our objectives in Southeast Asia. CinCPac and JCS believed that we should seek to destroy North Vietnamese will and capability as necessary to compel them to cease providing support to the insurgents in South Vietnam and in Laos. This was the strong course of action. However, the Secretary of Defense and, I believe, certain people in the Department of State, and probably certain members of the White House staff visualized a limited military action which, hopefully, would cause the North Vietnamese to decide to terminate their support of the insurgents. This objective is a lesser one and is not geared to the destruction of the North Vietnamese capability, and I always thought that while that might be a useful course of action, it would not be as sure a way of terminating the war as the way we recommended.

Q: Did you ever have a chance to appear personally with the JCS?

Adm. S.: Yes. So what we thought should have been done would be to set down what our objectives were precisely, with supporting courses of action, recognizing that we wanted to get this war over with as soon as possible, the assured way to do it would be through destruction of North Vietnamese will and capability to continue the aggression. I thought and told the JCS that any lesser objective, if it is adopted, should recognize there might be a change in United States outlook and determination to continue to take steps to achieve the objectives.

Q: In other words, what actually happened you were afraid would happen?

Adm. S.: Yes. This kind of exchange went on frequently in 1964 and 1965.

Q: Wasn't that frustrating to you?

Adm. S.: Oh, no. Frustration is not a thing that I'm concerned with very much. I'm concerned with doing my job properly and informing my superiors what I think and continue to inform them. Then I consider I'm doing my job.

Q: Well, you must have been the right man in the right job.

Adm. S.: I don't know about that. In the latter part of

1964, of course, we had some of our aircraft participating in overt action against the infiltration routes, and we were assisting the VNAF - the Vietnamese Air Force - by supplying them with advice, leadership to a certain extent, and having one squadron of Air Force A-1 aircraft, the old propeller-driven Navy aircraft of the Korean War, working with the VNAF in attacking targets in Laos and in South Vietnam. There was a tendency to try to cut back on all U.S. military actions in some quarters. Ambassador Maxwell Taylor in Saigon had a tendency to hold down on actions that U.S. forces could take, although it was obvious that the situation was fairly critical so far as South Vietnam was concerned. Nevertheless, he was recommending courses of action that involved only gradual application of U.S. power.

Q: How much authority did he have?

Adm. S.: He had a lot of authority. He was the President's representative in Saigon. So, although our action after the Gulf of Tonkin incident was a strong one, we then lapsed into a period of relative inaction and use of our forces in only a minimal way. CinCPac and, I think, the JCS also felt that failure to resume action such as we took after the Gulf of Tonkin and to maintain pressure on the enemy could be misinterpreted as a lack of resolve, insofar as the United States was concerned. We still continued to recommend that the military course of action which offers the best chance of success would be the destruction of the North Vietnamese will and capability, as necessary to compel them to cease providing support.

In late October of '64 CinCPac and the JCS were in agreement that strong military action was required to prevent the colapse of the U.S. position in Vietnam. We thought that there should be attacks on lines of communication in North Vietnam over which the troops in South Vietnam were being supplied, and we recommended, too, that targets in North Vietnam should be attacked. There was a target list which we had submitted which included targets which contributed to the economic viability of North Vietnam.

Q: Not just barracks?

Adm. S.: Not just barracks, no. They included a lot of military targets, such things as oil installations and power plants.

Q: You never were permitted to do that, were you?

Adm. S.: Not at that time. And there was much exchange of thinking about whether the Chicoms would come into this, and it was CinCPac's opinion and the JCS that the Chicoms were not likely to get into this affair unless their own bases were attacked, and we had no intention of attacking them.

I don't know whether we covered this or not, but in

October of '64 the air base at Bien Hoa was attacked . . .

Q: Yes, we did.

Adm. S.: We covered that? Yes, and then after that we were told to send the Marine Landing Force to Da Nang?

Q: Yes.

Adm. S.: Yes, we got that. There was another item that went on in November of 1964 which I'm not sure we covered. This was a dialogue between CinCPac and the JCS, and the JCS and then on to the Secretary of Defense.

And this called for a program of systematically increasing military pressures which we would recommend be taken against North Vietnam, and this was more or less the pattern of our actions throughout the war.

As I recall it, we recommended at that time that the most minor action that we should take would be to attack the lines of communications in North Vietnam, systematically moving north from the DMZ. Then we should also hit targets that were associated with infiltration, and we had a whole series of those targets which ran from the DMZ right on up to Hanoi. We also recommended aerial mining of various ports in North Vietnam, including Haiphong, of course, and along with mining, a naval blockade. Then we wanted to step up the air attacks and make them stronger and increasingly severe. Of course, as time went on, we thought that we should strike all the military and industrial targets in North Vietnam. We also pointed out that it might be necessary to control shipping into Cambodia, because the North Vietnamese could resort to moving supplies from North Vietnam to their forces in South Vietnam via Cambodia, and actually, at this point in time, they are doing exactly that.

Of course, CinCPac had in existence a whole series of plans for the conduct of operations in Southeast Asia. This is the normal military procedure and these plans are constantly changed to keep them up to date, and new plans are made up as time goes on. It must be recognized, however, that plans like the various ones we had for Southeast Asia are only a framework upon which to take action. You don't have to have a written plan for everything you intend to do. The idea is to have general plans that take care of a situation in a broad context, and then you issue operational orders to carry out specific operations or tasks under the general broad context of the plan. In early 1965 we were pretty much using our existing operations plans as a framework for our actions. However, or course, no one plan was ever just implemented completely, but rather, using the framework of the plans, we issued message op orders that took care of situations, as they came along. We had a plan for air attacks against targets in North Vietnam and the target annex of this plan was constantly revised as we selected targets which would inflict the maximum level of damage to the enemy. The target list kept being revised and refined as we found new targets and as others came to be considered unimportant.

Of course, we had two forces engaged. We had the Navy air force in the carriers, and then we had the U.S. Air Force involved. There were now airplanes and bases in both South Vietnam and Thailand. Whenever the Vietnamese Air Force was involved or the so-called Farmgate forces - Farmgate squadrons were U.S. Air Force squadrons of A-1 aircraft based in South Vietnam. Whenever these squadrons were involved, ComUSMACV was the coordinator between Farmgate squadrons and the Vietnamese air force.

Of course, there were no U.S. ground combatant forces in Southeast Asia at the beginning of 1965, and also there were no other friendly combatant forces to aid the South Vietnamese. At the beginning of 1965 the Viet Cong had the military initiative and they were making progress - very significant progress - towards destroying the armed forces of the Republic of South Vietnam. Throughout 1965 there were deployments of not only our own forces, but also combatant forces from Australia, from New Zealand, and from South Korea. And by the end of '65 we had enough forces deployed there so that the Allied forces combined with the Vietnamese forces had pretty much achieved at least a stalemate. The progress of the North Vietnamese and Viet Cong forces had slowed down so that the situation was much better, although I don't think it could be said that we were winning, at least we had stopped the enemy from winning.

The VC on 7 February struck the U.S. facility at Pleiku

and several other installations and there was considerable concern that the aircraft at Da Nang were apt to be struck by North Vietnamese aircraft, so that a U.S. Marine Corps Hawk battery was airlifted from Okinawa to Da Nang and became operational at the Da Nang airfield in early February. I believe it was about the 8th of February. Then the rest of this battalion, that part that wasn't airlifted, came by sea, so the whole battalion was installed at Da Nang by the 18th of February, and there was a small Marine security detachment there at Da Nang which provided local security for the anti-aircraft battalion as well as a certain amount of security for the airfield. The United States responded to the attack on the U.S. installations on the 7th of February with a series of air strikes against targets in North Vietnam.

Q: Were those off carriers?

Adm. S.: I think there were some from carriers and some from land-based aircraft, and we'll get into the air strike business a little later.

In early February a national decision was made by the United States for limited commitment of U.S. ground forces, U.S. ground combat forces, in South Vietnam. At this time the JCS approved a recommendation that I had made many times to deploy U.S. Marine Corps combat troops to Da Nang.

It was about the 7th of March when I got the go-ahead to deploy the 9th Marine Amphibious Brigade. This was the command and control elements of the brigade and, at the same time, a BLT - a Battalion Landing Team - which was at that time afloat off Da Nang. The BLT also was augmented by a helicopter squadron and some logistics elements, and at the same time, we started moving a second BLT from Okinawa to Da Nang by air and surface. As we depleted the Marines in Okinawa, the First Marine Brigade of about 7,000 people, was moved from Kanehoe to Okinawa on the 31st of March. Then, I guess it must have been April or May, we moved more Marines from Da Nang to - I mean from Okinawa to Da Nang, and one of the BLTs at Da Nang moved up to the Hue-Phu Bai area. Then in late April and May the Viet Cong initiated more large-scale attacks and ambushes and they were apparently bent on destroying the armed forces of the South Vietnamese and taking advantage of the instability of the South Vietnamese government to undermine the civilian will to continue fighting. There were many routes that were closed because of Viet Cong action, and many of the population centers were cut off from the agricultural areas so that they had difficulty getting food in and some of the areas had to be supplied by air. The situation was generally pretty bad. This, in turn, caused increasing concern in the United States and we had more deployments of forces to Vietnam.

On the 6th of May, 1965, the Third Marine Amphibious Force was established. It was composed of the Third Marine Division and the First Marine Aircraft Wing which were then ashore at Da Nang. During this time we also built up an expeditionary airfield at Chu Lai. This was built by the Seebees and naval mobile construction battalion No. 10, and with the assistance of Marine engineers, they put down an aluminum-matting airfield. We had two BLTs down at Chu Lai providing security for this construction. Then also during May we moved an amphibious - Marine Amphibious Brigade - from California to Okinawa to build up a reserve in the forward area.

I should say also that in April I proposed to move the 173rd Airborne Brigade from Okinawa to Bien Hoa. This brigade had the mission of securing the Vung Tau-Bien Hoa area. Of course, about this same time the Marines were landing troops at Chu Lai to secure the site for the construction of the airfield. There was some thought of taking the 173rd Brigade out of Vietnam as soon as it was relieved by another unit in order to reconstitute the reserve at Okinawa. However, it never was taken out while the buildup continued.

I think we might mention the Australian and New Zealand force. The Australian Minister of Defense was in Washington in February and gave some indication that his country might consider providing combat forces in South Vietnam, and the U.S. did invite them to talk to CinCPac about the possibility of deployments, so Air Chief Marshal Sir Frederick Scherger headed an Australian planning group, and New Zealand also accepted an invitation. Their group was headed by Rear Admiral Sir Peter Phipps. The talks were scheduled at CinCPac headquarters on 31st of March and the 1st of April. These talks included briefings on the situation in Southeast Asia and consideration of deploying Australian and New Zealand forces to Vietnam. They also mentioned that naval units might be supplied to augment the sea anti-infiltration force which was called Market Time. So we indicated that we could use any forces they had, air, sea, or ground, and would welcome them. We sent the summation of what we had accomplished in the talks to JCS, and we recommended that their offer of assistance be accepted. So Australia about the 1st of May announced that they would contribute one infantry battalion, and the New Zealand contribution was to be an artillery battery. The Australians arrived about between the 10th of May and the 10th of June, and the New Zealand artillery battery arrived about the end of July. Air Chief Marshal Sir Frederick Scherger, who is a friend of mine, and was the Australian military adviser to SEATO, and of course I was the U.S. military adviser, so we had participated in SEATO meetings together and had become acquainted in that way.

Now I'll go back and look over what was going on at Honolulu during 1965 up to this point.

Q: Speaking of going back to Honolulu, did you by chance find it difficult, the distance to be in over-all command and you had to be at such distance from Vietnam?

Adm. S.: No. It wouldn't make any difference whether you were 50 miles away or 5,000. Radio communications were just the same. It takes just as long to get to one place as it does to another. Communications were very good, and I got out there quite frequently.

Q: And of course you had excellent people on the ground.

Adm. S.: On the 9th of January 1965, Japanese Prime Minister Sato came through Honolulu. I was asked to meet him and talk to him. This was a contact that was very valuable.

On the 13th of January Australia's Prime Minister Sir Robert Menzies came to Honolulu and I had a chance to talk with him.

Then Prime Minister Sato came through again on the 15th of January and I had a chance to talk to him again.

On the 18th of January Prime Minister Huong of South Vietnam reshuffled his government and included a pair of generals in his government, trying to stabilize the government which he had little success in doing. This was a period where there was always a coup or a threat of a coup being talked about in Vietnam. During the month of January they were having Buddhist demonstrations in South Vietnam also. In early 1965 it became apparent that the North Vietnamese were not just supporting the insurgency. They were now sending North Vietnamese Army units into South Vietnam.

On the 27th of January a group of generals ousted Prime Minister Huong and set up an armed forces council, and made Lieutenant General Khanh the Prime Minister. They also had a minor coup in Laos on January 31st. General Phoumi Nosavan tried to regain power and was unsuccessful. On the 2nd of February our ambassador to Japan, Ed Reischauer, came through Honolulu and we had a briefing for him, also had a reception for him and for Mrs. Reischauer. This was a friendship that was very valuable to me in the years I was CinCPac. Ambassador and Mrs. Reischauer are good friends of ours and I've had many opportunities to discuss the situation very frankly with Ed.

Q: He was an awfully knowledgeable man about the Far East.

Adm. S.: Very knowledgeable about the Far East, that's right. I didn't agree with all of his thoughts on the Vietnam War but nevertheless we did have many good discussions.

On the 7th of February we had a Viet Cong attack on the U.S. helicopter base at Pleiku, in which eight U.S. personnel were killed and 108 wounded. In retaliation for this raid carrier-based fighters bombed and strafed the barracks and staging areas at Dong Hoi in North Vietnam. Also about this time the President ordered evacuation of all dependents from South Vietnam, since it was the estimate that dependents were in some danger and they were a hindrance to our over-all operations, so they were moved out. On the 9th of February Premier Kosygin of the Soviet Union declared that his government had reached an agreement with North Vietnam on measures to strengthen North Vietnam's defense potential, and this was probably the time that they started moving air defense weapons into North Vietnam.

Q: The Russians?

Adm. S.: The Russians, yes.

There was another air attack on North Vietnam on the 11th of February. On the 19th of February we started using B-57s to attack Viet Cong in the Binh Dinh sector of South Vietnam. That was the first time that we'd used our own aircraft to bomb in South Vietnam. On the 21st of February, the South Vietnamese Armed Forces Council tossed out General Khanh and named Major General Tran Van Minh as temporary chairman of the Council.

On the 26th of February Kosygin announced that North Vietnam - that the agreement they made with North Vietnam to increase its defense potential was now being implemented, which indicated how fast the Soviets responded to the North Vietnamese request for help.

On the 27th of February the State Department issued a White Paper <u>Aggression from the North</u> which was the first of many papers put out to demonstrate to the American public and to the world that North Vietnam was directing the aggression and actually was the aggressor in South Vietnam.

On the 2nd of March there was another raid on North Vietnam by U.S. and South Vietnamese planes. On the 6th of March I went from Honolulu for a trip to WestPac - Philippines,

Saigon, Da Nang. The first Marine Corps unit landed at Da Nang on the 8th of March 1965. On the 8th of March the International Control Commission published a report. Actually the report was published by the British Foreign Office. This report was initiated by the Indian and Polish members of the ICC for IndoChina, and they were condemning U.S. air strikes against North Vietnam as violations of the Geneva Agreement. The minority member of ICC, the Canadian member, criticized the report, called it misleading, and placed the blame on North Vietnam for the aggression. However, this was indicative of the impotence of the ICC with an Indian and a Polish member, and the Indian might as well have been a Communist. The ICC was never able to function to do what it was supposed to do, namely, determine the facts and report them. The Indian and the Pole never reported anything that pointed out any problems that the Communist side had generated. So it should be a lesson, which I don't know whether we'll ever learn or not, that any kind of an international body, if it's dominated by a combination of Communists and neutrals, can never function in a way that would make it useful. It actually is a great disadvantage to the United States to have that kind of a commission set up.

Q: Was this set up at the Geneva Conference?

Adm. S.: Yes. Whenever we give in to the extent of having an Indian and a Pole be two-thirds of a committee . . .

Q: I think it's important that you say a <u>neutral</u> and a Communist.

Adm. S.: Well, so-called neutral, but the Indians were right with the Communists all the time.

On the 9th of March I attended a Conference of the Chiefs of Mission in the Philippines, at Bagio. These are the U.S. ambassadors for all of our countries in the Far East. I left Bagio and arrived in Saigon on the 11th of March for a conference with General Westmoreland and his staff. On the 13th of March President Johnson declared that there was no possibility of the United States entering negotiations to end the war in Vietnam until North Vietnam displayed a willingness to end its aggression in South Vietnam. That was a fine strong statement, and it's too bad that we didn't stand by that policy for the whole war.

All during March there was a series of raids, air raids, on North Vietnam and I'll get into them in more detail later.

I returned to Honolulu on the 14th of March, and on the 21st of March departed on a trip to Washington, to the Army War College, and to the Naval War College. On the 22nd of March I met with the Joint Chiefs of Staff in Washington, discussed the war with the Chiefs. The Joint Chiefs of Staff were most cooperative throughout the war, we agreed on the same over-all concepts and they supported my suggestions one hundred per cent. The relationship couldn't have been more useful. It's just unfortunate that the recommendations that I initiated and the Chiefs approved to the Secretary of Defense got chewed up by a lot of people that really didn't — on the Secretary's staff — that really didn't understand military operations at all.

Q: Was it politically motivated also?

Adm. S.: I don't know. They thought they were military experts when they weren't.

Q: Were they civilian people?

Adm. S.: Yes. While I was in Washington, on the 23rd of March, I testified before the House Foreign Affairs Committee on the foreign aid bill and proceeded to the Army War College and talked to the students there, then to the Naval War College and talked to the students there. Then on the 26th returned to Honolulu.

On the 27th of March Ambassador Taylor came through Honolulu and we had a meeting with him at Keehi Lagoon, the site of many impromptu meetings when contingents from Washington and Vietnam came through Honolulu.

On the 30th of March, VC terrorists exploded a bomb in the U.S. Embassy, killed two U.S. personnel and 18 South Vietnamese.

On the 1st of April 17 non-aligned nations appealed to the U.S., South Vietnam, and North Vietnam for immediate negotiations without any pre-conditions. This was typical of the pressure that was generated by so-called non-aligned nations throughout the whole war, of making it appear that the United States and South Vietnam and the United States and our Free World allies were negligent in not trying to end the war. Of course, the way the war could be ended properly would be for the North Vietnamese just to stop their aggression. On the 4th of April two U.S. jets were shot down by North Vietnamese MIGs, the first time that MIGs had gone into battle with our planes, and it was a serious thing that these jets were shot down as easily as they were.

Q: Where were they?

Adm. S.: I don't remember what planes they were, but we may get into that later.

Now, talking for a moment about the air war against North Vietnam. It was typical of the direction and detail that Washington was exerting on the air war that I would be told to develop air strike plans based on three different alternative solutions, for example, and they'd specify that one option would have 130 sorties, another one would have 200 sorties, and one would have 275 sorties. So that they were getting into great detail in deciding just how these strikes would go, and where they would go, and when they would hit, what was the composition of the strike force, and this was due, apparently, to a desire by the Secretary of Defense and, perhaps, by the White House, I don't know, to get into the greatest of detail on these strikes because they felt they had such political connotation.

Q: They came to you from JCS?

Adm. S.: Right.

Q: Would you have been able to do anything on your own?

Adm. S.: Yes, to a certain degree. I'll get into that.

During February we were running occasional patrols of destroyers up into the gulf of Tonkin, called the Desoto patrols, as I recall it, and each time we sent a destroyer up there we were expecting them to be attacked and were ready to retaliate, if necessary. I mentioned that on the 6th of February there was an attack on a helicopter base at Pleiku, and in retaliation for that, we did execute an attack. I made numerous attempts to get more freedom of action during the early part of '65. I tried to get authority to use U.S. aircraft inside of South Vietnam on a continuing basis. I asked permission to run patrols in the Gulf of Tonkin on a continuing basis and also to run reconnaissance flights whenever I needed to. The JCS, I'm sure at the Secretary of Defense's instigation, even controlled reconnaissance flights in great detail.

Q: That's hard to believe.

Adm. S.: On about the 10th of February the VC destroyed an enlisted billet hotel at Qui Nhon. Three U.S. were killed and several injured, and General Westmoreland and I wanted to retaliate for that bombing with some air strikes against North Vietnam. However, we were turned down on that request, and were told to use the Vietnamese Air Force to strike a target.

Q: To strike a target?

Adm. S.: To strike a target in North Vietnam - I can't remember what it was now - and I was authorized to use our Farmgate aircraft for navigational assistance. This was another example of the great detail of direction during this period. During the middle of February there was consideration given to what kind of a program of air strikes should be taken against the North Vietnamese, and naval gunfire was considered along with more armed ship patrols up the coast. And in connection with commenting on this the JCS indicated that the Soviets would probably provide military support for North Vietnam and perhaps provide SA-2 missiles to North Vietnam. It was also about this time that we started a recommendation to use our bases - air bases - in Thailand to launch the strikes against North Vietnam. About this time also I recommended that I be given further latitude in planning for targets in North Vietnam, and recommended a progression northward of the targets we were using - we were hitting at that time. In the middle of February of '65, we made a recommendation to land a Marine expeditionary brigade at Da Nang to protect our investment there, and to use Da Nang as a base from which to launch strikes against North Vietnam. There was a considerable amount of worry here that the South Vietnamese troops were not adequate to protect our U.S. air squadrons and other installations that we had on the beach.

In February of '65 we launched the first air strike that was nicknamed "Rolling Thunder." Rolling Thunder became the name for our air strikes against North Vietnam, and Rolling Thunder No. 1 was planned for the 22nd of February. Toward the end of February there was real concern about the U.S. position in South Vietnam. The position was deteriorating to the extent that it was thought possible that the South Vietnamese would be unable to continue the battle if they did not stabilize their government and get on with fighting the war with less diversions. And it was apparent that we had a very large investment in South Vietnam and would need to get on with augmenting our effort of gain our objectives in South Vietnam. This, of course, involved deploying the first Marine ground forces into the Da Nang area, augmenting the fleet, augmenting the land-based air, and making increased strikes against North Vietnam. There was the continuing problem of instability in the South Vietnamese government, and this was to prove a continuing problem for at least another year. There was the continued mention, however, of a gradual increase in military pressure.

By mid-March 1965 the United States was applying additional pressure against the Viet Cong and also against North Vietnam, as I mentioned previously. ComUSMACV's logistic capability was being expanded and, of course, two Marine Battalion Landing Teams were ashore at Da Nang. Still, the VC was enjoying continuing success in efforts to divide the Republic of Vietnam and to weaken the government. So, to improve the security and general strength in Vietnam the JCS proposed deploying a Marine Expeditionary Force, a U.S. Army division, and a Korean division. The Army division wasn't ready to go but the Marines were, and so in early April orders went out directing two additional Marine battalions into South Vietnam. Because of this buildup that was about to take place, we had a conference in Honolulu in early April with representatives from JCS and from the Army, the Air Force, and the Navy, and people from ComUSMACV staff, looking to the necessary logistic action to support this force that we could see coming. While this conference was in session, CinCPac generally gave them a briefing on CinCPac's concept and this was that forces would first occupy and secure coastal bases, from which they would move out and engage in counter-insurgency operations, with the assistance and coordination of the South Vietnamese. The idea was that these bases were supportable from the sea and would be utilized as a way of getting around the problem of land-based communications in South Vietnam. The thing was that from these - from the security of these enclaves with their logistics coming in from the sea, which we controlled, our forces could fan out with the assistance of the Vietnamese and take on the enemy. Then, as our forces expanded, of course, our operations would expand in the area. And it was important to note that we had to build up our bases before we could do anything on a sustained scale because the operations that we were contemplating would require a lot of logistic support.

We also gave out our concept of command arrangements.' The conference was told that CinCPac was to exercise over-all operational control through his component commanders and through ComUSMACV, as appropriate. ComUSMACV would be the operational joint commander for operations in South Vietnam. Commander, Second Air Division, in Saigon wouldbe a component commander under ComUSMACV and he would be the operational commander under MACV for air operations in South Vietnam. On the other hand, for air operations against North Vietnam, operational control for U.S. Air Force forces in Southeast Asia was to be exercised by CinCPacAf, Commander-in-Chief, Pacific Air Forces, through the Commander, Thirteenth Air Force, and then again through the Commander, Second Air Division. CinCPacAF would also operation in support of ComUSMACV when directed. This was the first time that this command arrangement had been set forth in detail. It was the command arrangement that held throughout the war, despite many attempts by a lot of people to change it, and it turned out to be the best possible command arrangement. There were and still are many criticisms of this command arrangement but I think it is and was the best that could be generated and it actually was a model for use in the future.

Q: Did you and General Westmoreland get along personally?

Adm. S.: Yes, we got on fine, and of course that was one thing, we did have a close personal relationship. Westy was frequently pinged on by his staff to try to gain over-all control of the whole operation - and he came in to me frequently trying to get control of the whole operation and I politely but firmly told him that it wasn't going to work that way, it was going to work like I had laid it out. He finally got to the point where he recognized that that was the way to run it.

Q: But you had to have that cooperation personally, really, as well as professionally, don't you?

Adm. S.: Yes, personal cooperation was important, but just the firm, reasonable attitude was more important. But you'll still find army colonels that say that command arrangements were the reason we didn't win the war.

Q: Not really?

Adm. S.: Oh, yes. Sure. You ought to read U.S. News and World Report this week. They have some Army colonels in there whoever they were - maybe they weren't colonels - but they definitely thought that that was one of the reasons we weren't winning the war. They couldn't have been more wrong.

To continue with the command arrangement deal: in Vietnam the naval component commander functions in South Vietnam was to be exercised by the commanding general of the Third Marine Expeditionary force, reporting to ComUSMACV. And of course other operations outside of the country, other naval operations, were conducted under the operational control of CinCPacFlt through ComSeventhFlt, and I told CinCPacFlt to support ComUSMACV when it was required and when I directed. I also directed at that time that amphibious operations in Southeast Asia would be conducted under CinCPacFlt's operational control. Actually, there were no amphibious operations outside of South Vietnam, so all the amphibious operations were actually controlled by CinCPacFlt in support of ComUSMACV. Of course, for operations - on land, Com USMACV was in operational control of commanding general, Third Marine Amphibious Force, and he also exercised opcon of the Australian and New Zealand forces in the republic of Korea when they finally came in.

Also there was a considerable amount of talk about having a combined staff of U.S. and Vietnamese to correlate activities and perform liaison for the combat operations in which U.S. and Vietnamese forces were involved. Actually, ComUSMACV supervised the U.S. operations, had op control. The Commander-in-Chief of the Vietnamese armed forces had control of their operations, and they coordinated closely, and actually, as the war went on the Vietnamese came to pretty much do what General Westmoreland recommended. We did not want to set up a big combined command because we felt that, if we did, the Vietnamese would react by considering that now the U.S. had taken over, because, of course, in any combined staff the U.S. would have to have the majority of the positions because of their superior amount of experience and their superior numbers. We felt that if this happened, why, the Vietnamese would be apt to lay back and let the U.S. fight the war, and that was one of the problems anyway. So there wasn't any use setting up a command arrangement which would generate this kind of action. We felt that if the Vietnamese were in command of their own forces and responsible for their actions, they would go on and take action to improve these armed forces. That turned out to be, in my opinion, a very fine arrangement.

In 1965 we also set up ComUSMACThai as Commander, U.S. Military ?Assistance Command Thailand. This was done to have a command setup in Thailand in case we had to get into action in that area. During this period, of course, there was a very heavy buildup of base development because of the deployments and those deployments that were anticipated for the future. It was very important that we very rapidly generate a base structure from which these forces could operate. I think in FY '65 funds there were something like 125 million which we thought was necessary and then it got up to about 150 million, I think, by '66. There was a great deal of work to be done by the Seebees at Da Nang and also Chu Lai, and there was even more work to be done by the Army engineer units all over the country. First, they had to do a lot of construction in order to establish an adequate base for POL support as this force expanded. There also had to be an emergency POL capability afloat, and there was considerable dependence - as a matter of fact, when we moved in there the POL system was completely a commercial system. As we went along we got more and more capability for ourselves, so at the end the system was pretty much completely a military system.

We also had to do a lot of work in Thailand during this period to bring the logistics facilities in that country up to what was required to support the large number of forces that we eventually had in there, in Thailand, and the large amount of strike effort that was going out from our Thai air bases.

On the 16th of April U.S. planes bombed some bridges near Nanoi and also on that date the first North Vietnamese surface-to-air missile site was reported under construction near Hanoi.

On the 17th Ambassador Taylor flew to Honolulu and there we had a meeting of General Wheeler, Chairman of the JCS, General Westmoreland, Ambassador Taylor, and CinCPac, and we went over the whole spectrum of U.S. policy in the Pacific, with particular emphasis on Vietnam, of course. Then on the 20th of April Secretary McNamara, Assistant Secretary Bill Bundy, John McNaughton, Assistant Secretary of Defense for ISA, joined the conference. This conference went on for a few days.

Q: Did Maxwell Taylor ever change his attitude? Which you expressed earlier of always wanting to hold back?

Adm. S.: Yes, he did. On the 24th of April I left Honolulu for a trip to the continental United States and then on to London for a SEATO meeting. On the 26th of April I spoke at the Air War College and the Armed Forces Staff College and met with CNO and SecNav in Washington, and met with the Joint Chiefs, I guess. I don't remember but I always did when I went to Washington. Then went on to London. There we had a military advisers' meeting and then a SEATO Council meeting, and we had an audience with the Queen . . .

Q: You did?

Adm. S.: Well, all of the military advisers. As a matter of fact, we had dinner in Buckingham Palace.

Q: With the royal family?

Adm. S.: With the Queen.

Q: Wasn't that kind of exciting?

Adm. S.: Oh, I guess so.

Q: What did you wear? Of course, you wore/full dress uniform.

Adm. S.: Mess jacket, I guess it was. I don't know. Mess jacket, I'm sure. I also had a luncheon with Admiral Lord Louis Mountbatten and numerous other friends in London.

Q: Were any of the conversations memorable?

Adm. S.: Oh, they were just the usual SEATO meetings and that sort of thing. It was a good meeting.

Q: I meant with the Queen.

Adm. S.: With the Queen? Just official.

In that SEATO meeting we did get the Council to condemn North Vietnam for aggression. France abstained from voting on this, and I think we probably had to twist England's arm a little bit, since the English were not great supporters of our Vietnam action. After the SEATO meeting in London, we went over to Paris and called on General Lemnitzer, had lunch with him in his quarters, stayed with Air Force General Jake Smart, and then arrived in Washington again on the 7th of May and met with the JCS, and talked to the National War College, and returned to Honolulu on the 8th of May.

On the 11th of May the Viet Cong overran a provincial capital, Song Be, which is north of Saigon. They were finally driven off by U.S. air strikes, and this was a fairly serious attack.

On the 12th of May the Philippine House of Representatives voted the necessary money to send a Philippine contingent to South Vietnam, but that was delayed because the Senate on the 12th of July voted to defer action on the Vietnam question. During this period the United States was performing a little stronger than they had before in North Vietnam, but on the 13th of May they had a bombing pause, a five-day standdown of their own counter operations and - to see if they could get any reaction from the North Vietnamese, and of course they didn't. Meantime, we were, of course, building up our forces in South Vietnam. On the 18th of May the air attacks on North Vietnam were resumed after this five-day pause because the President had no response from his latest offer.

On the 21st of May Air Chief Marshal Dawee Chullaspaya, Royal Thai Air Force and Deputy Minister of Defense of Thailand, visited with me in Honolulu. Air Chief Marshal Dawee was, by this time, a very close friend of mine since we had participated in a number of meetings and I visited him in Thailand. On the 26th of May the Minister of defense of New Zealand, Dean Eyre, received a briefing from our command center, and the same day Kim Song Um, Minister of Defense for the Republic of Korea, had a briefing. At the end of May the VC launched an offensive in the central provinces of Vietnam and also U.S. and South Vietnamese planes began the three-day bombing of Hoai An, which is 45 miles from Hanoi.

On the 31st of May and the 1st of June Ambassador Martin

from Thailand - I mean the U.S. Ambassador to Thailand visited Honolulu, had a briefing, then a discussion. At the end of May and first of June we were having problems in Saigon with Catholics demonstrating against the government which was then - what was his - the Prime Minister's name was Quat. The chief of state was named Suu. And it was an unstable government. Nobody was very happy with it.

On the 4th of June the South Korean Defense Minister announced that South Korea would send 15,000 combat troops to South Vietnam. I see a note here that on the 15th of June the U.S. State Department said that U.S. troops in South Vietnam are engaging in combat only to defend key installations, and U.S. troops only advise South Vietnamese government troops to carry out combat operations. In my opinion, this kind of announcement from our State Department is unfortunate, unnecessary, and doesn't help the United States a bit.

Q: It wasn't even true, was it?

Adm. S.: Well, it wasn't very accurate, no. I guess, you could say, yes, we were only engaging in combat operations to protect U.S. bases there because that's about all we could do at that point. But to make that kind of a statement and to subsequently get into large combat operations doesn't make much sense.

In early March of 1965 I made some comment to the JCS on the military and political situation in South Vietnam and, among other things, said that the single most important thing we can do quickly to improve the security situation in South Vietnam is to make full use of our air power. And I emphasized that removal of constraints upon use of U.S. air power is urgent. I told them that even if we start using our air power without constraint, it will take time to build it up to its maximum effectiveness. This is typical of the continued requests for authority to make proper use of our air power. In general, Rolling Thunder operations were initiated under strict control and specific guidance. The strike day was specified as well as the number of sorties by task and by target. Strikes were dependent initially upon Vietnamese Air Force participation prior to or concurrent with the United States strikes. We finally got over that hurdle, however, because being dependent on Vietnamese Air Force participation really hampered our strikes.

Q: I was wondering, you said also you had to even ask the Vietnamese Air Force if you could hit certain targets. Was that ever true?

Adm. S.: No. We had just a very restricted list of targets that we could hit and sometimes we had an alternate and sometimes we didn't, and frequently they - the planes came off the primary targets because they couldn't get in to them because of the low clouds - they couldn't get in to the other, to the secondary targets, so they were prohibited from dropping their bombs on enemy territory, and most of them dropped their bombs in the ocean, which I think is kind of a sad way to run a war. Another problem was that they wouldn't let us do prestrike reconnaissance so that frequently we went in with a minimum of information. At one time bomb-damage-assessment aircraft were required to accompany the strike aircraft or immediately follow strike aircraft so that this would sometimes mean that the bomb-damage assessment was no good because the smoke over the target obscured the target so that the pictures were no good.

Well, as the Rolling Thunder campaign progressed, restrictions were gradually reduced and we had a lot more latitude in air operations. Finally, with the approval for areas to operate in, they didn't tell us when we could do armed reconnaissance in detail. We were restricted as to the number of strike aircraft wecould use for a long time, but finally, I think, that restriction was lifted, as I recall it, in 1966, or maybe it was '67, when we could go ahead and use as many strike aircraft as we had available. Then there were all kinds of restrictions as to the number of times we could go back to a target, and this went on throughout the war. Finally, North Vietnam was divided into seven regions, which we called route packages, for these Rolling Thunder operations. They were designed for the purpose of assigning responsibility for target development, collection of intelligence data, and target analysis, and the idea was to ensure economical and effective use of our resources and to ensure that there was not interference from one outfit and another in Northern Vietnam. We did have very fine operational procedures developed between the Second Air Force and the Seventh Fleet, so that there was always full coordination and cooperation in these air ops.

As a result of the meeting in Honolulu, which Secretary McNamara, Ambassador Taylor, General Westmoreland, and General Wheeler attended, there was some discussion at the meeting that tasks for our air power in South Vietnam must get the first call on air assets. Any time there was not enough air in Vietnam to take care of the air requirements in Vietnam, more air would be brought in. This is an indication of Secretary McNamara's feeling that South Vietnam is all-important and North Vietnam is a - the requirement for striking North Vietnam is of lesser importance. At that conference there was considerable discourse about restricting the strikes to the north. Ambassador Taylor made some comment about it is important not to kill the hostage by destroying the North Vietnamese assets inside the Hanoi doughnut.

Q: What does that mean?

Adm. S.: Well, that means don't strike inside the Hanoi-Haiphong circle because you would, what he calls kill the hostage, then they wouldn't have anything to worry about because they'd all be dead anyway. And that, of course, is a theory of war that I completely and utterly disagree with.

Q: I couldn't even understand what it meant.

Adm. S.: The idea was that there'd be slow improvement in the South and the strategy for victory over time is to break the will of the North Vietnamese and the VC by denying them victory. Of course, that, again is this gradualism concept which didn't work and never does work. In May of '65, I commented on a proposal to try to get negotiations started, with a general comment on the situation in Southeast Asia, and I said our objective must be to maintain a position of strength, to thwart Chicom expansion. Cessation of fighting in South Vietnam does not solve all our problems in Southeast Asia. I said I had three general observations. First, the Communists might unilaterally suspend the insurgency without benefit of any negotiations, shift their attentions elsewhere, and wait for a suitable occasion to make a new effort in South Vietnam. And I said that if we're going to have some kind of effort at negotiations, that possibility should be covered. And I said, secondly, we have had enough experience in negotiations with the Communists to know that pressure must be maintained during negotiations. We must, therefore, maintain air and naval action against North Vietnam during any negotiations, despite expected pressures to suspend such military actions in order to provide a propitious climate for talks. The alternative would be to hold off negotiations until we and the GVN had established a strong military position in South Vietnam, such a strong military position in South Vietnam that we could maintain a strong bargaining position without continuing military attacks against North Vietnam. Given the uncertainty, however, as to when or under what circumstances we might become involved in negotiations, we should plan on maintaining air attacks on North Vietnam during negotiations. And third I believed that more effective control mechanisms would be needed to ensure that North Vietnam fulfills promises made during the negotiations. That comment which was made in May of 1965, and it was a pretty good comment and bears on negotiations today, 1970.

CinCPac recommended in early April to the JCS a concept and schedule for deployment of forces to Southeast Asia. The JCS passed this plan on to the Secretary of Defense with a schedule for deployment of three divisions and certain other forces to Southeast Asia, and these were the first deployments that were discussed during the conference in Honolulu on 20 and 21 April. The JCS decided to recommend eight U.S. battalions as an early reinforcement to the Vietnamese ground effort, and an additional 12 battalions - U.S. battalions - were required at a later date. They also included four third-country battalions and equivalents as appropriate deployments with the possibility that they would get six more battalions from this source. Three U.S. air squadrons and certain logistic support forces were also recommended. During the first half of 1965, with the increasing force deployments to Vietnam, there was frequent interchange of comments regarding the strategy for the situation, and in

June I said that the focus of strategy should be on control of the important coastal areas of central and northern South Vietnam, and also the Mekong Delta. I felt that our strategy should aim at reducing the mobility of the Viet Cong as well as their morale and offensive capability, forcing the VC to the defensive by progressively increasing the size of the tactical areas of responsibility and connecting one friendly area to another by means of cleared zones. Later on, in August, I was asked to comment regarding a JCS concept for South Vietnam and said then that the JCS listed almost all South Vietnam as being of major significance, while I thought that the relative importance of the various areas should be recognized to provide direction and thrust for the strategy and to guide employment and positioning of forces, and again I said I thought the Saigon area and the Mekong Delta were of primary importance, the coastal plains second, and the highlands third. I also said I thought it was important to control food-producing areas so as to feed the people that were under friendly control and to export the surplus, thus causing the VC to either import their food or to fight for it. I also emphasized the necessity for the basic U.S. military strategy to include Thailand, where we had to have a buildup of logistic support bases and improvements of our existing air bases, and we needed to construct new airfields, and also needed to improve the lines of communication and the state of readiness of the Thailand forces. It had become apparent by this time that the lines of communication in Thailand would not support . . .

Interview No. 6 with Admiral U.S. Grant Sharp

Place: San Diego, California

Date: 7 February 1970

Subject: Biography

By: Etta Belle Kitchen

Adm. S.: What I said at the end of the last tape there - we could see by now that our lines of communication in Thailand were inadequate in case we had to move ground forces into that area in any size. So we started a program to improve lines of communication in that area and there was a lot of work done over the next three or four years.

Another point that I made in my discussions with the JCS was that we must consider Southeast Asia as a single, integrated U.S. strategy, which would include North and South Vietnam and Thailand and Laos, in that military operations must be conducted in concert with major political, economic, and social programs. CinCPac on numerous occasions made statements to the JCS reminding them of the need for an integrated strategy for the area.

In early June of 1965 we were very concerned that the Communists might be about ready to increase the intensity of the conflict. We thought that the Viet Cong were capable of mounting regimental-size operations in any of the Corps areas, and battalion-size operations almost any place in South Vietnam. Further, that Viet Cong units were now equipped with a new family of weapons which represented a great increase in in their fire power. These weapons they had received, of course, from Communist China and from the Soviet Union. At this time there were elements of one North Vietnamese regiment and, perhaps, two additional regiments in the northern zone of the II Corps area, and it appeared that another NVN division was in southern Laos capable of moving in to South Vietnam quite rapidly. There were only two of the nine VC regiments in South Vietnam that had been heavily engaged, and it seemed, at that time, that the commitment of their separate battalions was in about the same proportion. The highlands, at this point, were virtually isolated and there was a siege of Saigon going on that was causing serious military and economic consequences. The South Vietnamese armed forces, at this point, were being chewed up pretty badly and were not in good position, and we were worried whether they would continue to fight. Although we had authority to go ahead with an increase of the Vietnamese armed forces, it was deferred because the available men were needed to reconstitute forces that had suffered heavy battle losses. As a result of all this, it was considered that there was required a further buildup of U.S. and Allied forces in South Vietnam at the most rapid possible rate. We recommended then that the immediate remaining ground forces of the Third Marine Amphibious Force be deployed and, along with U.S. Army logistics support units, and then we wanted the - an air mobile division with all of its combat and logistic support forces to close as early as possible. And, at that time, it recommended four additional tactical fighter squadrons be brought in. At the same time, it was recommended that we have intensified air action against North Vietnam.

By early July - oh, first I should go back and say that there was a Seacord meeting - coordinating committee for U.S. missions in Southeast Asia. This consists of the U.S. ambassadors to South Vietnam, Laos, and Thailand, CinCPac, and ComUSMACV. This meeting was held in Bangkok on the 23rd and 24th of July 1965. We had a general discussion of the situation, including how arms were being infiltrated into South Vietnam and we felt that Thailand needed to be careful to detect any insurgency in their northern provinces - any increasing insurgency in their northern provinces.

As a result of these recommendations to increase the forces as rapidly as possible, the Secretary of Defense went out to Saigon and asked General Westmoreland for a shopping list of what he needed to facilitate the accomplishment of his mission. Well, the list that General Westmoreland gave the Secretary differed from the recommendations that were made to the JCS by CinCPac and MACV, so they decided they needed to have another conference in Hawaii to prepare a coordinated program of deployments. So a planning conference was conducted on the 3rd to the 6th of August with representatives from almost everywhere, joint staff of the JCS, the services, OSD, Military Air Transport Service, MSTS, the PacCom component commanders, CinCStrike, and everybody else, even ComUSKorea. The resulting program covered the movement to South Vietnam of both United States and Republic of Korea military units, and personnel and materiel, which we thought was necessary to achieve a military stalemate with the Viet Cong.

Q: Not victory, just stalemate?

Adm. S.: Stalemate, yes, because we thought we were going downhill at this point.

So we came out with everything that we needed in the way of forces, troop list, deployment priorities, airfield construction that was necessary, transportation schedules, and all this sort of thing. Very comprehensive recommendations came out of this conference. There were a few problems concerned with this requirement for forces. First of all, we had to have an early decision to deploy the U.S. forces - some of them were ready to deploy, but we had to have a decision to get them there in a hurry. And, of course, the Republic of Korea division was dependent on the Korean government making a decision to deploy, and they would be unable to close South Vietnam as fast as U.S. forces. Then there was a problem of port capacity in Saigon and the other ports. Saigon was a port of very poor facilities and apt to get jammed up, and it wasn't very well managed. We had to use other ports in Vietnam, although Saigon was the only port that was really developed, so we had to start developing the ports, and about this time there was a very large program started on developing facilities in ports.

The JCS shortly after they received CinCPac's recommendation, recommended to the Secretary of Defense the major portion of the deployments that we had recommended. However, we had recommended the deployment of Army troops to Thailand, and they recommended against that.

Shortly after the August conference, CinCPac issued preliminary guidance for later conferences to be held both at Saigon and in Honolulu. These conferences were to address the force requirements for the next stage of operations, when we would resume the military offensive and get on with pacifying the high-priority areas in South Vietnam. The idea was to develop ComUSMACV's concept of operations at the Saigon conference, and then together with the courses of action, force requirements, and so forth, and have a broader conference in Honolulu where we developed plans for all of Southeast Asia, after which CinCPac would submit his recommendations to JCS.

Incidentally, in these conferences, we talked of three phases of action. The first phase was to include forces to halt the Viet Cong offensive and stem the tide. Here, we would defend the major bases and the minor bases, have reaction offensive operations, secure the province capitals, and we hoped that by the end of 1965 this phase would terminate and phase two could start. This phase included additional forces with which we would resume the military offensive, then re-institute pacification measures in high-priority areas where they would be highly visible, and then we'd also need reserve forces and support forces. We hoped that Phase Two would embrace the period from 1 January of 1966 to 30 June 1966, and then we'd go into Phase Three, which would require additional forces in South Vietnam to defeat the remaining organized VC and to pacify the country.

In February of 1965 I established an ad hoc study group with the mission of producing a concept and initial program for the optimum use of air weapon systems to attrite, harass, and interdict North Vietnamese support of insurgency in Laos and South Vietnam. This group consisted of members of my staff and also of the component commanders staffs. They came up with findings. One of the important ones was that in northern North Vietnam all road traffic to Laos and South Vietnam was channeled through four funnels: the Barthelmy, Mugia, and Nafe passes in the route structure approaching the DMZ. Each of these funnels is susceptible to effective disruption with attendance development of a new series of targets at cut points, such as backed-up convoys, temporary truck parks, and supply troop staging areas, and they said that disruption of these LOCs and destruction of developing targets will require constant and unrelenting surveillance and attack. And they said that the forces presently deployed in Southeast Asia have the capability to interdict the LOCs and harass and attrite DRV activity supporting the insurgents. They said they needed more target intelligence in some cases so that they needed to expand their intelligence-acquisition program. They also recommended that CinCPac reiterate to the JCS that the pressure program against North Vietnam and complementary Laotian areas should be constant and unrelenting to keep the LOC network cut and harassed in depth, and that fleeting and targets dictate a requirement to strike rapidly, so therefore delegation of authority to appropriate commanders to execute strike missions was necessary to exploit these targets.

This brings up again the fact that Rolling Thunder was not a military campaign in the classical sense. It was a limited campaign designed by Washington to place enough military pressure on North Vietnam to halt their support of insurgents in South Vietnam and Laos. The initial JCS restrictions, which were put out by higher authority, were designed to tighten control of all facets of the air strikes. For example, the strike day was specified and it was mandatory that the Vietnamese air force participate, the number of sorties by task on each target was specified, and you couldn't vary from this without prior justification, only the primary target or one or two alternates would be attacked, pre-strike reconnaissance was prohibited, maximum feasible damage had to be achieved by a single strike, you could not re-cycle your aircraft - that is, you could not send them back to land and take on fuel and ammo and come back - bomb-damage assessment aircraft had to accompany strike aircraft, and then subsequent bomb-damage assessment had to be accomplished without escort and at medium altitude, otherwise you had to get approval from the JCS. And there could be no armed reconnaissance. As Rolling Thunder went on and in accord with repeated requests to ease off on these restrictions, we gradually gained operational flexibility to some degree. It was a step-by-step thing with each Rolling Thunder hopefully containing a few less restrictions. I repeatedly had to inform the JCS that their restrictions were denying the full benefit that operations might achieve, and of course, the JCS knew this full well, but they were being held down by higher authority in Washington.

Q: I wonder what would have happened if you'd gone ahead and done what you wanted to.

Adm. S.: You just don't do that.

Some of the suggestions I made was that we shouldn't try to conduct U.S. and VNAF strikes on the same day and the same hour, but be flexible about it. We should be able to conduct our strikes on more than one day, picking the strike day by the weather over the target. It was very important that the schedule get sufficiently flexible to take advantage of good weather conditions, because weather was usually very bad. And these restrictions were removed gradually but never completely.

For example, in Rolling Thunder Six, they authorized the use of napalm which we'd been asking for. Then the next Rolling Thunder, Rolling Thunder Seven, they assigned more than one target to U.S. forces and they allowed a limited amount of armed reconnaissance on a very few sections of one route. And then, in the same RT 7, they permitted strikes to be conducted over a seven-day period, as dictated by the judgment of the tactical commander. Then in Rolling Thunder Eight, a program of strikes against radar installations was authorized, which we'd been trying to get, and the area for armed reconnaissance was extended to 20° North in North Vietnam, and for the first time they allowed us to arm reconnaissance aircraft to attack North Vietnamese naval craft. In Rolling Thunder Nine, they eased off the restrictions a little bit more. This time they allowed additional armed reconnaissance, and they allowed us to expend ordnance which should have been expended on the main target against rolling stock. This was a change because previously we'd been dumping unexpended ordnance into the ocean.

Q: Did you have to go back and ask for this each time?

Adm. S.: Yes. And in Rolling Rhunder Ten they let us do armed reconnaissance against locomotives and what was called infiltration support structures. Then, the next Rolling Thunder they allowed us to strike military targets in the immediate vicinity of armed reconnaissance or fixed targets. This just goes to emphasize the very heavy restrictions which made it very difficult to get the most effective use out of our air power.

Q: And this air power was in both Navy, off carriers, and ground . . . ?

Adm. S.: Yes.

To continue with the restrictions on Rolling Thunder, Rolling Thunder Twelve - and I should explain that each one of these Rolling Thunder numbers means a new - they would come out once a week or maybe once every two weeks, with a new Rolling Thunder operation. These came out from Washington where they took recommendations that we sent in and massaged them and tried to get them approved, then sent them on back out. Rolling Thunder Twelve, they gave us fifteen fixed targets which was more than we'd ever had before and for the first time they permitted us to strike in waves against the target, so that you could strike more than once a day. However, if you wanted to strike the following day you had to get JCS approval. They were still restricting us very carefully to the number of sorties of armed reconnaissance. I think at this time we were allowed 24 armed reconnaissance sorties or something like that. And they lifted the requirement so that we could now expend unexpended ordnance against any armed reconnaissance route, and they allowed a few more targets per armed reconnaissance aircraft.

Then in Rolling Thunder Thirteen, they allowed a few more kinds of targets for armed reconnaissance aircraft. For example, they could hit lighters and load repair equipment and bivouac and staging areas. In Rolling Thunder Fourteen they added a new target for armed reconnaissance. This was any surface craft that fired on a friendly aircraft. You would think, of course, that anybody who fired on a friendly aircraft would immediately be a target, but this wasn't so until this point. Then in Rolling Thunder Fifteen they allowed us to strike one North Vietnamese surface-to-air missile site, but later on the JCS directed that surface-to-air missile sites be avoided.

Q: Oh, really! That I don't understand.

Adm. S.: They said to go around them rather than go after them. Then that changed. And in Rolling Thunder Sixteen they allowed us to conduct strikes in small increments over a ten-day period, giving us a little more leeway, but not much. Rolling Thunder Seventeen concentrated on armed reconnaissance without any fixed target. Throughout this Rolling Thunder program, in one week you'd have a lot of fixed targets, the next week they wouldn't give you any. So it went up and down. Rolling Thunder Eighteen they added barges to the list of authorized armed reconnaissance targets. Rolling Thunder Nineteen they expanded the armed reconnaissance area a little bit and allowed us to strike three fixed targets north of 20°. Rolling Thunder Twenty they authorized seven fixed targets, and five of them were in the northwest part of North Vietnam. The armed reconnaissance area was also expanded into the northwest.

Q: That's away from Hanoi?

Adm. S.: Well, it's west of Hanoi, yes. At CinCPac's request, we were authorized to re-strike Dong Hoi and Vinh airfields. In RT 21, we had ten fixed targets and seven of them were north of 20°, and the armed reconnaissance was extended a little bit. They also allowed us to make a few more sorties. In RT 22 and 23 the period to strike specified targets was extended to two weeks, and the armed reconnaissance area was expanded a bit more, and armed reconnaissance aircraft were authorized to strike airfields or any previously struck JCS target. When I say "strike airfields," that is, any airfield that had been authorized and there weren't very many. RT 24 and 25 there were a few more armed reconnaissance targets. For example, area approaches, ford, pontoon bridges, and pontoon construction sites. RT 26 and 27 armed reconnaissance was permitted against naval berthing areas. RT 28 and 29 the number of armed reconnaissance sorties was expanded to a thousand, and they allowed the armed reconnaissance aircraft to strike SAM systems in the mobile mode, and they also gave us several more additional fixed targets. Then, in RT 30 and 31, which was now getting to the end of 1965, the armed reconaissance area was further increased and the number of sorties was increased to 1,200, and any JCS target could be struck if it appeared that is was recovering from a previous strike, but this was only if the target had been authorized in the first place. So, although this may sound as though a lot of restrictions were lifted, there were still tremendous restrictions on what could be done.

Q: Did Rolling Thunder go on into '66?

Adm. S.: Yes, went right on till they stopped the bombing. I think, as I've said before, as we got a little bit more flexibility I had to tell the operational commanders to be careful not to overstep the still-tight boundaries, because, if they did, why, we'd get cut back again. There never seemed to be any desire to unleash our forces and get on with the war. It was always, hold them tight and use any excuse to cut back the bombing.

Q: I like the explanation of your April message to your commanders.

Adm. S.: The April message that you're talking about I sent to my subordinate commanders. I said in the day-to-day pressure of an operational environment, it was not easy to remember that the air campaign in North Vietnam was not just another war with the objective of inflicting maximum damage to the enemy. Rather, Rolling Thunder was a precise application of military pressure for the specific purpose of halting aggression in South Vietnam. And I commented that there was no doubt that the strikes had accomplished a lot of damage, but emphasized that the commanders could continue to expect various types of restrictions on their operations, and said that some would be explicitly stated while others would be indicated. I said I realized that the restrictions would not always be understandable at the operating level, but nevertheless they had to be obeyed. And I also said that because the air campaign was so fundamental to success, the air crews must continue to demonstrate extraordinarily high professional standards. All of these instructions were important because the air campaign was fundamental to success but certain people in Washington didn't recognize that fact, therefore you had to be very careful and not make any mistakes.

Q: It must have been tough for the guys out there.

Adm. S.: It was. Very tough. They had to fly over a good target and go after a lesser value target.

Q: And knowing they were risking their lives . . .

Adm. S.: Risking their lives to do it, that's right.

Q: Do you know whether anyone ever disobeyed it, or not?

Adm. S.: I guess there were a few but not very many.

I submitted a great many recommendations on the Rolling Thunder campaign almost once, or more, a week, as a matter of fact, throughout my whole tour there, and one of the things I said to the JCS was that I recognized that an assessment of the achievements of the air campaign are still inconclusive, however, there was more danger of underestimating rather than overestimating the results. And I said that it was important in developing the future course of the air campaign to carefully weigh the capabilities and limitations of air power - U.S. air power - operating within the existing political parameters, and the vulnerabilities of North Vietnam within that framework, and I proposed a concept of demonstration of U.S. air power characterized by an around-the-clock program of immobilization, attrition, and harassment. This was one of the many messages sent in in a desire to get more and more freedom and more and more horsepower supplied on the targets. And, of course, as I noted the lifting of restrictions in each succeeding Rolling Thunder I could have said that they were the result of continued requests for easing of restrictions from CinCPac. I must say the JCS did their best to comply with my requests, but they were held down by higher authority.

Q: That's Mr. McNamara!

Adm. S.: Yes.

I continually recommended, of course, increasing the zone in North Vietnam we were permitted to strike, always trying to move up to the north so that we could get up into the important areas of North Vietnam, and I also continually had to request that the numerical limit on reconnaissance sorties - armed reconnaissance sorties - be lifted so that the commanders in the field could go ahead and strike to the extent of their capabilities, rather than be held down by a specific number.

In September of 1965 the JCS study group assessed the Rolling Thunder achievements and revealed that despite the widespread damage to North Vietnam, there was no indication of any willingness to negotiate or terminate support for the Viet Cong in North Vietnam. In commenting on these - on this study - CinCPac emphasized that increasing pressure was basic to the concept of Rolling Thunder and that increasing pressure had not been maintained in either armed reconnaissance or fixed target strikes. I pointed out that the armed reconnaissance sorties had leveled off over the two previous months before September, and that strikes on fixed targets had actually been decreased. The over-all decrease in pressure was in part because the armed reconnaissance area that was authorized had fewer lucrative targets than previously, and further that the reduced number of fixed targets for each succeeding Rolling Thunder period had lessened pressure on North Vietnam, rather than increased it. An additional factor, of course, was that improved surface-to-air missile and gun and antiaircraft defenses tended to reduce the effectiveness of air operations. We had delayed striking these areas until they had time to build up their air defenses. I also noted, as I had many times before, that the lucrative targets were in the northeast part of the country and in the large sanctuaries round Hanoi and Haiphong, and we always had to avoid those sanctuaries. On the 26th of November I stated that it was necessary to destroy the source targets in the northeast, including those in the Hanoi-Haiphong area. I also recommended disruption of major port facilities and subsequent increased reconnaissance directed at road, rail, and coastal lines of communication from China and the inland waterways. Nevertheless, until the end of August North Vietnam had been subjected to steadily increasing pressure from Rolling Thunder operations, but then it eased off. After September I would recommend target options designed to close in on the external supply lines and also proposed destruction of basic fuel, power, and other resources which supported North Vietnam's aggression. I never got permission to hit those targets in '65, instead the assigned targets were primarily bridges and the armed reconnaissance operating areas and sortie levels remained constant, so that pressure really decreased on North Vietnam after about 1 September, which, of course, is completely foreign to the proper way to conduct a war. And, it must be remembered that all during this time the Soviet Union was shipping surface-to-air missiles and antiaircraft guns into North Vietnam, and the people were getting trained, so that it got tougher and tougher as time went on.

Also throughout 1965 there was consideration given to mining North Vietnamese harbors. Mining was generally favored by me rather than a blockade, because I thought mining was more effective and would do the job just as well as blockade without the attendant risk to the blockading ships. There were various recommendations to mine various ports, and of course we had plans ready to mine any port in North Vietnam on practically a moment's notice. While we received approval for planning for various jobs there was no mining and the ports went on functioning without hindrance, and, of course, in the meantime the air defenses of these ports increased quite rapidly.

Q: How many ports were there besides Haiphong?

Adm. S.: Oh, there's HongGai - there are roughly four or five ports that were worthy of mining.

To continue with the Rolling Thunder to the end of '65, on the 24th of December, all Rolling Thunder operations were suspended for an indefinite period. Just previous to this suspension, I had told JCS that the program, conducted as it was without increasing the pressure and at a level to which military and civilian activities had accommodated, was not accomplishing its purpose and we should step it up and get on with it.

It was during 1965 that we had our first aircraft shot down by a surface-to-air missile. This was on the 24th of July. Of course, this loss didn't come as a surprise because we'd known for several months that the missiles would be operational pretty soon. We'd made many requests for authority to destroy the missile installations while they were under construction, but did not get authority to hit them. We did get permission to attack surface-to-air missile sites in the latter part of July, and this attack was not successful. They had their missile sites surrounded with enough conventional antiaircraft fire that made the low-level attacks expensive, so we started looking for effective ways to destroy these SAM sites and also went into a reconnaissance program to get better information. We got some restrictions lifted on reconnaissance in August so that we could go in and get better coverage of the sites once they were located. In August some aircraft did attack - Air Force aircraft - attacked a site that had a missile in it the day before, and found that the missile installation had been moved, and this was the first time that we discovered that these people were going to move the missiles around as soon as they thought they were discovered. Later on in August we got permission to destroy SAM sites as they were discovered, except for sites around the Hanoi-Haiphong area, around Fukien airfield and within 30 miles of the Chicom border.

The component commanders mounted a campaign on these SAM sites, but they really didn't have very much effect, and they decided that the tactics had to be refined. In the meantime we concluded that we shouldn't make SAM sites our primary target, but go after targets important to the continued functioning of the support of the aggression, and one of the targets we wanted to go after was the Haiphong POL stores.

Q: Did you get permission to do it?

Adm. S.: No, not at that time. There were a few successful

missions against SAM sites where the strafers would strike a missile and of course that would set the missile off to running around the ground, but the SAM sites were a difficult target. They did very well at camouflaging them, so they were hard to find. The program against the SAMs did, however, decrease the effectiveness of the surface-to-air missile.

So, in summary of the year 1965, we operated under great restrictions, and the time schedule allowed the other side to build up their defenses to such a degree that it was very difficult to get at the surface-to-air missiles sites and our aircraft had to - were under considerable hazard at striking targets. Nevertheless, there was not a target in North Vietnam that we couldn't strike any time we got authority to do it, and the buildup of surface-to-air missile batteries and antiaircraft batteries was a considerable drain on the manpower available to the North Vietnamese. And, of course, there were still very many important targets that we had not hit. And at the end of 1965, the air operations were suspended for the Christmas cease-fire and they were not started up again until 1966. On the 26th of December 1965 I commented on the difficulties faced by a commander in the field in the presence of an enemy when the cease-fire was extended on short notice. I also said that the advantage of a cease-fire accrued to the enemy and suggested that any future cease-fires should be planned in detail well in advance. I further proposed that aerial observation of enemy installations in North Vietnam should continue during the cease-fire, then went on to say that I thought enemy morale and tenacity were supported by a strong conviction that U.S. patience would expire before their own. Hanoi officials had stated that the enormous cost and future casualties would persuade the U.S. to negotiate on North Vietnamese terms. They also boasted that they had had some victories in South Vietnam during 1965. I said that I thought their statements about persuading the U.S. to negotiate might be true in a strategic sense unless U.S. strategy made full use of superior air power to reduce casualties to our own people and foreshorten the time required to achieve the limited objectives sought by the United States.

I should also indicate that during this ferment of '65 I traveled to Vietnam a number of times. I was out there on the 18th, 19th, and 20th of July for a conference with Secretary McNamara and General Wheeler, then went on to Bangkok, and returned to Honolulu on the 25th of July. In early August we had another conference in Honolulu attended by General Wheeler, General Westmoreland, and other military people in the Pacific.

On the 9th of August, General Taylor on television said he sees no need to bomb Hanoi, which didn't help the situation very much as far as I was concerned.

On the 17th of August Ambassador Lodge came through Honolulu on his way to Vietnam for his second tour as ambassador, relieving Ambassador Taylor. On the 23rd of August I left Honolulu for a tour of military installations in the Western Pacific. This time I visited Taiwan, Hong Kong, Okinawa,

Japan, and South Korea.

We missed a point here - that in June of 1965 Prime Minister Quat had decided that he couldn't continue on in his post and General Thieu was proclaimed chief of state, and Air Vice Marshal Ky was installed as premier. The inauguration of this government marked the end of a long period of political turmoil which was very debilitating for the government. The Thieu-Ky government, of course, remained in power until the general elections in 1967, when Ky became Vice President instead of Premier, and they are still staying on and this marked the initial stabilization of the government that was so important to success of the war.

I got back from this trip to the Western Pacific on the 4th of September. The Minister of National Defense of the Republic of China, Chiang Ching Kuo, stopped in Honolulu on the 20th of September and called on me. On the 25th of September General Westmoreland came back to Hawaii for a week of conferences.

On the 10th of October I left for the SEATO military advisers conference in Bangkok, and on this ten-day trip, I stopped at Saigon and in the Philippines. While in Saigon I met with General Westmoreland, Ambassador Lodge, and visited several military installations in Vietnam, then flew out aboard the USS Independence in the Gulf of Tonkin. I returned from that trip on 19 October.

On the 26th of November I departed Honolulu again to go out to Saigon for a periodic visit and while there met again with Secretary of Defense McNamara, General Wheeler, and General Westmoreland. Returning from that trip on the 2nd of December, on the 10th of December General Westmoreland came back to Honolulu for further talks.

On numerous occasions in 1965 we were questioned regarding the priority of the air effort. Many in Washington were apprehensive that we were putting too much of our effort on striking North Vietnam and not enough on supporting the forces in-country. This was partly a concern for the forces in-country, but probably a more important aspect of this was the desire by certain people in Washington to hold down on the air effort in the north, since that, to them, was escalation and they were, per se, opposed to escalation. We were frequently asked how many requests for strikes in-country were turned down due to lack of aircraft. And, incidentally, there weren't very many. We tried to be sure that the in-country effort was satisfied although, in the opinion of many members of my staff, some of the requests for strikes in-country were not against worthwhile targets. We always had to be sure that we were having the in-country requests reasonably satisfied before we set up strikes against North Vietnam.

Q: Would those have been from General Westmoreland?

Adm. S.: No, they would have been from some of the organization, not necessarily from him.

I remember one time when the Secretary of the Navy,

Secretary Nitze, questioned how the CVAs were being used, what was the division of effort between in-country and the Rolling Thunder strikes. We sent him a very complete analysis of where the strikes were going which seemed to satisfy him.

Then in 1965 there was considerable thought given to the buildup of airfields in Southeast Asia. We knew that we needed more land-based air and this involved an analysis of how many CVAs we would be able to keep available, and we at CinCPac were desirous of building up our capability to the point that we were sure to be able to meet the requirements for air power, which we believed would go up very rapidly. So we told the authorities in Washington that it was not prudent to plan for just enough capacity with no leeway for possible contingencies. There was also the possibility that at some point the Thais would deny us use of their airfields, in which case the airfields in South Vietnam would become even more important. Then, too, we had to recognize that there might come a time when the CVAs would be needed for action in other areas, for example, Korea or, perhaps, the offshore islands. So it was necessary to get airfields built up very rapidly. Then, too, the Secretary of Defense had said that he wanted all requests for air strikes in South Vietnam filled, and this gave the ComUSMACV sort of a blank check which could mean that the requirements for air strikes would sky rocket. This desire to have all the requests for air strikes in South Vietnam filled I mentioned before, and I thought was partly a desire to be sure that they had ample air strikes in South

Vietnam, and partly a desire to hold down on the air effort in North Vietnam.

We eventually built up a requirement for five CVAs in the Western Pacific at all times, which was very difficult for the Navy to maintain, but nevertheless they did maintain it, indicating the flexibility of carrier air power. I repeatedly told the planners in Washington that I was not going to get caught with marginal capability if I could avoid it. I wanted the maximum flexibility, so I wanted plenty of land-based as well as sea-based air power available to me. The land-based airfields in South Vietnam, of course, were built up very rapidly by the use of aluminum matting which went down very rapidly and was used throughout the war. Some of the airfields in South Vietnam had aluminum matting at first, and then, as time went on, we would build a parallel runway of concrete, and as soon as the concrete runway was ready then we would lift the aluminum matting runway and put in another runway of concrete, so that we would end up with duel-runway fields of very high potential. I had a great deal of difficulty convincing Washington that the Da Nang airfield was going to be one of the busiest airfields in South Vietnam and that, therefore, we should put in a second runway at Da Nang as soon as possible. We were finally authorized to put in a second runway and Da Nang turned out to be one of the busiest airports in the world.

There was also a desire in Washington to have strikes go into Laos against the infiltration trails, rather than into

North Vietnam, and there was an immediate question from Washington any time that there was any indication that there were not sufficient strikes going into Laos. Actually, of course, the targets along the trails in Laos were so elusive that the planes were frequently just bombing the trails, which in any informed person's opinion, I believe, would indicate that they were practically useless. There were very few targets along these trails, or perhaps I should say, you couldn't find the targets along these trails if there were any. But they were certainly minor because the traffic was mostly on foot or perhaps by bicycle. The people pulled off the trail during daylight so that there was never anything on the trail when it could be seen and the concentrations alongside the trail were so small that they also could not be seen. So we had airplanes flying up and down these trails looking for targets and usually not finding them, and then dumping their ordnance on a trail just to crater the trail, and this was a pretty futile operation, and, of course, meant that you were diverting sorties from North Vietnam where good targets were available into an area where the airpower was being used to little effect. Nevertheless, this pressure to keep the maximum number of sorties in South Vietnam and in Laos did cause us to divert many strikes from North Vietnam into these two areas.

During 1965 there was opposition from many in Washington to a buildup of force in South Vietnam. In the meantime, the situation in South Vietnam in mid-1965 was critical enough that it was pretty obvious that we would have to put more forces in if we were to stay in the country long enough to get the Vietnamese government stabilized and the Vietnamese armed forces built up to the degree necessary so that they could oppose the Viet Cong. General Westmoreland and General Wheeler and I saw eye to eye on this, and General Westmoreland send numerous messages to Washington outlining the problem and saying that he believed that adequate forces would have to be deployed to permit the Vietnamese, with our help, to carry the war to the enemy. It was necessary, in his opinion, to neutralize enemy power and get the tide running in the other direction. So he could see the need in the immediate future of considerably increased U.S. forces in South Vietnam. And this was a period where people were worrying that if we got in there in force we would just be creating an image in South Vietnam that here were the French back again - I mean, here was the United States in here in the same way as the French had been. Of course, the United States had no desire to get in and stay in South Vietnam as the French had tried to do. Our only interest was getting in there to rescue the Vietnamese, to keep them from being overrun by the Communists. General Westmoreland was saying in mid-1965 that he could see a need for many more army helicopter companies and for at least another division - Army division, and it appeared that we would need to increase our forces to the point that perhaps mobilization would be necessary in the United States.

During 1965 also it should be reported that the B-52 effort was increased considerably, and these bombers with their heavy load of bombs and their capability to bomb accurately on instruments from high altitude became a very potent force in the war. It was during this period also that our policy of limited action against the DRV was becoming fairly firmly set. There were frequent requests for what could be done, what military actions we could take short of destroying North Vietnamese economic and population targets. Of course, we never went after population targets. We were under strict orders to avoid killing civilian people, under such strict orders, in fact, that the pilots frequently hazarded their own lives in order to avoid killing civilians in North Vietnam.

One of our general policies, and this was formulated in 1965, was that we would always let the Vietnamese know that this was a Vietnamese war, that the Vietnamese must fight it, and that they were the ones that would have to win it. So that we were always careful not to usurp their basic prerogatives as a nation, nor to assume the basic responsibilities which the maintenance of their sovereignty would require them to accept. In other words, we would give them heavy support in this war, but we would not take over the fighting completely. Thus, the composition of our forces tended to be heavy in the support role, because we were not only supporting the United States combat troops but we were supporting the Vietnamese as well. There has been criticism of the fact that there were so many U.S. support troops in Vietnam compared to the number of combat troops, and this was one of the criticisms leveled at the United States Army and at ComUSMACV. I consider it an unjust criticism made by people who fail to grasp the idea that we were basically supporting the Vietnamese, and not trying to take over the whole combat job ourselves.

In late June of 1965, Air Marshal Ky took over as Prime Minister, or Premier, in South Vietnam and immediately took positive steps to generate reforms in the government and general unification of the country which was badly needed. Ky had the support, of course, of the armed forces which was essential to maintain a government in this country. He turned out to be an excellent leader and did succeed in unifying the country and in bringing along economic reforms and general progress at a rate that was unheard of before he took over. This, of course, was a great advantage to our effort and the first sign that the Vietnamese would eventually unify their efforts and make it possible for them some day to run their country and hold off the VC without our assistance.

Toward the end of 1965 there was some discussion on whether we were getting involved in Vietnam to the point that U.S. forces were taking over the primary responsibility for combat and replacing the South Vietnamese forces who were going back to something of a support role. I expressed my thoughts to the Chairman of the Joint Chiefs of Staff. I said that in my opinion the U.S. military forces in South Vietnam were there to assist the army of Vietnam to win their war and not to supplant them in any of these processes, that our forces should assist the Vietnamese through advice and also to coordinate combat operations. And also they should help the GVN in the pacification of the countryside. Of course, one of the principal objectives was to expand and consolidate military and political control of key food-producing and population areas, because if we could control the food-producing areas we would not only be assuring the South Vietnamese of food but we would be denying food to the Viet Cong. Of course, we also had to recognize that the Vietnamese combat capabilities were not very strong at this point, while of course U.S. combat forces had very strong combat capability, so that we had to be careful that we didn't take over the bulk of the fighting. At the same time, to get the war over with as soon as possible, U.S. forces did have to take the offensive and carry the war to the enemy. We had to emphasize the necessity of developing Vietnamese armed forces, both as to equipment and as to operational techniques, so that they would become more and more efficient as time went on.

Part of the psychological warfare campaign included the leaflet program that was aimed at the North Vietnamese and the concept of this was approved in April of '65. The idea was that we would warn the populace by leaflet drop and by radio that certain categories of target were considered military objectives and the people should evacuate all the targets of the type described. We dropped leaflets to this effect. The idea was that the leaflet missions would complement the Rolling Thunder target strikes. In July of '65 I recommended that leaflet operations be conducted on the major North Vietnamese population centers, including Hanoi and Haiphong. This was approved in Washington, but there was a proviso that the leaflet aircraft could not penetrate a 40 nautical miles circle around either Hanoi or Haiphong, which, of course, made it very difficult to get leaflets into these highly populated areas. However, we continued to drop leaflets and other objects. One of the missions by C-130s dropped packets containing toys and all sorts of things that were useful to the citizens of North Vietnam. We were operating under considerable restrictions, of course, in this leaflet drop and we continued to try to get less stringent constraints, and finally on the 17th of December 1965 we were allowed to broaden the area of operations. However, aircraft were still restricted from entering a 25-nautical-mile radius round Hanoi and a 10-nautical-mile radius around Haiphong. During 1965 a total of 77 million leaflets and 15,000 gift kits were distributed under this program, and we received indications that the material was reaching the populace and the North Vietnamese authorities were forced to take counterpropaganda actions to counter the lowering of morale of the people of North Vietnam that was being caused by our leaflet drops. So that these operations were considered worthwhile.

One of the areas where we integrated our activities with the Vietnamese was in the intelligence field. General Westmoreland did have an integrated U.S.-Vietnamese intelligence activity. This was done in order to take advantage of all the Vietnamese talents, resources, and information, so that what he did was pool U.S. and Vietnamese intelligence resources in a combined intelligence center. This center had four major functions: interrogation of prisoners, exploitation of captured enemy material, exploitation of captured documents, and the preparation of intelligence reports for both U.S. and Vietnamese commands. This intelligence activity, which was set up in Saigon in '65, got to be very capable. It supplied information that was essential to our success in this war. Of course, as our troop strength increased and the operations became more widespread over the country and we captured more prisoners and more documents, the intelligence technicians had a lot more to work on and they provided a great deal of information which was of the greatest value in prosecuting the war. One of the problems they had was identifying appropriate enemy targets for air and artillery strikes, particularly the strikes of the B-52s. Our B-52 strikes, of course, covered rather a wide area because of the number of bombs involved and we had to be careful to hit areas that were actually populated by the enemy and not by loyal South Vietnamese. This process became very well refined and it became a very fine operation. B-52 strikes were a very great factor in gaining a position of superiority over the Viet Cong.

I don't believe I've indicated before when the first North Vietnamese regular army force entered South Vietnam. Our intelligence indicated that the first North Vietnamese Army Regiment entered South Vietnam in December of 1964. This was the 95th Regiment of the North Vietnamese regular army, and it was joined within the first two months of '65 by the 32nd and the 101st Regiments. During the same period the North Vietnamese 6th Regiment was being activated in Quang Tre province. The infiltration rate at this time was something over a thousand men per month.

The first major battle involving United States forces occurred in August of 1965. The Third Marine Amphibious Force commanded by Major General Lewis Walt discovered and engaged the Viet Cong Second Regiment on the Batangan Peninsula, just south of the Marine air base at Chu Lai. The Marines surrounded this Viet Cong unit, pinned it against the sea. In a bitter fight, much of it was hand-to-hand, the Marines killed 700 of this force in this operation which was called Starlight. This battle, which, of course, was the first time U.S. troops faced the Vietnamese, proved that U.S. troops - in this case, Marines - could defeat any Viet Cong or North Vietnamese force that they could corner so that they couldn't fade away into the jungle.

At Qui Nhon in September the Second Battalion of the 7th Marines, which had been placed at Qui Nhon to secure the port and logistics complex which was under development there, first employed the riot control agent called "CS". This was a type of tear gas that has a temporary harassing effect, and it was of great assistance to Allied troops in gaining control of an area with a minimum use of fire power, and thus enabled troops to avoid civilian casualties. This technique also was very effective in clearing the enemy from underground tunnels and caves which, of course, they dug in profusion and used to great advantage.

On the 27th of October General Westmoreland directed the First Cavalry Division to seek out and destroy the enemy force in Pleiku province. This province, in the highlands, had become the hiding place for three North Vietnamese army regiments. They were backed up against Cambodia and getting their supplies through Cambodia, and were able to retreat into Cambodia in case the going got too tough for them. The enemy opened a campaign on the 19th of October with an attack on the Plei Ne Special Forces camp, which is about 25 miles southwest of Pleiku. He attacked this fortified camp with a regiment, while holding the rest of his force in reserve. The Vietnamese Army countered this attack with the assistance of our air power. One brigade of the 1st Cavalry was moved into the area to block any further enemy advance and stand in readiness as a reaction force. Then on the 27th of October General Westmoreland directed the 1st Cavalry Division to get in there and seek out and destroy this force, and thus started the month-long campaign known as the Battle of the Ia Drang Valley. The principal engagement in the campaign was fought in the period 14 to 19 November along the base of Chupong Mountain. The 1st Cavalry Division did a fine job of combating the enemy in this very close-combat situation, and the over-all effect was that the enemy withdrew the assault regiment from Plei Me, suffered severe casualties from air strikes and from the pursuing Air Cavalry Division. The Cavalry Division put a blocking force behind the enemy. The enemy was withdrawing toward the Cambodian border. When the Cavalry Division put this blocking force in, the North Vietnamese commander committed his two remaining regiments in an attempt to redeem his failure, Plei Me, and to destroy this U.S. unit. The 3rd Brigade of the 1st Cavalry Division was the target in this battle, and this brigade decisively defeated each enemy regiment in turn, as they were thrown against the U.S. troops. This was a very hard battle and enemy loss estimated at 1,800 troops in this fight. Our troops took fairly heavy casualties. Right at the moment I can't recall what they were, but they did drive off the enemy with heavy effect on him. These troops, of course, had only been in Vietnam about 30 days, but this was a very timely victory for it produced a sharp upturn in the morale of the South Vietnamese government and its armed forces. This was the first time that the M-16 rifle was used in battle in Vietnam, and it turned out that this lightweight and, of course, very rapid-firing rifle was more than a match for the Communist AK-47 assault rifle.

After this battle General Westmoreland strongly recommended equipping all U.S., Free World, and Vietnamese forces with the M-16 rifle as soon as possible. And eventually all of them were equipped with the M-16 rifle, but it was quite a long time because in the United States they did not commit enough industrial capacity to manufacturing this rifle to get it out as fast as they should have, in my opinion.

Another important engagement in 1965 was the one around

the Michelin plantation to the northwest of Saigon. The ARVN Seventh Regiment was operating in this area, and was engaged by the Viet Cong 271st Regiment. The South Vietnamese inflicted a heavy defeat on this unit. However, five days later another regiment, the 272nd, overran the South Vietnamese troops inflicting very heavy casualties and rendering the regiment ineffective. The Vietnamese regimental commander was killed in this battle.

Q: I'd like to finish up 1965 with reading a comment by General Westmoreland as relating to his relationship with Admiral Sharp. He says the system of command which was established in the Pacific worked because of the judicious and skillful assignment of priorities by Admiral Sharp throughout the four and a half years of my service in Vietnam, Admiral Sharp provided counsel and support which were invaluable to me and the war effort. His management and direction of complex interrelated air and naval operations were made vastly easier and more effective by the high professional competence of the successive naval and air commanders involved.

And that ends 1965?

Adm. S.: Let's see. At the end of '65, insofar as the Rolling Thunder program is concerned, that is, the air strike program against North Vietnam, which had been going on for about eleven months, still Hanoi demonstrated no willingness to terminate support of the military struggle, although there were some signs that the North Vietnamese economy was being affected by the air strikes. During November, air operations had, for the first time, concentrated on the transportation system connecting the major industrial areas of North Vietnam, and additional injury to that system was inflicted during December when several spans of the Hanoi-Dong Dang railroad bridge were dropped and the Uong Be thermal power plant was damaged. These strikes disrupted the production schedules and created further drains on the resources of manpower and material. Yet, material continued to move over the highways and the waterways and the makeshift rail lines, and there were many transportation targets that we hadn't hit, and, of course, there were other sources of electrical energy that we hadn't hit. However, maintaining a flow of material under these conditions was costly to North Vietnam and was a drain on men and material resources which took them away from other economic programs and therefore made the whole thing very difficult for them.

Late in 1965 two Chinese railroad engineer divisions came in to North Vietnam to help keep the transportation lines open, and there was a large influx of trucks and construction material, most of them coming in through the port of Haiphong that we had not been permitted to mine. But as 1965 drew to a close, there wasn't any indication of a significant decline in North Vietnamese morale or any softening of their attitude toward negotiations, and they appeared to be preparing for a prolonged struggle.

Q: During this last part of 1965, Ambassador Lodge replaced Ambassador Taylor. Was his attitude similar or different from Ambassador Taylor's relating to your carrying on in North Vietnam?

Adm. S.: Well, relating to the war in general, Ambassador Lodge was more inclined to let the military run the war than was Ambassador Taylor. Ambassador Taylor, of course, being an Army general and ex-Chairman of the Joint Chiefs of Staff, naturally felt completely capable of running the war himself, and I must say, in view of his great knowledge of military affairs, he did leave the running of the war to General Westmoreland and to me more than you would expect. But he still did have many opinions on military matters, naturally, and he was always against any strong use of air power in the north, I think, so he held down on our use of air power. Ambassador Lodge, on the other hand, pretty much left military strategy and tactics to General Westmoreland and to me, and, I must say, supported us very well. He was an advocate of strong action and frequently said so.

Q: And the use of air power?

Adm. S.: And the use of air power. Right.

One of the most formidable tasks in 1965 was to create a logistical organization in Southeast Asia to support the very heavy buildup that we could see coming and to develop bases which would support the forces that we were going to put in the country. Supply and distribution of petroleum products required an expanding military effort, and was a very difficult problem at times, and involved major construction and much difficult effort. We were moving all these men and equipment and supplies over the whole Pacific, so it was a long distance and it required a great deal of airlift and sealift. Most of the military facilities that were constructed in these Southeast Asia bases were constructed under the Military Assistance Program, under a concept of joint-use bases, and they were sponsored by the host nation, but it was recognized that they had a possible U.S. contingency application. And it was a good thing that we had spent some money in these areas because when we started moving in in 1965 we really needed it very badly.

In the fall of 1964, OSD recognized that future construction to support U.S. forces was required and decided that it should be service funded rather than going through the Military Assistance Program. So, under this concept, the Navy was charged with funding the first item that we got in 1965, which was a parallel runway at Da Nang which I insisted was very necessary in view of the very heavy use we could see of this very strategically located airport. And also the Navy was charged with putting in a new major air base at Chu Lai, and these were the first major U.S. installations put in under this concept, service-funded. The JCS, in March of '65, directed that unified commanders would take a more direct part in joint base development to ensure that existing facilities were properly used and that program facilities were in fact required to support an approved operation plan and approved deployment. And also that the funding requirement was accurately stated. This was a very good move by the JCS and was made at my request to support me in taking direct charge of logistic planning and execution in the Pacific. So that with this, CinCPac's role in facility planning and programing was expanded from monitoring and supervision, to an active role in stating the validity of the operational requirements and stating the priority that I thought was necessary for funding. So we set up a facility section in the J-4 division of the joint staff under Brigadier General White, U.S. Army, a very dedicated and knowledgeable and outstanding Army officer. A large construction program within the Pacific area was coordinated and forwarded to the JCS by CinCPac after I had assumed an active role in this area.

We attempted to accomplish this mission with a flexible, dynamic program which would not inhibit the operational commands with administrative restrictions, and yet would provide sufficient information so that we could be responsive to the inquiries and requirements of higher headquarters.

During 1964 Military Assistance funds were used to put in a deep-water pier at Camranh Bay. This was constructed with Military Assistance funds for the use of the Vietnamese Navy. This pier, however, during the Vietnam buildup, became a major unloading facility and was used very heavily to start the base construction at Camranh Bay. Camranh Bay, of course, was the best natural deep-water harbor in Southeast Asia. It had been used many times over the years. It was used by the Russian Fleet in 1905 before their battle with the Japanese at Tushima Strait. It was used by the Japanese in World War II. It had been used by the French. This area, however, was still undeveloped and the only thing there was a very small Vietnamese Navy base - that is, on the Camranh Bay Peninsula - and this deep-draft pier which would take two ships alongside.

During April of '65 there was discussion about developing Camranh Bay as a major U.S. logistics base and transhipment area. We had in mind the fact of the deteriorating rail transportation system in South Vietnam and the need to transport much of the supplies by sea. We were going to use LSTs to move up and down the coast hauling supplies. So that in '65, we, recognizing that we had to have another port to supplement Saigon, because Saigon was so inadequate, we recommended to the Joint Chiefs of Staff that we develop Camranh Bay as a major U.S. port and logistics complex to support the war. We also proposed that we construct on the Camranh Bay Peninsula, a major jet capable combat and logistics air field, so that we would then divert to Camranh Bay some of the logistics and combat forces planned for the Qui Nhon-Nha Trang areas. In approximately 90 days, Camranh Bay was transformed from sand dunes - and the sand there was the most abrasive kind of sand that you can imagine - into a major port and the logistic complex was starting to build. We moved in a prefabricated De Long pier - it's a floating pier. Well, it didn't go in in '65, it went in in '66, but we made plans to move this pier in and to develop very rapidly the harbor and waterfront facilities. I flew over Camranh Bay in '65 and visited it early in '66 when I got down there to their airfield. Speaking of airfields, at the beginning of 1965, there were only three jet-capable airfields in South Vietnam. These were Binh Huoa, Ton Son Nhut, and Da Nang, and each of these airfields was crowded with a variety of U.S. and Vietnamese aircraft. The force increases and the plans for expanded air operations in North Vietnam made it essential that jet-capable airfields be expanded, and also we recognized that we had to have other airfields to accommodate helicopters and propeller-type aircraft. So, as a partial solution to this problem, new permanent facilities were planned at Camranh Bay, at Chu Lai, and at Chang Ran. Then, of course, we got authority to put a parallel runway in at Da Nang, and the Army built an airfield on the peninsula of Da Nang called Da Nang East, or subsequently it was called the Marble Mountain Air Facility. Then we had an airfield at Pleiku with an excellent 6,000-foot runway, which was completed, I guess, about October of that year. This field was used for logistic support aircraft, and we put in additional airfields at An Khe and Dong Ba Thin. These were assigned high priority in the FY '66 supplemental military construction program.

We also decided that the situation was so critical in

South Vietnam that it was obvious that air aupport requirements couldn't wait until contractors completed these permanent-type air bases, so the Marines and Seebees were landed at Chu Lai in early May and started construction of the jet-capable airfield utilizing aluminum matting in techniques developed as part of the Marine Corps short airfield tactical system concept called SATS. The Seebees and Marines built an 8,000-foot aluminum-matting airstrip less than 30 days after the initial landing the first aircraft landed on the new field, and the total facility was completed in approximately 60 days, and at that time we moved in four A-4D squadrons to operate from the base. The success of this operation stimulated an intense interest in jet-capable expeditionary tactical airfields, so that we put in the same kind of airfield at Camranh Bay and at Phan Rang. We started to put one in at Qui Nhon, but it was later changed to Tui Hoa. Of course, there was only a very limited quantity of this aluminum matting manufactured, so that we took all the Marine Corps AM-2 matting and allocated it, after the Chu Lai airfield, to Camranh Bay. Contracts were let immediately to manufacturers for an additional 12 million square feet of matting on a very urgent basis, and, I must say, that this aluminum matting saved our lives in Vietnam and was a very important part of the program. Right now we have aluminum matting airfields all over the country in Vietnam.

The Camranh Bay airfield was completed in about 100 days by a combination of contractor and U.S. Army Engineers effort, or was it the Seabees - and the base was operational the 1st of November 1965, and I landed there about that time and participated in laying the last strip of matting on that 10,000 foot runway. The U.S. Air Force had a very fine method of moving in support facilities. They had what they called a Gray Eagle kit, and they brought in bladder tanks for POL, inflatable maintenance shelters, tent camps, and all sorts of equipment needed to establish a temporary air base. So, our experience with the Camranh Bay airfield and the Chu Lai airfield indicated to us that this was the way to go and that we must get on with building more of these matting airfields.

Also during 1965 it was recognized that MACV's headquarters in Saigon was completely inadequate. He had his staff scattered all over about 10 or 12 sites in Saigon area and it was very difficult to manage a staff all scattered around. So SecDef approved construction of a headquarters in Saigon and that construction started at the end of 1965.

INDEX

for series of interviews

with

Admiral U.S. Grant Sharp, U.S.N. (Ret.)

ABRAMS, General Creighton W.: relieves Westmoreland on June 11, 1968 as ComUSMACV, p. 627; p. 639; p. 647.

ALLIED FORCES IN SOUTH VIETNAM: (1967), p. 549-550.

ANZUS - Council: meeting in Washington on July 15, 1964, p. 210-211; employment of Australian-New Zealand Military forces in Vietnam, p. 260-1

ARMED SERVICES COMMITTEE - U.S. Senate: Sharp testifies before Preparedness Investigating Sub-committee, Aug. 9/10, 1967 P. 504-8; McNamara testifies on August 25 and tried to 'shoot down' some of Sharp's testimony, p. 509; JCS statement on mission of air effort - similar to McNamara testimony before subcommittee, p. 519 ff.

B-52: first strike with these planes against North Vietnam, p. 361; SecDef repeats his directive that bombing operations in North Vietnam shall not be carried on to the detriment of combat operations in South Vietnam, p. 361-2. Washington agrees to use of B-52s in June 1965, p. 402-3. See also - despatches of CINCPAC to JCS.

BAY OF PIGS: p. 164

BOWLES, Chester: visits Sihanouk in Cambodia, p. 560.

USS BOYD - DD 544: Sharp puts her in commission - Jan. 1943 - assigned for escort duty out of Noumea, p. 62; participation in Baker Island landings, Wake Island raids, Gilbert Island landings, p. 63; damage sustained in engagement with shore batteries of Nauru, p. 66 ff; escorting the Cruiser DENVER, P. 74; installation of CIC, p. 75; participates in Battle of Philippine Sea, p. 77 ff; life on a DD during prolonged periods at sea, p. 82 ff; invasion of Guam, p. 85 ff; other island operations, p. 86ff; rescue operations of personnel from the HOUSTON, p. 89 ff; relieved of command on Guam, p. 92-5.

USS BUCHANAN (DD-131): Sharp becomes torpedo officer on board p. 20; p. 23.

BUNKER, The Hon. Ellsworth: U.S. Ambassador to South Vietnam, p. 465-6.

BURKE, Admiral Arleigh: CruDiv Commander, Atlantic, 1953, p. 138; takes Sharp with him on Pac tour after selection of CNO, p. 145 ff. p. 150, p. 155.

BU SHIPS: Sharp assigned as DD Eng. Maintenance Officer (1940) p. 44-45; turning over the 50 DD's to the British, p. 45-7.

CAMRANH BAY: In 1964 Military Assistance Funds used to put in a deep water pier, p. 327; In 1965 CINC PAC recommends that Camranh Bay be developed as a major port and logistics complex, p. 327 ff; successful experience with matting points way to others in Vietnam, p. 331.

USNS CARD: MSTS ship used to transport airplanes - sunk in Saigon harbor, p. 200.

CASABLANCA: U.S. landing (1942), p. 55ff.

CHICOMS: used as a designation of the Red Chinese government.

C.I.A.: gives estimate of civilian casualties in case of air attacks on certain targets, p. 376.

CIC: installation of an early CIC in DD BOYD, p. 75.
Note: see entry under COMMANDER, DD's, PAC:

CINC PAC: (Note: see entries under Admiral U.S. Grant Sharp - CincPac 1964-68);

Sharp relieves Adm. Felt on board the USS RANGER June 30, 1964) p. 202; scope of the CincPac Command, p. 202; Sharp' first trip as CincPac to ANZUS Council meeting in Washington p. 210-211; visit of Sharp to Far East - dinners in Taiwan and Japan - attendance at meeting of Japan - U.S. Consultative Committee on Security, p. 238; Sharp's discussion of command relations in the Pacific theatre and especially in Vietnam, p. 244-5; the problem of air support for ground troops, p. 246; statistics on military strength of command at beginning of 1965, p. 249; attitude of CincPac and JCS on how war should be conducted - contrasting philosophy of SecDef, State Dept. and White House p. 251-2 ff; plans for operations against North Vietnam, p. 255-6; series of visits to headquarters by Far East political leaders, p. 262; CincPac begins to experience more detailed control by SecDef (through JCS) on air sorties, patrols in Gulf of Tonkin, p. 268-9; conference in April 1965 with JCS, Army, Air Force, Navy on need for greater logistical action, p. 272-3; development of command arrangements, p. 273; efforts to encourage S. Vietnamese to great effort, p. 276; CincPac Conference (Apr. 17, 1965) withMcNamara, Wheeler, etc. p. 277; Sharp's comments on enemy possibilities, p. 285-6; his insistence on maintaining pressure on North Vietnamese, p. 285-7; his comments on relative importance of areas in South Vietnam, p. 287-8; Sharp's insistence on consideration of SE Asia as a single, integrated U.S. Strategy, p. 288 ff; Sharp's explanation of ROLLING THUNDER operations to Washington, p. 301-3; Sharp's response to special study group assessment, p. 303-4; summary of activities in 1965,

p. 307 ff; Sharp's travels in 1965, p. 308-9; gives much attention (1965) to build up of airfields, p. 311; difficulty in keeping 5 CV's in Western Pacific at all times, p. 311-12; comments of General Westmoreland on effectiveness of Adm. Sharp, p. 323 logistics in 1965, p. 325-6; facility section established in J-4 for construction programs, p. 327; airfields in South Vietnam, p. 328-30; given authority (July 1965) to attack certain SAM sites p. 341; CincPac advises JCS of relationship between military operations against North Vietnam and overall strategy of war in S. Vietnam - p. 344-55; Sharp sees clearly nature of political battle and propaganda campaign being waged by North Vietnamese in 1966, p. 349; reviews for JCS changed circumstances surrounding Rolling Thunder Operation, p. 349 ff; CincPac directs component commanders (Jan. 13, 1965) to be prepared for precise attacks when Rolling Thunder resumed, p. 355; CincPac goes over same area as on Jan. 13 to JCS - in effort to get more flexibility in Rolling Thunder operations, p. 358; frequent directions to component commanders, p. 372; asks Washington for authority to strike all airfields, p. 373; tried a new technique on Washington to get prompt answers to request for authority, p. 374; Oct. 166 another CincPac message to JCS to emphasize critical importance of air operations over North Vietnam, p. 385-6; p. 390-1; CincPac message to Gen. Wheeler (Dec. 1966) on effect of enemy propaganda, p. 394-5; asks permission of JCS (12/30/66) for use of surfact-to-air missiles against MIGs, p. 396-8; CincPac's summary of operations (Jan. 1967) to emphasize point U.S. air power not being used properly, p. 405-6; concern expressed over reports of special study to determine alternatives to present efforts in Vietnam, p. 410-11; p. 420-22; sends message of Feb. 1967 to underscore advantages of closing ports of Hanoi and Haiphong, p. 416-420; Sharp's reactions to proposals of special study group on alternatives, p. 421-2; Sharp's comments on restrictions placed on Rolling Thunder 53, p. 438; p. 445-6; Sharp draws up Rolling Thunder target list, p. 453; Sharp tries for lifting restrictions on targets within ten miles of Hanoi, p. 455; tells how targets are selected, p. 463; Sharp briefs McNamara on air war in Vietnam, Sharp's comment on no need for stalemate in Vietnam, p. 497; Sharp discusses restrictions on bombing, p. 499 ff; Sharp testifies before Subcommittee of Armed Services Committee of Senate (Aug. 9-10, 1967) p. 504, answers request of JCS for optimum air campaign outline against North Vietnam - 1967-8, p. 510-19; Sharp attempts to get JCS to change 'statement of mission' on bombing over North Vietnam, p. 519 ff; prepares an assessment for JCS on cessation of bombing, p. 523-29; gives JCS (Dec. 1967) assessment of closure of North Vietnamese port complexes, p. 529 ff; Sharp sends JCS (Jan. 1968) progress report on 1967 and standing at beginning of 1968,

p. 537-52; his plans for 1968, p. 552-4; Sharp's efforts to obtain a better press in 1968, p. 534-5; p. 559; visit Danang (Jan. 1968) for look at situation in KheSanh, p. 567; reactions to bombing cessation order, p. 594-5; Sharp not informed of cease bombing decision in Washington his reactions, p. 603-4; supports Westmoreland recommendations on retaliatory attacks on North Vietnamese cities, p. 623 ff; Sharp due for retirement on May 1, 1968 but retained until July 31, p. 627, sends his estimate of situation (July, 1968) to JCS before conference of Clark Clifford (SecDef) in Saigon, p. 629 ff; Sharp sends his last situation report on July 31, 1968, p. 635 ff; Sharp' problem with Westmoreland, McNamara on close air support, p. 637-9; problem over operational control of First Marine Air Wing, p. 641 ff.

CINC PAC CONFERENCES: p. 277; after conference of Aug. 1965 CincPac issues guidance for future conferences, p. 292-3.

CINC PAC FLEET: Sharp becomes Deputy Chief of Staff for Plans, Operations and Intelligence - Aug. 1954 - p. 141, Adm. Stump's top notch staff, p. 142-3; the process of separating CincPac and CincPac Fleet commands, p. 143; Sharp leaves staff in July 1956 for command of CruDiv 3, p. 149. Sharp takes over from Admiral Sides (Sept. 30, 1963), p. 180; activities during first days of his command p. 180-1; tour of Western Pacific, p. 181 ff; 7th Fleet scheduling conference at Subic Bay, p. 182-3; travels in Nov./Dec. 1963, p. 187-8; Sharp mentioned as possibility for CincPac command, p. 190; chronology of visitors and travels in 1964, p. 192 ff;

CLIFFORD, The Hon. Clark - Secretary of Defense: named by President Johnson as SecDef on Jan. 19, 1968, p. 566; the attitude of Clifford on the Tet offensive, p. 592-3; p. 595.

CLOSE AIR SUPPORT - Vietnam: problems attendant thereto, p. 637 ff.

COMBAT BEAVER: p. 390-1p. p. 393

COMMANDER DD's, Pacific: Sharp ordered (Jan. 1945) to staff in Honolulu as Combat Information Center and Radar Officer, p. 96 ff; base transferred to San Diego (1946) - concern then with demobilization, p. 99.

USS COMSTOCK: (LSD-19): mother ship for ten of the river patrol boats in South Vietnam, p. 401.

COM USMAC THAI: set up in 1965 in case of military action in that area, p. 276.

COM USMACV: Command set up and General Westmoreland named as Commander, p. 201; p. 272; Westmoreland objects to continued stand-down on North Vietnam bombing efforts, p. 356; wanted authority to take charge of air campaign in lower part of North Vietnam, p. 360; given that authority by Adm. Sharp in April 1966, p. 360; p. 372; instructed in some detail by CincPac on air war in Laos and North Vietnam, p. 373. Has command of T.F. 116 (river patrol), p. 400; has command of MARKET TIME to prevent waterborne infiltration into South Vietnam, p. 402; Jan. 1967 gives command guidance to subordinate commanders on conduct of war in 1967, p. 414-6; a new headquarters complex (1967) outside Saigon, p. 551.
(Note: See additional entries under WESTMORELAND)

CRU DES FORCE, PACFLT: Sharp takes command, Feb. 1959, p. 154.

CRU DIV 3: Sharp takes command, July 1956, p. 149; operation for evaluation of REGULUS I missile, p. 149-150.

CUBAN MISSILE CRISIS: p. 165

CURTZ, Adm. Maurice E. (Germany); p. 143.

CUSHMAN, General Robert E. Jr.: Commandant U.S. Marine Corps; question raised by Gen. Westmoreland over operational control of First Marine Air Wing, p. 641 ff.

DANANG: p. 258; deployment of Marine Corps combat troops, p. 258-9; addition of a second runway, p. 312; p. 326. Sharp visits there to discuss situation at Khesanh, p. 567.

DAWEE, Air Chief Marshal: Deputy Minister of Defense in Thailand, p. 280.

DCNO for PLANS: p. 155, p. 160 ff; Sharp's citation for his duty as DCNO, p. 166-7.

DD SQUADRON 5: Sharp takes command in San Diego (1950) p. 105-6; p. 125-130.

DE SOTO PATROL: Name given the DD patrol in Tonkin Gulf, p. 226-7; p. 234; retaliatory strikes were readied by the U.S. for possible enemy action against the DeSoto Patrol p. 240-1; p. 269.

DIEM, Ngo-dinh - President of South Vietnam: p. 195; overthrown and assassinated, p. 196.

USS ENTERPRISE: her involvement in PUEBLO incident, p. 572-3; p. 580-3.

FARMGATE FORCES: U.S. Airforce Squadrons in Vietnam, p. 257; p. 270.

FELT, Admiral H.D.: p. 190; p. 193;

FIRST FLEET: Sharp takes command as Vice Admiral, Apr. 1960, p. 156.

FULBRIGHT, Senator Wm.: his remarks in Feb. 1970 on Tonkin Gulf and the Senate Resolution, p. 299-50.

GAME WARDEN: (T.F. 116): The River Patrol, p. 400; used to halt Viet Cong actions on the inland waterways of South Vietnam... first boats in April, 1966, p. 401.

GUAM: p. 85-6; Sharp detached from BOYD on Guam, p. 92.

HANOI: See numerous references under: NORTH VIETNAM, CINC PAC JCS. Hanoi frequently used in dispatches, summaries, etc when reference is actually to North Vietnam, North Vietnamese policies and actions, etc.

HARKINS, General Paul: Feb. 1962 becomes head of MAAG in Saigon, p. 175; p. 191; MAAG abolished (May 15, 1964) and Harkins departs, p. 201.

HELICOPTERS: history of their use in South Vietnam, p. 174-6; NOTE: see occasional references to them in Adm. Stark's summary of operations - CINC PAC.

USS HENDERSON - transport; Sharp serves as officer of the deck (1928), p. 14 ff.

HERRICK, Capt. John J.: DD Division Commander in Tonkin Gulf, p. 218; p. 220-1; DD TURNER JOY joins his patrol, p.222 p. 226-7; p. 230.

USS HIGBEE: designated to take position off Wonsan during PUEBLO incident, p. 582-; p. 585.

USS HOGAN (DD-Minesweeper): Sharp becomes skipper (May, 1942) p. 51; his difficulties with Adm. Hoover in San Juan, p. 53-4; the landing at Casablanca, p. 55-7.

HOLYOAKE, The Hon. K.J.: Prime Minister of New Zealand (1967), p. 203 p. 211; p. 238.

HOOVER, Admiral John: p. 53-4.

HOP TAC OPERATION: Pacification effort in areas out from Saigo p. 236.

USS HOUSTON: DD BOYD participates in rescue of personnel who had abandoned the HOUSTON, p. 89-90; helps take the Houst in tow, p. 91.

HYLAND, Admiral John J. - Commander, 7th Fleet: Sharp enlists his aid in briefing SecDef on value of bombing program on North Vietnamese targets, p. 463-6; p. 477.

IA DRANG VALLEY, Battle of: (Oct.-Nov. 1965), p. 321

INCHON, Korea: See entry under Admiral STRUBLE: landing operation, p. 116 ff; MacArthur and Struble inspect operation (night of Sept. 15), p. 118; Sharp and companions land - attempt to visit Kimpo Air Base, p. 120-1.

INDONESIA: her claim to territorial sea areas - a 12 mile limit instead of 3 miles - p. 205; complications - for U.S. and Great Britain, p. 206-7.

INTERNATIONAL CONTROL COMMISSION: March 1965 - puts out paper (through British Foreign Office) condemning U.S. air strikes against North Vietnam, p. 265. p. 565.

IRON HAND: surface-to-air missile suppression strikes over North Vietnam, p. 364.

JOHNSON, President Lyndon: asks Gen. Westmoreland (Oct. 166) for estimate of bombing campaign, p. 384-5. His statement in Manila (Oct. 1966) on getting out of Vietnam - causes CincPac to launch post hostilities planning study in Jan. 1967, p. 416; p. 430, p. 558; p. 563; names Clark Clifford as SecDef (Jan. 1968), p. 566; calls up some reservists Jan. 25, 1968, p. 586; March 31, 1968 announces additional forces for Vietnam - cessation of bombing over North Vietnam - a new peace offensive, p. 594.

JOINT CHIEFS OF STAFF (JCS): p. 165; first meeting with Sec Def McNamara, p. 167 ff; attitude towards picture in Vietnam, p. 170-2; join in recommendations of CincPac for action to destroy will and capability of North Vietnamese, p. 252-4 Sharp before the JCS p. 266-7; p. 279; p. 281; JCS concept for South Vietnam in 1965, p. 287; Rolling Thunder directions p. 294-5; attempt of JCS to comply with request of CincPac on air strikes, p. 302; March, 1965, directed unified commanders to take more direct part in joint base development, p. 327; CincPac sends message (Jan. 1966) outlining strategy to get air war underway again, p. 344-55; Sharp reports assistance from JCS (1966) in getting his ideas across, p. 357; p. 374; Sharp sends urgent message Oct. 26, 1966 urging extension of air warfare, p. 389; p. 394-6; Sharp asks permission to use missiles against MIGs, p. 396-8; JCS did not give good support to Sharp in his request for naval gunfire against North Vietnam targets, p. 398; Sharp sends summary message of operations, Jan. 14, 1967; p. 403-9; Sharp sends message to Wheeler, Jan. 20, 1967 dealing with anti-infiltration measures, p. 411-13; Sharp's message of

Feb. 1967 recommending closing of North Vietnam ports, p. 416-20; JCS asks for Sharp's comments on key questions formulated by Gen. Taylor, p. 422-27; refers to Adm. Joy' book on "how communists negotiate" as applicable in Vietnam, p. 427-8; Sharp comments on restrictions placed on Rolling Thunder #53, p. 438; JCS gives Sharp resistance on his proposals to use Talos missiles, p. 440-1; p.445-6; expresses concern over build-up of debate on U.S. bombing in North Vietnam, p. 447-8; permission granted Sharp for further targets near Hanoi-Haiphong, p. 449 ff; Sharp's briefing of McNamara very similar to messages send JCS previously, p. 483; JCS answers McNamara's memo of May 20, 1967 on alternatives in Vietnam - presents a new one, p. 484 ff; Sharp recommends targets in buffer zone near China (Aug. 1967), p. 488 ff; JCS asks Sharp for outline of optimum air campaign against North Vietnam (Nov. 1967-68), p. 510-519 ff; Sharp questions JCS proposed statement on 'mission' of air warfare over North Vietnam - similar to statement of SecDef, p. 519 ff Sharp's assessment of cessation of bombing, p. 523-29; Sharp's assessment of port closures, p. 529; Sharp again asks JCS for authority (Sept. 1967) to bomb certain targets, p. 533; Sharp sends (Jan. 1, 1968) review of 1967 operations, p. 537-52; Sharp continues his report of Jan. 1, 1968 with intensions for 1968, p. 552-54, for role in PUEBLO incident see p. 569 ff; p. 606; ask Sharp for assessment of capability of U.S. and Allied Forces to achieve objectives in S.E. Asia, p. 607 ff; when peace negotiations start JCS asks Cinc Pac for periodic assessment of military position - reports no longer requested by them after a month, p. 613-16; Sharp's recommendations on what we should do as result of attacks in S. Vietnam p. 616-19;

JOY, Admiral Turner: his book on "How Communists Negotiate", p. 427-8;

KHANH, General: ousts Gen. Minh and becomes Prime Minister, p. 198; p. 209; his address to a mass meeting on July 19 Ambassador Taylor's reaction, p. 211-212; renames Gen. Minh as Chief of State, p. 236.

KHESANH: Attack on (1968), p. 567; p. 587; p. 589; p. 643.

KIMPO AIR BASE - South Korea: Sharp visits a short time after the Inchon landings, p. 120-1.

KOREA: Sharp uses Korea as example of what to avoid in negotiations with communists, p. 427-8;

KRULAK, Gen. Victor H.: In 1964 becomes Commander of Fleet Marine Force, Pacific, p. 192; trusted adviser of Sharp, p. 192.

KY, Air Vice Marshal Nguyen cao: installed as Prime Minister of South Vietnam in 1965, p. 309; success of his efforts, p. 316. p. 374-5.

LAMBERT, Comdr. V.G.: Assistant Planning Officer on staff of Adm. Struble for Inchon landing operation, p. 109; p. 120-1.

LAOS: Washington's interest in air strikes on trails - difficulty involved, p. 313; see other references to Laos in CINC PAC summaries and despatched to JCS.
Note: See numerous entries under: CINC PAC, NORTH VIETNAM, SOUTH VIETNAM, WESTMORELAND.

LODGE, The Hon. Henry Cabot: Aug. 1965 resumes his second tour of duty as U.S. Ambassador in Saigon, p. 308-9; tended to leave military operations to military men - in favor of strong action against North Vietnam, p. 325;

USS LONG BEACH: p. 440; Sharp seeks permission to use her in TALOS MISSILE attacks against enemy MIGs, p. 440-1; p. 457.

M-16 RIFLE: New U.S. Rifle 1965 - effective use of, p. 322; first issued to South Vietnamese forces in 1967, p. 548; Note: see numerous references in dispatch summaries of CINC PAC.

MAAG - Saigon: p. 175; abolished on May 15, 1964, p. 201.

USS MACON: Sharp takes command - Aug. 1953, p. 137; Adm. Burke uses MACON as flagship, p. 138; midshipman cruise of June 1954, p. 138; Sharp leaves MACON for duty with CincPac in Aug. 1954, p. 139.

USS MADDOX: p. 213-221; p. 226-8; p. 249-51.

U.S. MARINE CORPS: question about operational control of First Marine Air Wing in Vietnam, p. 641 ff.

MARK 36 DESTRUCTOR: Comes on stream in August, 1967, p. 489.

MARKET TIME - Operation: p. 261.
See other references in reports of CincPac to JCS.
Task Force 115 - under command of US Macv - a patrol effort to prevent the waterborne infiltration of men and material into South Vietnam, p. 402.

McMahon, The Hon. Wm.: Minister of Labor and National Service in Australia, p. 209.

McNAMARA, Robert S.: Secretary of Defense: his first meeting with the Joint Chiefs, p. 167-9; arrives with Gen. Taylor

to attend CincPac Conference in Hawaii - terminated because of assassination of Pres. Kennedy, p. 186-7; selects Sharp to succeed Adm. Felt as CincPac, p. 191; on July 15, 1964 announces no evidence of North Vietnamese troops in South Vietnam, p. 210; p. 227; telephone conversation with Sharp on Tonkin Gulf incident, p. 229-230; reinforces Pacific forces, p. 232; p. 238; begins to get involved (April 1965) in details of air strike plans of CincPac, p. 268 ff; visits Gen. Westmoreland - gets list of his needs, p. 290; calling of another conference in Hawaii (Aug. 3-6, 1965) for coordinated program of deployment in Vietnam, p. 290-1; tendency to underestimate bombing results in Vietnam, p. 337; his emphasis on importance of South Vietnamese theatre, p. 302; in Saigon Nov. 1965 with Wheeler and Westmoreland, p. 310; p. 336; gives Westmoreland approval to conduct bombing on package #1 p. 360; p. 369; never fully convinced air war over North Vietnam getting results, p. 370-1; requests info from CincPac on what steps to be taken to minimize civilian casualties in north Vietnam, p. 377-8; apprehension on part of SecDef and President over results of bombing - leaks from Washington on proposed missions - difficulty for U.S. pilots, p. 379; p. 390-1; more on his thesis that war effort should be focussed on anti-infiltration efforts, p. 411-12; continued reservations about air war over North Vietnam, p. 454; proposes alternate plans to present bombing campaign, p. 461-2; p. 464-5; Sharp's briefing of him in Saigon (June 1967), p. 465 ff; his reaction to Sharp's presentation, p. 481; substance of his memo to JCS, SecNav, etc. on alternatives in North Vietnam, p. 485 ff; he gives CincPac permission to hit certain targets - the night before CincPac testifies before Senate Committee, p. 505-6; Republican's Task Force report ascribes policy of gradualism in Vietnam a 'brain child' of McNamara, p. 611;
Sharp indicates his difficulty in keeping McNamara from ordering air offensive off of North Vietnam and into South Vietnam, P. 637-8; p. 648.

MIGs: They offer increasing threat to U.S. air operations over North Vietnam, p. 445-6; p. 447, p. 451; p. 457; In Sharp' briefing of McNamara (June, 1967 - Saigon) he deals with change in manner of employment of MIGs, p. 469 ff.
see also - entries; ROLLING THUNDER: NORTH VIETNAM.

MINH, Major Gen. Duong Van: heads provisional government following Diem, p. 196; ousted in Jan. 1964 by Gen. Khanh who names him Chief of State on Feb. 10, p. 198.

MINING Operations - North Vietnamese harbors: p. 304-5: see also entries under CincPac - especially in his summaries to JCS on operations.

USS MISSOURI - BB: in Korean waters, p. 126-7.

MOMYER, General Wm. Wallace - Commander, 7th Air Force: Sharp enlists his aid in briefing SecDef on value of North Vietnam bombing, p. 463-6; p. 477; p. 641-2; p. 646.

MOORE, RADM R. B.: Carrier Division Commander in Tonkin Gulf at time of the incident, p. 217; p. 221.

MOORER, Adm. Thos. H.: CincPacFlt., p. 221-3; p. 230.

MORSE, Senator Wayne: on the Tonkin Gulf incidents in the U.S. Senate, p. 227.

MUSTIN, Vice Admiral Lloyd: In 1966 served as J-3 of the Joint Staff, JCS - helpful to Admiral Sharp, p. 357.

NAURU: See entry under DD BOYD.

NAVAL WAR COLLEGE: Sharp spends a year (1949-50) in residence, p. 104-5.

USS NEW MEXICO - BB: First duty for Sharp after graduation from N. Academy, p. 12 ff;

NITZE, Paul: Secretary of the Navy; shows interest in air strikes in support of in-country forces, p. 311.

NIXON, President Richard M.: Sharp's statement of what he might have done when he took office as regards Vietnam, p. 621-22.

NORTH VIETNAM: response to Rolling Thunder pressure in 1965, p. 308; dropping of leaflets and toy packets, p. 317-8; first regular army units enter South Vietnam, p. 319-20; CincPac and the necessity for maintaining pressure on the north, p. 344 ff; efforts to improve logistic supplies in the Tet stand-down, p. 435; p. 437-8; cumulative efforts of bombing (1967), p. 444-5; Sharp delineates North Vietnam strategy for the JCS, p. 445-6; p. 452-3; no shortage of targets in North Vietnam, p. 460-1. Sharp discusses restrictions under which he operated, p. 498 ff; a tentative peace overture from North Vietnam, p. 558-9; Sharp's remarks to General Wheeler on conditions that should be met first before peace discussions p. 561; bombing attacks over North Vietnam cease on April 1, 1968; p. 594 ff; North Vietnam agrees to meet with U.S. peace delegation in Paris on May 10, 1968, p. 610; North Vietnam exploitation of bombing cessation, p. 615-6 ff.

OP - 06 (Strategic Plans Division): Sharp serves (Sept. 1957) under Adm. Libby and Adm. B. Austin, P. 150 ff.

USS ORISKANY: serious fire on board - Oct. 26, 1966, p. 365

PARIS PEACE NEGOTIATIONS: Begun in May, 1968 (May 10), p. 610; Sharp's reasons why negotiations continued even though North Vietnamese were taking advantage of cessation of bombing, p. 610-1; p. 629.

POL Targets (Fuel oil installations): see entries under ROLLING THUNDER, CINC PAC: p. 363; p. 375; Washington gives permission for strikes on POL targets around Hanoi and Haiphon ...success of strikes...explanation offered by State Department to the world, p. 380; p. 381-2; p. 388; p. 438; p. 458; p. 473; p. 600-1; p. 630-1;

POST GRADUATE COURSE: p. 33 ff.

USS PUEBLO: Background to the mission of the PUEBLO, p. 567-8; Sharp's story of the capture, p. 569 ff; Sharp's comments on book about PUEBLO incident by Admiral Dan Gallery, p. 575-6.

RAHMAN, Tengku Abdul - Prime Minister of Mayala, p. 212.

REGULUS I: p. 149-150.

REISCHAUER, Edwin Oldfather: U.S. Ambassador to Japan, 263.

REPUBLICAN PARTY - Task Force of Military Experts: writes report on "The Failure of Gradualism in Vietnam", p. 610-12.

USS RICHMOND: Sharp ordered to her from P.G. school, p. 38 ff; wins the Engineering E, p. 41.

USS ROCHESTER: Adm. Struble's flagship - 7th fleet, p. 110-111; p. 115-6.

ROLLING THUNDER: (name given U.S. air operations over North Vietnam): Feb. 22, 1965 - first in series, p. 271; p. 282; discussion of restrictions placed by Washington on U.S. air operations, p. 282 - 4; JCS restrictions (representing ideas of a higher authority) p. 294-5; illustrations of gradual relaxation of restrictions, p. 295-9; operations suspended Dec. 1965 for indefinite period, p. 305; SAM missile sites and restrictions placed on their attack, p. 305-6; concern in Washington over priority of the air effort, p. 310; summary of operations Nov/Dec. 1965, p. 323-4; overall look at operations in 1965, p. 332-344; chronology of air operations against North Vietnam in 1966, p. 344 ff; p. 349 ff; bombing resumed Jan. 31, 1966 with Rolling Thunder #48, p. 357-8; Rolling Thunder #49 gives CincPac more freedom with armed reconnaissance, p. 358-9; Rolling Thunder #50 - SecDef gives fixed targets, p. 359; Rolling Thunder #51 (July

1966) armed reconnaissance extended to all North Vietnam, p. 363-4; Rolling Thunder #52, p. 365-8; Nov. 1966 Cinc Pac published ROLLING THUNDER (ed. #1-66) - Sharp notes good effects of this summary with pictures, p. 371-2. p. 388-9; Rolling Thunder #52 got approval for certain targets - then approval withdrawn because British Foreign Minister was visiting Moscow and Washington didn't want complications, p. 390; p. 392; Sharp's outline of objectives of Rolling Thunder Operations - message to JCS Jan. 14, 1967 - p. 404; air war over North Vietnam in first quarter of 1967, p. 431-6; p. 438; air efforts in 2nd quarter of 1967, p. 441-2; cumulative effects of bombing efforts, p. 444-6; p. 448; p. 452-3; p. 459-60; p. 463-4; p. 507; p. 532-6; bombing over North Vietnam comes to halt, p. 594-5; review of Rolling Thunder attacks in first three months of 1968, p. 596 ff.

ROUTE PACKAGES: term used for ROLLING THUNDER armed recco areas, p. 441;
See also - ROLLING THUNDER Operations.

RUSK, The Hon. Dean - Secretary of State: p. 494; his ideas for an all-out effort in South Vietnam, p. 494; General Westmoreland's reply, p. 495-7; p. 595.

RUSSIAN ASSISTANCE - for North Vietnam: p. 263-4.

SAFI, Morocco: p. 58.

SAIGON: Note: see numerous references in the story of U.S. activities in Vietnam - under SOUTH VIETNAM, CINC PAC, WESTMORELAND, McNAMARA.
focal point for North Vietnamese attacks in 1968 - during bombing cessation of north p. 624; Gen. Abrams, as USMACV gives his estimate (June, 1968) of morale in Saigon - effects of North Vietnamese attacks, p. 627-8.

SALISBURY, Harrison: New York TIMES correspondent - visits Hanoi (Dec. 1966) and reports on results of U.S. bombing, p. 447.

SAM threat: becomes increasingly difficult in middle of 1966 for U.S. bombers, p. 382-4.

SANGLEY POINT: p. 583-4.

USS SARATOGA: Sharp (July 1932) becomes division officer, p. 24-27; plane types on board, p. 29; the baseball team, p. 31-2.

SCHERGER, Air Chief Marshall Sir Frederick: Australian Military Advisor to SEATO, p. 260-1.

SEACORD Meeting: July, 1965 in Bangkok - coordinating committee for U.S. missions in SE Asia, p. 290.

SEA DRAGON: (naval gunfire operations): p. 398; use of naval gunfire in support of friendly forces in South Vietnam began in May, 1965, p. 398; authority was never given by Washington for shore bombardment of North Vietnam, p. 398-9; p. 433; p. 500.

SEATO: Sharp at semi-annual conference in Bangkok (Oct. 1964), p. 239; airpower demonstration aboard the USS CONSTELLATION p. 239-40; p. 261; meeting in London (Apr. 1965), p. 278-9p. 309; meeting in New Zealand, p. 595.

SEC DEF (Secretary of Defense): See entries under name of Secretary - Robert S. McNamara and Clark Clifford.

SECOND FLEET: Sharp becomes operations officer on staff of Comdr. 2nd fleet, Jan. 1951, p. 131-2.

SEVENTH FLEET: activities of DD Task Force along North Vietnamese coast line, p. 443.

SHARP, VADM Alexander: p. 38-9; p. 42; p. 54.

SHARP, Adm. U.S. Grant: Personal data, p. 1 ff; entrance to Naval Academy, p. 6 ff; interest in aviation, p. 12; meets his future wife, p. 19; marriage, p. 20-21; family difficulties in Long Beach earthquake, p. 27-28; p. 33; incident involving selection, p. 39-40; objects to assignment orders, p. 44-5; p. 96; family information, p. 101-2; marriage of daughter (1954), p. 139-40; promotion to Admiral and CincPac Fleet, p. 178-9; his discussion of recommendations made to Washington on Vietnam strategy, p. 242-3; his discussion of problem of command relationships in Pacific, p. 244; his response to remarks of Senator Fulbright on Tonkin Gulf incident, p. 249-50. present activities (1970), p. 653 ff.

SIHANOUK, Prince - Chief of State in Cambodia; p. 560; p. 564-5.

SIRI, Vice Admiral - Thai Navy: his orientation visit to Hawaii, p. 187-8.

SMART, Gen. Jacob B.: PacAir Force Commander, p. 190-1.

SONAR SCHOOL: (AWS school); Sharp in command at San Diego from 1948-9, p. 100.

SOUTH KOREA: Defense Minister (June, 1965) announces despatch of 15,000 combat troops to South Vietnam, p. 281; p. 291.

SOUTH VIETNAM: Developments in Vietnamese picture, p. 169-173; joint communique of VP Johnson and Pres. Diem on Defense and Economic program, p. 172; introduction of U.S. helicopter companies, p. 173-5; chronological summary of Vietnam situation in 1963, p. 194 ff; summary of major events in first six months of 1964, p. 197 ff; south Vietnamese patrols in Tonkin Gulf, p. 218-9; Note: see entries under TONKIN GULF for full story of this incident; recommendations of Adm. Sharp, p. 232 ff; summary statement of Sharp on final months of 1964, p. 241-2; Sharp recommends landing marines at Danang (Oct. 1964), p. 242; cooperation of Cinc Pac with the Vietnamese airforce, p. 253; account of activities in South Vietnam in 1965, p. 257 ff; more political changes in Saigon, p. 262-4; activities in March - April 1965, p. 267; p. 271-2; attempt to encourage South Vietnam military effort, p. 276; p. 279-80; more governmental instability, p. 281; situation in June, 1965, p. 288-9; (Aug. 1965) a large program instituted for development of port facilities, p. 291; Thieu-Ky in power with more stabilization, p. 309; Westmoreland tells Washington of need for more troops, p. 313-4; U.S. Policy - formulated in 1965 - let South Vietnamese know it is their war and they would have to win it - with U.S. assistance, p. 315; Sharp reiterates to JCS - U.S. forces are in supporting role, p. 316-7; integrated U.S. - Vietnamese Intelligence activity, p. 318-9; first encounter U.S. Marines and Viet Cong 2nd Regiment, p. 320; battles in Pleiku province, p. 321-2; service-funded construction inaugurated in 1965 - to facilitate, p. 326; development of airfields (1965-6), p. 328-30; Sharp underscores necessity of continuing pressure on North Vietnamese, p. 344-5; more political turmoil (mid 1946) Ky finally becomes Prime Minister and stabilizes things, p. 374;

STRUBLE, Admiral Arthur D.: asks Sharp to join his staff (tempo) as head planner for Inchon operation, p. 108 ff; Struble enters Inchon harbor and supervises landing forces, p. 116; with Gen. MacArthur inspects landing night of Sept. 15, p. 118-20; p. 123.

STUDY GROUP (State, CIA, Defense): on alternatives in the North Vietnam conflict, p. 410-11; p. 420-2.

STUMP, Admiral Felix: becomes Commander, 2nd fleet, March, 1951, p. 133-5; p. 137; p. 140; See other entries under CINC PAC FLEET.

USS SUMNER: Sharp serves on her, p. 17.

TALOS MISSILES: Nov. 1966 CincPac fleet recommends use of missile cruisers - CHICAGO and LONG BEACH - to interdict North Vietnam aircraft, p. 390: p. 440-1 p. p. 457.

TAYLOR, General Maxwell: p. 193; p. 201; p. 208; becomes U.S.

Ambassador to Saigon, p. 208; disagrees with aggressive attitude of Gen. Khanh, p. 212; p. 238; his letter from the President of the U.S. giving him over all responsibility for the entire military activity in South Vietnam, p. 244; his tendency in Saigon to recommend courses of action involving gradual application of U.S. power, p. 253 p. 267; at CincPac Conference, Hawaii, April 1965, p. 277-8; his theory of warfare as it concerned the Hanoi-Haiphong area, p. 284-5; statement on TV (Aug. 9, 1965), p. 308; relieved by Henry Cabot Lodge as Ambassador (Aug. 1965), p. 308; poses key questions regarding settlement of Vietnam conflict - Sharp gives his reactions to the JCS, p. 422-428; tours SE Asia with Clark Clifford (July, 1967) - given briefing by Gen. Westmoreland, p. 490 ff.

TET OFFENSIVE: p. 432, p. 435; p. 437; p. 525; the Tet Offensive of Jan., 1968, p. 586 ff; results of this offensive, p. 586-7; Clifford reports on reaction to Tet Offensive, p. 592.

THAI NGUYEN STEEL PLANT: becomes a desireable target for bombing operations in 1966, p. 382-3.

THAILAND: p. 276-7; p. 280; p. 287; p. 290.

THAILAND Based Planes: Thais would not agree to their use in South Vietnam, p. 639-40.

THANAT KHOMAN - Foreign Minister of Thailand: his statement on Dec. 10 (1964) about future of various countries in SE Asia should U.S. Withdraw from South Vietnam, p. 240.

THIEU, General Nguyen van: becomes Chief of State in South Vietnam - June, 1965, p. 309.

USS TICONDEROGA: supplies air support to the Maddox in Tonkin Gulf, p. 217-8; p. 230.

USS TOLEDO: with ROCHESTER in Inchon harbor, p. 116.

TONKIN GULF INCIDENT: attack on the USS MADDOX, p. 213-p. 221 influence of South Vietnamese patrol craft on the MADDOX incident, p. 218-9; the Second encounter, p. 224-5; retaiatory attacks by Task Force 77 on various North Vietnamest targets, p. 231; aftermath - reinforcement of forces in Pacific - the Tonkin Resolution in Congress, p. 232-3 Senator Fulbright's remarks in 1970 and Sharp's reaction p. 249-251.

TONKIN RESOLUTION: p. 232; note: see also entries under Tonkin Gulf Incident.

TURNER, Adm. R. Kelly: Exec on the CV SARATOGA (1932), p. 24, p. 31; p. 33.

USS TURNER JOY: joins the MADDOX for Tonkin Gulf patrol, p. 222; p. 227-8.

U THANT: Secretary General of the United Nations: first in his series of recommendations on the Vietnamese conflict, p. 208.

VIET CONG: for their activities in South Vietnam see entries under SOUTH VIETNAM.

VIETNAM: The Geneva Treaty of 1954 results in shifting of population from north to south, p. 147; U.S. Navy provides transportation, p. 147-8.

VIETNAM - LOGISTICS COMMAND: Navy had first obligation for logistic support - as involvement grew establishment of Army Logistic Command, p. 247-8.

WESTMORELAND, General Wm. C.: Becomes Commander, U.S. Military Assistance Command (June 20, 1964), replacing MAAG, p. 201; p. 212-213; p. 235; p. 238; p. 240; p. 246-7; p. 266; p. 270; p. 274-5; attends CincPac Conference (Apt. 1965) in Hawaii, p. 277; a week of conferences in Hawaii - Sept. 1965, p. 309; tells Washington (1965) about need for more troops in South Vietnam, p. 314; p. 321; recommends widespread use of M-16 rifle, p. 322; his comments on effectiveness of Adm. Sharp, p. 323; asks authority to take charge of bombing operations in lower part of North vietnam, p. 360; Sharp says Westmoreland fully understands importance of bombing over North Vietnam by end of 1966-67; p. 369-70; President asks (Oct. 1966) for his views on bombing campaign - p. 384-5; message to subordinate commanders in Jan. 1967, p. 414-6; p. 465; p. 480-1; briefs Clark Clifford and Maxwell Taylor, July 1967, p. 490; on his objectives in Vietnam, p. 490 ff; his reply to Secretary Rusk's for all-out push in South Vietnam, p. 495-6; p. 530-1; efforts to secure better press in 1968, p. 554 ff; has plan for putting combat forces into Laos (Jan. 1968), p. 562-3; tells Gen. Wheeler what his optimum needs are - resultant furor in Washington, p. 587-8 ff; sends message to JCS (May 26, 1968) pointing out extent of North Vietnamese preparation under cover of peace restraints, p. 622-3; proposes we retaliate on North Vietnam cities, p. 623; Sharp supports his recommendations, p. 623; Sharp prevented Westmoreland from taking over attack carriers for close air support - Sharp kept them in supporting role, p. 636-7;
See also - entries under Com USMAC V.

WHEELER, General Earle Gilmore: Chairman of the Joint Chiefs of Staff (1964): p. 223; p. 229; p. 277; p. 310; p.314; p. 381, p. 383. p. 391; Sharp sends message Dec. 1966 dealing with enemy use of propaganda, p. 394 ff; Wheeler's communication to Sharp in Feb. 1967 stepping up pressure on North Vietnam, p. 429-31; p. 445; Sharp expresses concern over proposed remarks of Secretary of State, p. 451; p. 457-8; p. 481; p. 488; Wheeler asks for Sharp's reaction to Secretary Rusk's suggestion of an all-out effort in South Vietnam, p. 494 ff; Westmoreland's reply to Rusk via Wheeler, p. 495-6; p. 519; p. 521-2; p. 530; p. 559-60; p. 562; his trip to Vietnam (Feb. 1968) and decisions by-passing CincPac, p. 587-8; Sharp commends Westmoreland - makes comments on what should be done in Vietnam (March 1968), p. 590-2; reports to Sharp and Westmoreland on attitude of new SecDef- Clark Clifford, p. 592-3; Sharp's message to him about Cease Bombing order, p. 603-4; involved over question of operational control of First Marine Air Wing in Vietnam, p. 641; p. 648-9.

WHITE PAPERS - U.S.: first one issued Feb. 27, 1965 - titled: AGGRESSION FROM THE NORTH, p. 264.

WONSAN, Korea: destination of the PUEBLO after capture, p. 573.

www.ingramcontent.com/pod-product-compliance
Lightning Source LLC
Chambersburg PA
CBHW080619170426
43209CB00007B/1469